# Bolstering Student Resilience

## Creating a Classroom With Consistency, Connection, and Compassion

JASON E. HARLACHER

SARA A. WHITCOMB

 **MARZANO** Resources

555 North Morton Street
Bloomington, IN 47404
888.849.0851
FAX: 866.801.1447

email: info@MarzanoResources.com
MarzanoResources.com

Visit **MarzanoResources.com/reproducibles** to download the free reproducibles in this book.

Printed in the United States of America

Library of Congress Cataloging-in-Publication Data

Names: Harlacher, Jason E., 1977- author. | Whitcomb, Sara A., author.
Title: Bolstering student resilience : creating a classroom with
    consistency, connection, and compassion / Jason E. Harlacher, Sara A.
    Whitcomb.
Description: Bloomington, IN : Marzano Resources, [2022] | Includes
    bibliographical references and index.
Identifiers: LCCN 2021057636 (print) | LCCN 2021057637 (ebook) | ISBN
    9781943360598 (Paperback) | ISBN 9781943360604 (eBook)
Subjects: LCSH: Students--United States--Social conditions. | Children with
    social disabilities--Education--United States. | School improvement
    programs--United States. | Affective education--United States. |
    Resilience (Personality trait)
Classification: LCC LC205 .H36 2022  (print) | LCC LC205  (ebook) | DDC
    370.15/340973--dc23/eng/20220218
LC record available at https://lccn.loc.gov/2021057636
LC ebook record available at https://lccn.loc.gov/2021057637

---

**Production Team**

*President and Publisher:* Douglas M. Rife
*Associate Publisher:* Sarah Payne-Mills
*Art Director:* Rian Anderson
*Managing Production Editor:* Kendra Slayton
*Copy Chief:* Jessi Finn
*Senior Production Editor:* Tonya Maddox Cupp
*Content Development Specialist:* Amy Rubenstein
*Acquisitions Editor:* Sarah Jubar
*Copy Editor:* Mark Hain
*Proofreader:* Elisabeth Abrams
*Text and Cover Designer:* Rian Anderson
*Editorial Assistants:* Sarah Ludwig and Elijah Oates

# ACKNOWLEDGMENTS

As graduate students, we spent our time researching and studying social and emotional learning. We had the pleasure of doing so under a great mentor and educator, Dr. Kenneth W. Merrell, whose work laid the pathways for our careers and the core concepts of this book. This fueled both of our passions for creating safe environments for students and careers focused on data-based decision making, systemic reform, and the well-being of students. Now, since we left the town of Eugene in 2008, we are thrilled to share a book on bolstering the social and emotional learning competencies of the students. This collaboration has been a bright light in an otherwise stressful and unique time in history. We are grateful that we could pull this book together and provide practical advice, and in doing so, we hope we have made social and emotional learning practices both tangible and manageable for educators.

We want to thank our colleagues, former classmates, and professionals in the field of school psychology for their contributions to our careers and to this book. We have built on the work of many others by pulling together information, best practices, and research from professionals that we respect greatly. We want to credit the following organizations for their research and materials from which we consistently draw in our work, including the Center on Positive Behavioral Interventions and Supports, National Center on Intensive Intervention, Collaborative for Academic, Social, and Emotional Learning (CASEL), and Center on Multi-Tiered System of Supports (MTSS) at American Institutes for Research.

—Jason E. Harlacher and Sara A. Whitcomb

Marzano Resources would like to thank the following reviewers:

Mandy Barrett
Principal
Gravette Upper Elementary School
Gravette, Arkansas

David Huber
Principal
South Side School
Bristol, Connecticut

Andrew Mather
Principal
Karen Western Elementary School
Omaha, Nebraska

David Pillar
Principal
Jackson Creek Middle School
Bloomington, Indiana

Julie Wallace
Principal
Quitman Elementary School
Quitman, Arkansas

Visit **MarzanoResources.com/reproducibles** to download the free reproducibles in this book.

# TABLE OF CONTENTS

*Reproducible pages are in italics.*

## Chapter 1

# Chapter 2

# Chapter 3

# Chapter 4

# Chapter 5

## Chapter 6

### Adjusting Discipline for Compassion . . . . . . . . . . . . . . . . . . . . . . . .133

## Chapter 7

### Using Data Effectively to Tie It All Together . . . . . . . . . . . . . . . .153

# Chapter 8

# ABOUT THE AUTHORS

**J**ason E. Harlacher, PhD, is a senior researcher with American Institutes for Research. Jason began his educational career as a day treatment facilitator, teaching youths skills to build their social and emotional learning (SEL) competencies. Since then, he has worked as a school psychologist, district technical assistance provider, private consultant, adjunct professor, and state-level consultant.

With over fifteen years of experience in education across the school, district, and state levels, Jason presents nationally on topics related to classroom management and multitiered systems of support. He has been published in several peer-reviewed journals and has authored several books, including *Designing Effective Classroom Management, Practitioner's Guide to Curriculum-Based Evaluation in Reading,* and *An Educator's Guide to Schoolwide Positive Behavioral Interventions and Supports.*

Jason received his BA in psychology from Ohio University in 1999, his MA in school psychology from Utah State University in 2005, and his PhD in school psychology from the University of Oregon in 2009.

**S**ara A. Whitcomb, PhD, is a licensed psychologist and director of the School Psychology Doctoral Program at the University of Massachusetts Amherst. Sara began her career in 1998 as a special education teacher in a middle school structured-learning program and as a general education teacher in kindergarten and first grade. In 2009, she began serving as a consultant to over twenty school districts in the Commonwealth of Massachusetts.

Sara presents and publishes peer-reviewed articles on topics related to school-based behavioral health, consultation, positive behavioral interventions and supports (PBIS), and social-emotional learning (SEL). She has authored and coauthored a number of books, including *Behavioral, Social, and Emotional Assessment of Children and Adolescents* (fourth and fifth editions), *Merrell's Strong Start, Grades K–2* (first and second editions), *Merrell's Strong Start, Pre-K* (first and second editions), and *Clinical Interviews for Children and Adolescents* (third edition).

Sara received her BA in education and psychology from Boston College in 1996, her MEd from Harvard Graduate School of Education in 1998, and her PhD in school psychology from the University of Oregon in 2009.

# INTRODUCTION

*Mrs. Newbacker needed a large coffee today. As she climbed out of bed and got ready for work, she was fighting off the tethers from a late night of grading papers. The crisp air nipped gently as she stepped outside and opened her car door. She felt a slight sting on her face, but it was nothing compared to the stress and anxiety she felt as she thought about her classroom.*

*She was seeing a range of issues from her students, and she was struggling with how best to support them. There was Martin, who was always exhausted in the mornings because of having to stay up late tending to his baby sibling. There was Carly, a bright, overachieving perfectionist who, if she made one little mistake, would repeat negative self-talk to herself about her abilities. There was Matty, who lived in a hotel, and whose favorite pastime was making rude comments to his peers, and also Josie, who struggled with learning disabilities and who was mocked by her classmates, despite Mrs. Newbacker's efforts to stop the bullying. Each day, it was a toss-up regarding when, not if, students would argue or yell at each other. Drama among students constantly interrupted her teaching, and all of it was creating a chaotic classroom and making teaching difficult. Sometimes, she was elated if she finished just one lesson plan.*

*Mrs. Newbacker knew she needed stronger classroom management, but it was hard to enforce rules when students came to school beleaguered by their home lives. It was difficult to develop structure while also helping students navigate the stressors they faced. She had worked out a flowchart that reflected best practices in classroom management, but she often found it hard to discipline a student who she knew was dealing with significant life trauma. Sometimes she let it go, and other times she felt like she was being harsh. It was exhausting, and Mrs. Newbacker wasn't alone. Lunch in the staff lounge was often filled with fatigued teachers sharing their frustrations and strategies.*

*Mrs. Newbacker couldn't fault the school for a lack of help, but she was also feeling the burden from all of leadership's requests. She was trying to implement the school's student supports, teaching classroom expectations that reflected the school's positive behavioral interventions and supports (PBIS) framework. She was also trying to use the morning circles that a restorative practices (RP) trainer shared last year. She was conscious of trauma-informed practices (TIP) and knew they were important for several of her students, though she was confused as to how this was different from the resilience in school environments (RISE) strategies that she learned several years ago. She knew that her principal wanted to add social and emotional learning (SEL) instruction after winter break. She wondered if that would create a calmer classroom—and when all the new approaches would end. Mrs. Newbacker wished for a single approach to support all of her students and find ways to bolster their resilience. "Does that even exist?" she thought as she pulled into a parking spot at school and shut off the engine.*

## Bolstering Resilience

Many educators can relate to Mrs. Newbacker's experience with a classroom full of students who bring a range of backgrounds and life experiences to school, and the corresponding task of figuring out how best to support them. While some may refer to this ability as *grit* (Duckworth, 2016) or *growth mindset* (Dweck, 2006), we use the term *resilience*. In this context, *resilience* is a student's ability to manage and cope with life's stressors (Doll, Brehm, & Zucker, 2014; Goldstein & Brooks, 2013). We selected this term because it's commonly used, and it captures this book's focus succinctly: *creating a structured, supportive classroom that helps bolster students' abilities to cope with stress.* We've also selected the term *bolstering* because we feel all people, adults and students, have a range of resilience that can be nurtured. By creating a classroom environment that supports students' emotional growth and ability to navigate stressors, teachers can meet students wherever they are to bolster their resilience.

School leaders ask teachers to use all sorts of approaches to support students, and there's no shortage of acronyms for them to learn: RTI (response to intervention), MTSS (multitiered system of support), and the previously described PBIS, RP, TIP, and SEL, just to name a few. All of these can be helpful, but unfortunately, the piling up of these approaches can fill teachers' plates. In turn, teachers feel overwhelmed (Van Droogenbroeck, Spruyt, & Vanroelen, 2014), and schools can become fractured places in which things feel disorganized and misaligned (Elmore, 2000; Jimerson, Burns, & VanDerHeyden, 2016; Newmann, Smith, Allensworth, & Bryk, 2001;

Schmoker, 2006). Is it any wonder that roughly 40 percent of teachers leave the profession in the first five years (Gray & Taie, 2015; Ingersoll, Merrill, Stuckey, & Collins, 2018)?

So how does a teacher maintain personal sanity *and* create a classroom that bolsters resilience in students? There are various approaches that educators can use, making it difficult to discern which one is most helpful. In table I.1, we have listed some of the more well-known approaches, including a brief description of each approach and its key practices.

**Table I.1: Similarities Among Common Approaches to Bolster Resilience**

| Approach | Description | Key Practices |
|---|---|---|
| Positive behavioral interventions and supports (PBIS) | Organizes school into a multitiered system to support students' behavior and improve climate | • Teaching students between three and five schoolwide expectations<br>• Focusing on explicit lessons and reinforcement of schoolwide expectations<br>• Providing a clear discipline structure |
| Restorative practices (RP) | Focuses on building and maintaining relationships and repairing harm from conflict | • Morning meetings<br>• Classroom circles<br>• Repair conversations |
| Social and emotional learning (SEL) | Uses strong instructional practices to teach core social and emotional learning (SEL) competencies | • Explicit teaching of SEL with lesson plans<br>• Cooperative learning<br>• Other techniques to embed competency practice throughout school day and across school settings |
| Trauma-informed practices (TIP) | Ensures a safe environment for students to learn coping skills and to process their emotions | • Teaching and reinforcement of coping skills, such as mindfulness and deep breathing<br>• Creating relationships with students<br>• Developing predictable learning environments |

You can see there is considerable overlap among the approaches. For example, classrooms focused on both PBIS and SEL target prosocial skills (such as interpersonal and emotional skills and assets students draw on to interact with others, get their needs met, and benefit others; Eisenberg & Spinrad, 2014). With PBIS, a teacher may teach students three common classroom expectations, which are descriptors of expected behaviors or skills, such as *be safe*, *be respectful*, and *be responsible* (Harlacher & Rodriguez, 2018; McKevitt & Braaksma, 2008). This overlaps with SEL, which includes teaching students how to be responsible. Additionally, teaching students how to navigate and build relationships is a focus not just of SEL instruction but also of restorative practices. Furthermore, several approaches establish a predictable classroom by teaching routines or ensuring structure.

In fact, we noticed that all the named approaches in table I.1 (page 3) aim to establish, in one form or another, classrooms that do the following.

- Teach and strengthen prosocial skills in students.
- Build relationships between the staff and students and among students themselves.
- Create a predictable and safe classroom by teaching routines and establishing procedures.
- Allow flexibility and emotional space for students—particularly those with *social, emotional,* or *behavioral needs* (needs related to social adjustment, mental health diagnoses, learning difficulties, trauma, or short- or long-term issues related to social-emotional functioning).

As we reviewed these approaches and noticed so much alignment among them, we discovered that, at the heart of supporting students are classrooms that ensure consistency, connection, and compassion. So, while the bad news is that teachers experience exhaustion and frustration with fragmentation of approaches in school, the good news is that there's a way to synthesize many approaches to do what's best for students' emotional well-being. The acronyms may be alphabet soup, but it's a healthy soup that can be strained to find core concepts.

We have identified best practices from the literature on behavioral principles (Alberto & Troutman, 2013), PBIS (Center on PBIS, n.d.a; Dunlap, Sailor, Horner, & Sugai, 2009), trauma-informed practices (Eber, Barrett, Scheel, Flammini, & Pohlman, 2020; Pickens & Tschopp, 2017), restorative practices (Maynard & Weinstein, 2020; McCammon, 2020), and social and emotional learning (Dusenbury, Calin, Domitrovich, & Weissberg, 2015; Jones, Bailey, Brush, & Kahn, 2018) and our own experiences that span the approaches listed in table I.1, and put together this book to illustrate how teachers can use those practices to support students. Table I.2 summarizes our synthesis of these approaches into three concepts. We hope this book makes bolstering resilience accessible and practical for our readers, leading to classrooms that provide consistency, connection, and compassion for students. We expand on those three terms next before discussing how best to use this book.

**Table I.2: Key Features of Classrooms That Bolster Resilience**

| Feature | Description |
|---|---|
| **Consistency** | |
| Teaching prosocial skills | Teachers provide instruction related to prosocial skills, including skills that enable empathy, such as emotion regulation and coping skills. |
| Establishing clear structures for routines, acknowledgment, and discipline | Teachers implement classroom structures that promote consistency in routines and student and teacher responses to various incidents. |
| **Connection** | |
| Maintaining high rates of feedback | Teachers give high rates of feedback on prosocial skills to strengthen students' skills and build rapport. |
| Building relationships | Instruction highlights intentional efforts to create bonds among students, between students and teacher, and with families. |
| **Compassion** | |
| Adjusting structures to meet students' individual needs | Teachers adjust classroom structures and strategies based on specific student needs and students' current emotional states. |
| Providing support matched to the behavior's function (for example, teaching a student to express emotions assertively versus using passive-aggressive comments) | Teachers anchor additional support and specific plans for students around reteaching a prosocial skill to replace an unwanted skill or behavior. |

## Creating Consistency

Consistency is important in classrooms because of the structure and safety it can provide to students (Centre for Education Statistics and Evaluation [CESE], 2020; Harlacher, 2015; Simonsen & Myers, 2015). To create consistency is to ensure a predictable environment. This includes explicitly teaching prosocial skills to create a foundation of how the teacher and students can interact with one another. Consistency also includes clear and transparent structures in the classroom, such as how the teacher manages unwanted behavior and how students get their needs met. We use the terms *behavior* and *skill* interchangeably throughout this book, as both refer to observable acts that someone performs.

In this book, we offer two main approaches for consistency.

1.  Teaching prosocial skills through the establishment of classroom expectations and the use of instruction on SEL competencies

2.  Establishing clear structures for students

These structures include three pieces: (1) teaching routines so students can get their needs met, (2) providing acknowledgment of students' performance and growth with those prosocial skills, and (3) outlining a discipline structure for managing unexpected or unwanted behavior. We also discuss physical classroom setup.

To establish consistency, teachers begin by actively and explicitly teaching prosocial skills. They accomplish this by outlining and teaching classroom expectations, such as *be safe, be respectful, be responsible*. These expectations form the classroom's culture and outline general behavior or skills that the teacher expects throughout the various activities and routines for the classroom. Several researchers have linked the explicit teaching of expectations to decreases in problematic behavior in classrooms and increases in feelings of safety and academic performance (Algozzine et al., 2008; Bradshaw, Mitchell, & Leaf, 2010; Bradshaw, Waasdorp, & Leaf, 2012; Estrapala, Rila, & Bruhn, 2021; James, Noltemeyer, Ritchie, & Palmer, 2019; Taylor-Greene et al., 1997).

In addition, teachers can enhance use of the classroom expectations and further support students by teaching critical SEL competencies, which the Collaborative for Academic, Social, and Emotional Learning (CASEL; 2020) has outlined. Table I.3 lists these skills.

Teaching SEL competencies is associated with a range of benefits, including improvements in interpersonal skills, emotional and behavioral functioning in school,

**Table I.3: SEL Competencies**

| Skill | Description | Example |
|---|---|---|
| Self-awareness | Understanding and recognizing one's emotions | A student can identify situations that result in anxiety and the thoughts, feelings, and behaviors that go along with feeling anxious. |
| Self-management | Managing to self-soothe, and managing and monitoring one's responses to a range of emotions | A student can use coping skills (such as journaling) to reduce anxiety prior to taking a test. |
| Social awareness | Recognizing others' emotions and having empathy for different cultures and perspectives | A student can identify when others are feeling defensive by noticing their body language. |
| Relationship skills | Initiating and maintaining healthy relationships, including with diverse individuals or groups | When discussing a disagreement, a student mirrors another person's experience in order to reach a solution. |
| Responsible decision making | Making safe, thoughtful, and constructive behavior choices and activities to achieve goals or outcomes | A student can plan and stick to study time during the week to feel prepared for an exam on Friday. |

*Source: Adapted from CASEL, 2020.*

and academic performance (Durlak, Weissberg, Dymnicki, Taylor, & Schellinger, 2011; Taylor, Oberle, Durlak, & Weissberg, 2017).

After introducing and teaching prosocial skills, the teacher structures the classroom to provide a positive environment supporting use of those skills (CESE, 2020; Darch & Kame'enui, 2003; Harlacher, 2015; Simonsen, Fairbanks, Briesch, Myers, & Sugai, 2008). Part of this structure is active supervision and engagement on the teacher's part in the form of regular prompts, reminding students to use skills during key moments, and providing feedback to reinforce students' use of the prosocial skills. For example, imagine a teacher teaches students about perspective-taking as part of the SEL instruction targeting relationship skills in a seventh-grade classroom. Following teaching of perspective-taking in a brief lesson, the teacher can prompt students verbally prior to a group activity to use perspective-taking and to listen to their classmates' experiences. The teacher can then move about the room and use active supervision to acknowledge students' use of perspective-taking during the group activity. Feedback is instructional and helps students incorporate the skills into their repertoire (Burns, VanDerHeyden, & Zaslofsky, 2014; Daly, Lentz, & Boyer, 1996). By providing reinforcement and acknowledgment to students, the teacher can shape students' use of a skill and help them gain mastery of the skill (in this example, the skill being perspective-taking).

The teacher can also ensure consistency by teaching expectations and routines to students. Teaching students clear routines creates a consistent, unambiguous classroom environment. Specifically, this entails teaching students procedures to get various needs met, such as how to ask for help during class time, the procedure for entering the classroom, or the process for cleaning up lab equipment (Simonsen & Myers, 2015).

Additionally, when students need support or correction for engaging in an unwanted or unexpected behavior, consistency also includes a discipline structure. This structure (which we have labeled the supportive discipline framework and talk more about in chapter 5, page 101), is designed to reteach and strengthen the lacking skill. It also ensures a process that is instructional and supportive to students, which can reduce anxiety that a teacher or students may have about how behavior will be managed (George, Kincaid, & Pollard-Sage, 2009; Minahan, 2019; Pickens & Tschopp, 2017). By teaching expectations to students and providing transparent structures on how they will receive support, a teacher can establish a consistent, predictable, and safe classroom environment (Harlacher, 2015; Simonsen et al., 2008).

## Creating Connection

*Connection* refers to the relation students feel to school, to each other, and to the teacher. This is a critical concept, because students who feel positively connected to at least one adult are more engaged with their schooling and at lower risk for delinquent or risky behavior (Anderson, Christenson, Sinclair, & Lehr, 2004; Decker, Dona, & Christenson, 2007; Zolkoski, 2019). To create connection in the classroom, teachers can do two things: (1) build relationships among students and between the teacher and students and (2) create a supportive, positive environment where students receive more feedback on their strengths and skills relative to corrections or constructive criticism (Harlacher, 2015; Simonsen, MacSuga, Fallon, & Sugai, 2013).

While reading this book, you will learn specific relationship-building strategies, including the use of greetings at the door, using emotional check-ins, and morning circles for students to share their experiences and emotions. We also detail methods to create a supportive, positive classroom by praising students. We provide a way to frame acknowledgment that is strategic and comprehensive. Further, we provide a structure for how students earn praise and how praise also reinforces consistency.

## Creating Compassion

Compassion is the notion that even though classrooms have established structure and expectations, students need flexibility in that structure. To fully support students as they build resilience, teachers can't hold to a rigid application of practices that ignores students' life experiences (Pickens & Tschopp, 2017), but rather they can adjust the structure based on students' needs. This flexibility and acknowledgment of vast experiences are the art of teaching that many people refer to; we deal with students and parents who bring unique experiences, personal choice, and emotions to the classroom. Consequently, teachers need to adjust and adapt practices to fully support students.

To create a classroom that is compassionate, teachers can do two things, the first of which is to adjust their practices and strategies to fit the needs of students who have unique or challenging circumstances. This book covers practices that create a foundation of consistency and connection. However, for the sake of compassion, teachers may need to be flexible and adjust these practices at times for students with certain life stressors, mental health concerns, or histories of trauma (Cummings, Addante, Swindell, & Meadan, 2017; Minahan, 2019). That is to say, there are considerations when applying methods to students with certain needs, and the rigid application of all rules and structures without adaptations could lead to more stress for students if their personal needs aren't considered (Minahan, 2019; Pickens & Tschopp, 2017). All teachers can relate to this; you have seen a student act out but also know the student is emotionally overwhelmed by something personal. We offer guidelines on how to adjust these strategies while maintaining the integrity of the classroom structure.

Second, teachers can offer function-based support, which includes understanding what a student is communicating with behavior and teaching more adaptive skills that serve the same function or purpose as the student's current behavior (Crone, Hawken, & Horner, 2015). Some students need more time and attention for their needs related to social, emotional, and behavioral concerns or to increase their use and proficiency of adaptive and prosocial skills. This additional time or attention includes a sufficient amount of support that is matched to the function of a student's unwanted behavior or skill, thereby providing a more suitable skill to use instead of the maladaptive skill the student currently uses (Crone et al., 2015). For example, a high school student who has difficulty regulating emotions may engage in self-harm (cutting) to alleviate emotional pain. By understanding the function of this behavior (for example, to avoid uncomfortable feelings and get relief from emotions), support can be designed to teach a more adaptive skill that serves the same function. Because the behavior is serious, the support would need to be of sufficient intensity to ensure the student develops the more adaptive skill into their repertoire (which might include counseling, teaching of various emotion regulation techniques, and monitoring to ensure its use). To ensure students with such needs are addressed, we describe a function-based approach in which students' support plans, labeled *individualized support plans*, use behavioral principles to ensure students learn the taught skill (this process is analogous to a response to intervention process and aligns with an MTSS framework; McIntosh & Goodman, 2016). By providing students with function-based support designed to teach them more adaptive skills and by having the flexibility to adjust strategies to support all students, teachers can create a compassionate classroom.

## Understanding How to Use This Book

The knowledge that a classroom that bolsters resilience is built on creating consistency, connection, and compassion generates a fair question, For whom? Students come from different backgrounds and are educated in a variety of settings, so before we share the structure of the book, we want to point out that the approaches in this book can align with the diversity of student backgrounds and the settings in which students and teachers find themselves.

### Culturally Responsive Teaching

The practices in this book fit naturally with creating culturally responsive teaching environments. The U.S. federally funded Center on PBIS, which has led the field in research and training on developing supportive environments based on students' needs and context, has outlined culturally responsive components as the following (Leverson, Smith, McIntosh, Rose, & Pinkelman, 2021).

- **Identity:** Understanding and including student cultural identity within the classroom, but also the understanding of staff of their own cultural identity and how it may influence, shape, and interact with the students' identities

- **Voice:** Engaging authentically with family, community, and students such that their voice is heard and they are seen as collaborators with shaping the culture and climate in the classroom

- **A supportive environment:** Creating a positive environment that includes teaching students expectations and prosocial skills to be successful, as well as ensuring students feel valued

- **Situational appropriateness:** Understanding that some behaviors or skills are adaptive in one setting but not in others, and teaching students that understanding of when and where to use certain skills

- **Data for equity:** Using data to examine any biases or issues related to student populations or characteristics, including a willingness to have discussions of how practices may impact certain populations

We believe that creating a supportive, data-driven environment leads to equitable and fair environments that respect students' lives. By including student voice, respecting their identities, and creating a classroom built on consistency, connection, and compassion, teachers will align with culturally responsive practices. In table I.4, we provide some examples of the practices shared in this book and their relations to the five components outlined by Leverson and colleagues (2021).

**Table I.4: Culturally Responsive Practices and Bolstering Resilience**

| Core Components | Practice |
| --- | --- |
| Identity | <ul><li>Use connection strategies to allow room for student identity.</li><li>Provide space for students to express their identities.</li><li>Teach self-awareness in relation to student identity.</li><li>Understand your own cultural identity in relation to students' identity.</li></ul> |
| Voice | <ul><li>Include student and family voice when creating your classroom expectations (page 83).</li><li>Engage students with discussion around problem solving and behavior issues that may arise; enlist them as collaborators on solving the issue.</li><li>Use two-way communication efforts over one-way types of communication (page 92).</li></ul> |

continued →

| Core Components | Practice |
|---|---|
| A supportive environment | • Teach routines that allow students to get their needs met (for example, asking for help, asking for space to process emotions, and so on).<br>• Teach students missing skills so they are equipped to navigate stressors.<br>• Ensure students feel valued by engaging them in the issues that concern them.<br>• Respect and validate students' perspectives. |
| Situational appropriateness | • Acknowledge that students may live in different cultures, with differences between home and school.<br>• Allow grace as students learn and use skills within the classroom that may be new or not used in other environments.<br>• Incorporate students' perspectives and values into the classroom culture. |
| Data for equity | • Disaggregate classroom (or school) data between subgroups.<br>• Examine whether outcomes for one student are experienced by others. |

*Source: Adapted from Leverson et al., 2021.*

## Online Schooling

We believe that the methods in this book extend to all settings, in person and online. Students can learn expectations for any learning environment, so when creating a matrix for their classrooms, teachers can include a column or separate matrix for virtual learning and then outline rules for that setting. See figure 4.3 (page 96) for an example matrix; also see Center on Positive Behavioral Interventions and Supports (www.pbis.org) and Center for Parent Information and Resources (www .parentcenterhub.org) for additional examples.

Additionally, teachers can create clear structures and processes for remote learning, such as a clear sequence for beginning class or making comments in a virtual classroom. Teachers can foster connection by having students use the chat box to share information about their lives or by highlighting a student each class period. Teachers can also share information about themselves during class, which can assist with building relationships with students (Song, Kim, & Luo, 2016). Teachers can also have brief, five- to fifteen-minute connection calls with students and families. During these calls, teachers can share what the student is doing well and ask what support the family may need for ensuring remote learning is beneficial to the student. Such calls can be helpful for building relationships with families.

Teachers can extend compassion by adjusting remote learning to suit a student's life. Not all of our students will have the resources to connect online, so modifying one's strategies can demonstrate compassion and understanding. We highlight a few methods we've seen to make virtual learning and resilience possible in table I.5.

**Table I.5: Consistency, Connection, and Compassion for Virtual Learning**

| Principle | Examples |
|---|---|
| Consistency | • Outline the classroom expectations for online classes (that is, what the expectations look like within a virtual setting).<br>• Provide parents with sample routines for how to support their children during remote learning (see von Ravensburg [2020] and Center on Positive Behavioral Interventions and Supports [2020] for examples and tips). |
| Connection | • Allow space for students to share their day-to-day lives and process remote learning.<br>• Pair students up for projects and allow them to work remotely.<br>• Provide icebreakers at the start of each class by having students share in the chat box about themselves. |
| Compassion | • Allow flexibility for students to attend class or make up work, as they may need to work jobs or care for younger siblings during normal school hours.<br>• If possible, print materials or packets for students who may not have internet access to ensure they can participate in activities.<br>• Work with your school psychologist or counselor to provide resources to students who may need support.<br>• Adjust interventions for remote learning (for example, Center on Positive Behavioral Interventions and Supports [2020] offers one way to adapt a behavior intervention online). |

## Chapter Organization

We have structured this book to begin with universal practices that lay the foundation for a classroom that supports resilience. Here, *universal* refers to best practices that all students receive and have access to; these are best practices that lay the foundation for a classroom that bolsters resilience. Readers should approach the chapters in order, as each builds on the previous one. Readers will learn universal practices before digging into support for students with persistent needs. Jumping ahead to different chapters may mean missing out on foundational pieces that support resilience. Additionally, Practice in Action feature boxes throughout the chapters illustrate applied examples of the practices discussed.

Chapter 1 provides an understanding of the stress and risk factors that many students experience. We provide case studies to illustrate a school day from the perspective of a student with social, emotional, and behavioral needs and a teacher navigating those needs.

Chapter 2 is a foundational chapter that details setting up the classroom for consistency. We outline the physical layout of the classroom and how to teach prosocial skills to students, including classroom expectations and SEL competencies.

Chapter 3 reinforces the previously taught prosocial skills, as you learn how to promote use of the classroom expectations and SEL competencies, building off the previous chapter. We detail how to provide high rates of effective feedback and how to use prompts to ensure students use and retain the prosocial skills they are taught. Additionally, we offer a framework for reinforcement: a comprehensive reinforcement plan. We discuss feedback and reinforcement within its own chapter, as feedback is used to both reinforce consistency (that is, the prosocial skills) and to build connection with students.

In chapter 4, we discuss creating connections in a classroom, including building teacher-student relationships, student-student relationships, and relationships with caregivers.

In chapter 5, we offer a critical structure for building consistency, which is a supportive discipline framework. This framework offers a way to structure your responses to unwanted or unexpected behavior in a manner that reduces the chances of the behavior occurring again. This framework centers on teaching or reteaching nonproficient skills and offers a compassionate approach to helping students navigate their emotions and behaviors.

Chapter 6 discusses how to adjust discipline for compassion, as we outline how you can adjust the supportive discipline framework for students with persistent needs or those exposed to traumatic experiences. We also discuss modifying a response to students who display aggressive or explosive behavior that aligns with the escalation cycle (Colvin & Scott, 2015).

The first six chapters can be a lot to digest and manage, so we offer ideas for tying everything together in chapter 7. You will learn how to create classroom systems to implement the book's content, including how to use data to monitor one's effectiveness.

Finally, chapter 8 focuses on creating compassionate support for specific students with ongoing needs. There, we offer strategies for providing additional support to students using a function-based approach. We outline steps of the problem-solving model that you can use to support students with ongoing needs.

As you read through this book, we hope you see the alignment of your current practices into the three anchor points we will discuss: consistency, connection, and compassion. To support students and bolster their resilience can be a daunting task, but we consider a good starting point to be three simple questions. Within your classroom, what are you doing to ensure consistency for students? What are you doing to create connection with and among students? And what are you doing to show compassion as students navigate their lives? We offer answers to each of those questions in the following chapters.

# CHAPTER 1

# Understanding Student Risk Factors

I n the previous chapter, we introduced the concept of resilience and framed it as one's ability to cope with life's stressors. While we tried to distill this definition into digestible information, the reality is that resilience is a layered, multifaceted concept. In this chapter, we provide readers with an explanation of risk factors that may hinder resilience as well as protective factors that may serve to enhance resilience. We also explore the ways a consistent, connected, and compassionate classroom can be protective for students.

We start this chapter with a few scenarios of teachers aiming to effectively establish practices that support all students. We then share some rather alarming statistics related to the increasing social and emotional concerns that affect students and that may challenge teachers' practices to bolster their resilience. We share examples of various pathways that may shape these concerns. We close with a focus on strategies that promote resilience and consider how students as well as teachers might experience social and emotional concerns and resilience in a busy classroom environment.

## Ms. Vogt

Ms. Vogt has been a first-grade teacher for three years. She entered the profession because she loves to be around young children and finds that she learns something new from them every day. Ms. Vogt grew up in a middle-class suburb. She always enjoyed school and excelled, and she loved many of her teachers, which motivated her to be a teacher herself.

Ms. Vogt learned a lot in her first three years of teaching in an urban elementary school, but while she remains excited to help all students succeed academically, she also realized early on that social, emotional, and behavioral skills are equally important to foster in her classroom. Many of the students in her classroom come from neighborhoods that are very different from the one in which she grew up, and Ms. Vogt is aware that many of her students have been exposed to more challenges in their young lives than she has in her twenty-six years. She also learned that she could not make assumptions about what students are experiencing and that it is important for her to build authentic relationships with both her students and her students' families.

Ms. Vogt has created a number of strategies to connect with students and families. She makes sure to greet each student at the classroom door every morning. She greets students by name and with a smile. Each week, she writes an email or a note to about half of the students' families, so that she can communicate a quick, personalized, encouraging word about the students' week and a goal that students are working toward. During the following week, she sends similar messages to the other half of her class.

Ms. Vogt realized that while building connections with her students and their families is important, it is also critical that she creates a classroom environment that emphasizes consistency. She knows that such a classroom includes structured routines, clear behavioral expectations, and limit setting. Ms. Vogt always aims to ensure that students know what to expect from her and that they can trust that their teacher is always working to understand what they may be experiencing. Finally, Ms. Vogt places an emphasis on directly prompting, teaching, and reinforcing key social and emotional skills relevant to first-grade students. This includes lessons that help students understand and regulate emotions, practice coping strategies, and maintain friendships. These universal practices aim to support most students in her class, though some students will likely need further intervention.

## Mr. Matheson

Mr. Matheson has been a high school English teacher for fifteen years. He became a teacher because he really enjoys literature and likes to share this passion and critical understanding with his students. Mr. Matheson is a seasoned teacher and has an organizational structure for his curriculum as well as daily routines to ensure that he can cover all necessary material during a school year. Early in his career, he recognized that consistent classroom practices are key for keeping students engaged and out of trouble. As time has passed, however, he has noticed that more students are coming to school with a number of stressors and social and emotional concerns. He is concerned that students seem more anxious in general and less able to cope with emotions. Chronically absent students have a harder time passing his class, as do the students that are physically present but seem distracted or withdrawn.

More recently, Mr. Matheson has begun to incorporate a few key strategies into his daily routine to promote well-being and encourage engagement. One strategy engages students in a mood check each day. Usually, Mr. Matheson either asks students to share an adjective to highlight their current emotional state (for example, happy, angry, frustrated, nervous), or he shows pictures of people exhibiting different expressions and asks, "Which person do you identify with most today?" His goals for mood checks are to help students recognize their own emotions and to help himself gauge how students are coming to him. Understanding students' moods and energy levels helps him think about how to potentially adjust expectations or his delivery of content to ensure students stay engaged. Mr. Matheson also teaches prosocial skills to students through character studies in books that they read for class. He often assigns work that asks students to think through the social, emotional, and behavioral responses of characters and how such responses affect relationships, story lines, and other aspects of the book. While these strategies seem to be helpful and most of Matheson's students appear to appreciate his efforts and enjoy his class, there are still a few that seem to struggle socially and emotionally.

## The Statistics

For the teachers reading these stories, it may not surprise you at all that at least one in every five students in your classroom is struggling socially and emotionally, and these struggles are so severe that they could be diagnosed as actual disorders (Perou et al., 2013). Approximately 7 to 10 percent of students may be diagnosed with externalized concerns (Samek & Hicks, 2014); these are easy to see and may disrupt classroom environments and student learning. Attention-deficit/hyperactivity disorder (ADHD), oppositional defiant disorder (ODD), and conduct disorder (CD) are a few of these externalized concerns. Broadly speaking, these are the students who may have a hard time sitting still, whose desks might be overflowing with papers, and who might have difficulty staying on task. They may impulsively pull the hair of the person in front of them in line, and they may have trouble making friends. Some of these students may be argumentative, even defiant, and have problems getting along with others. Others may have a very hard time regulating their emotions and become explosive when they get upset, which could lead to safety concerns or property destruction in the classroom. These behaviors are hard to understand and manage, especially while working with twenty-five other students simultaneously!

Further, one in twenty students may suffer from internalized, harder-to-see concerns such as anxiety and depression (Bitsko et al., 2018). If you have been teaching for a while, you might also have noticed the increased prevalence of anxious behaviors in students (Ghandour et al., 2019). Though rates of depression seem to remain fairly stable, psychologists surveyed children and adolescents and found 30 percent of their respondents reported feeling sad or hopeless every day in the month prior to survey administration (Kann et al., 2014).

Internalized concerns like anxiety and depression may be a little harder to see than externalized concerns like ADHD and ODD because these struggles are generally less disruptive in a classroom. For example, common symptoms of generalized anxiety include consistent worry, inflexible thinking, restlessness, difficulty concentrating, and irritability. Symptoms of depression overlap with symptoms of anxiety and might also include feelings of sadness, hopelessness, and lethargy. There are some behavioral indicators of depressive and anxious behaviors that teachers can identify, however. For example, students who may be nervous or sad much of the time often end up in the nurse's office with a stomachache or headache. They often ask to leave the classroom for a bathroom break, or they might look to their teachers for more attention and reassurance than other students.

Students with anxiety, in particular, may appear visibly upset when something unexpected occurs, even simple changes in daily routines. Some students might also appear excessively shy or withdrawn, and they may choose to spend their time alone rather than with peers, even if that is not really what they want to do. They may respond well when invited to play a game at recess, for example, but if they are not invited, they may be unlikely to initiate a game or join in, resulting in a pattern of social withdrawal. As a teacher, working with these students can be a challenge, particularly because these behaviors can be silent or unnoticeable in a busy classroom environment.

Why is it that some students suffer from social, emotional, or behavioral concerns while others do not? How is it that some students grow up in healthy, functional home environments and struggle with behavioral health for a lifetime, while others grow up with barriers and hardship at every turn and still become productive and well-adjusted citizens? While there are certainly biological and genetic variables that contribute to the development of particular behaviors, children do not develop in a vacuum, and the environment in which they grow plays an important role in shaping both maladaptive and adaptive behaviors. Years of research have taught us that some factors students experience place them at incredible risk for poor outcomes (for example, harsh parenting, poverty, learning challenges, behavioral concerns) while other factors are protective and serve to buffer students from maladaptive behaviors (for example, trusted teachers; Buchanan, 2014; Cairns, Yap, Pilkington, & Jorm, 2014). Such factors serve as a buffer and encourage resilience. Here we discuss individual characteristics and environmental factors that influence student social and emotional behavior, and the roles and functions of risk and protective factors, so that you may approach students who exhibit challenging behaviors from a place of understanding and work to foster resilience.

## Nature and Nurture

The phrase *nature versus nurture* was first coined by a psychologist, Sir Francis Galton, in 1869, and after more than a century of research and debate on this topic, it has become more and more clear that students' behavior is predicted by both their physiology as well as the environment in which they develop over time (Biglan, Flay, Embry, & Sandler, 2012; Waldman, Rhee, LoParo, & Park, 2018). Infants are born with particular innate or inherited characteristics that are shaped over time through their attainment of typical developmental milestones and by their interaction with the environments in which they grow.

### Nature

Researchers Bornstein and colleagues (2015) find that caregivers can observe an individual's temperament characteristics from infancy and that such characteristics are stable over time.

Broadly defined, infant temperament includes tendencies toward demonstrating distress or positive affect, activity levels, and attention to or focus on stimuli (Rothbart, 2012; Rothbart & Rueda, 2005). Different infants may respond differently to the same situation. For an example from our personal experience, from very early on, Sara noticed that her son would tense up and cry whenever he heard an unexpected noise, like a doorbell, whereas her daughter was relaxed no matter what noises were happening around her. As her children developed, she noticed that while they changed and learned various social and emotional skills, their early indicators of temperament remained fairly stable. Her son continues to tense up and is more reactive to new stimuli, while her daughter is a bit more easygoing.

As they grow, most toddlers and young children become more able to demonstrate another aspect of temperament called *effortful control* or *self-regulation*, which means they are better able to hold back an immediate response to an uncomfortable emotion (Rothbart, 2012). They may be able to shift their attention away from something scary, for example, and they may become more able to self-soothe. This does not come easily for all children, however. For instance, some young children may begin to panic or cry when something unexpected happens, such as a thunderstorm, while others may be easily distracted or may find ways to calm themselves, such as snuggling on the couch with a favorite stuffed animal.

### Nurture

Student behaviors are not solely a result of their genetics or temperament (Plomin, DeFries, Knopik, & Neiderhiser, 2016). In addition to being able to understand students' various genetic and temperament characteristics, we can also rely on years of research (for example, Chung, Lam, & Liew, 2020; Denham, Wyatt, Bassett, Echeverria, & Knox, 2009; Sheldrick et al., 2019) from developmental sciences that have helped us understand developmental milestones or expected progression in children's social, emotional, and behavioral skills. Children achieve such milestones through natural cognitive processes and through learning. For example, toddlers begin to develop emotional awareness and, as their vocabulary grows, are able to label their emotions, which helps them to communicate how they are feeling and ask for help and support. As they grow into middle childhood, they are able to name the emotions of others and even regulate their responses to their own complex or confusing emotions, such as those they may experience when in conflict with peers. During adolescence, they learn cognitive strategies that may enable them to think positively, problem solve, and understand the perspectives of others. They also may become increasingly adept at coping strategies to help them relax, reframe negative thoughts, and communicate with trusted friends and family.

These examples of developmental milestones assume children will develop typically and attain social, emotional, and behavioral competencies that contribute to their overall resilience. Of course, this is not always the case, as we indicate in the statistics related to social and emotional concerns, such as depression and anxiety, presented

earlier in the chapter. Sometimes, children's "nature," in combination with less helpful nurture experiences, can facilitate negative outcomes. Regardless of their nature
or temperament, children can learn skills to navigate their day and regulate their
emotions. We cover this throughout the book.

Children's behaviors are constantly shaped by their interactions with the people,
symbols, and objects in their environments. (This is where building classrooms that
support resilience plays an important role!) As a model for understanding a child's
environment, consider psychologist Urie Bronfenbrenner's (1979) ecological framework, which is simplified in figure 1.1.

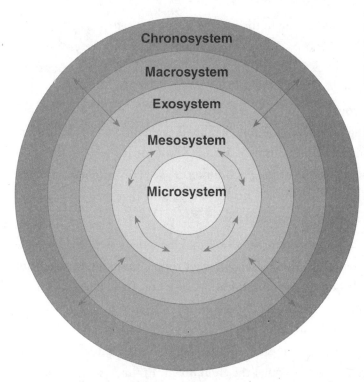

**Chronosystem**
Phase of life a child is
experiencing regarding
current situations: effects
of pandemic learning
environment over time

**Macrosystem**
Cultural elements that
affect a single child and
everyone around that child:
political climate

**Exosystem**
Factors that affect a child's
life but don't directly relate
to the child: caregiver's
work schedule, community
services, district curriculum
adoption practices

**Mesosystem**
Relationships between
microsystems: family-
school partnerships

**Microsystem**
Groups that most directly
influence a child: family,
school, and church

*Source: Adapted from Bronfenbrenner, 1979; Santa Clara University, n.d.*

**FIGURE 1.1:** Bronfenbrenner's (1979) ecological framework.

Children learn constantly from these interactions with their environment. For
example, according to Albert Bandura's social-cognitive theory, the adults in their
lives, such as parents and teachers, model particular behaviors and ways of being in
the world. Children see how adults behave, and they attend to such behavior, remember it, and often behave in similar ways (Bandura, 1986; Whitcomb, 2017). If they
see adults who work hard, engage in prosocial and communicative relationships, and

problem solve during conflict with others, then they will more likely adopt a similar approach; however, if they see coercive, harsh, or violent interactions, they may interact with others in the same way. When children behave in particular ways, they are often communicating a need. They may be communicating that they need attention or want an item, that they would like to be left alone, that they don't want to do something asked of them, or that they don't like feeling a certain emotion. Children who have learned adaptive communication skills can have their needs met in positive ways, but those who have not may misbehave to communicate, and sometimes the response to their behaviors reinforces this communication pattern, making it more likely to happen again in the future (Crone et al., 2015).

For example, imagine a child riding in the car and seeing the sign for an ice cream shop from the window as the car passes by. The child would love an ice cream cone and communicates that to Dad. In an environment in which a child has seen others or has been taught and encouraged to communicate his or her needs calmly, that child may ask, "Daddy, could we stop for ice cream today?" The dad may say, "Sure!" and pull into the parking lot, increasing the likelihood the child will communicate needs similarly in the future. The dad might also say, "Not today," leaving the child disappointed but, in an environment in which limits are set, this response may not be surprising. Children in such environments learn over time that they won't always get everything they want when they want it.

A child with an easygoing temperament, who can self-regulate well, may be able to roll with disappointment and think, "Maybe next time!" In an environment in which adults have modeled coercive communication, or with a child who has a more reactive and less regulated temperament, however, the response to not getting ice cream may be different. In this situation, if a parent says, "No ice cream today," the child may continue to push for ice cream, and maybe even scream for it, until the parent stops for ice cream, mostly to quiet the child down. In this case, the child has learned that screaming loud or long enough results in getting what he or she wants.

This behavior, which is often a combination of nature and nurture, will likely play out in classroom settings, too. For example, a middle school student, who does not like or feel particularly competent in mathematics, may put his or her head down when it is time to complete problems independently. The teacher may restate the expectation, "It's time to complete the problems." At this point, a student who has learned adequate coping strategies and has grown up in environments with clear expectations and predictable responses may give the problems a try. A student raised in a dynamic where he or she can push back on expectations until getting what he or she wants may continue to push back. When the teacher provides a prompt, the student may say, "I'm not doing the problems." If the teacher continues to engage with the student, the student may continue to escalate until asked to leave the room, successfully avoiding mathematics problems. Although students may enter your classroom with a range of nature and nurture experiences, we provide examples throughout this book to help you set up your classroom with a focus on consistency, connection, and compassion that supports all students with skills to increase their resilience.

## Risks and Protective Factors

For years, researchers have been intrigued by how it is that some children can be exposed to adverse experiences and still live healthy and productive lives, while others may struggle (for example, Buchanan, 2014; Rutter, 1985). In this section, we provide background on how risks and protective factors that are part of one's nature or interactions with the environment (nurture) interact and influence outcomes.

### Risks

For years, researchers have been interested in understanding biological, psychological, and social (nature and nurture) factors that contribute to poor outcomes or limited resilience, as well as in understanding protective factors that are most predictive of resilience. It is clear that there are individual personal characteristics, family characteristics, extrafamilial characteristics, and experiences that interact to shape a person's pathway. For example, one of the largest studies ever conducted on how adverse childhood experiences (ACEs)—in which children experienced or felt a threat of harm—relate to poor physical health, mental health, and academic achievement (Felitti et al., 1998). The study "was immensely beneficial as one of the first research reports to examine ACEs with a racially and socioeconomically diverse urban population and found clear differences in ACE exposure based on demographic characteristics" (Hanna Institute, n.d.).

ACEs may include poor physical or mental health of the child or parents, harsh parenting, child maltreatment, poverty, and domestic violence. ACEs may be chronic, such as poverty or abuse, or they may be one-time traumatic events, such as a parent's death or a natural disaster. The more ACEs one experiences, the more likely one will experience poor outcomes, such as poor physical health, mental illness, and limited educational attainment. For example, the Philadelphia Urban ACE Survey (Public Health Management Corporation, 2013) replicated the original ACE study; however, this study included participants with more socioeconomic and racial diversity, who endorsed experiencing more ACEs than in previous studies. Questions on the survey also included additional environmental factors related to experiencing racism and witnessing violence (Public Health Management Corporation, 2013). Approximately 70 percent of participants experienced one ACE, while 37 percent reported having experienced four or more ACEs; those who experienced four or more ACEs were more likely to be smokers, to experience mental health concerns such as depression, and to not complete high school than those with three or fewer ACEs (Public Health Management Corporation, 2013).

Living under adverse conditions can alter how a student understands the world. Such students may be more likely to develop social information processing deficits, where they experience interactions with others or cues in the environment as threatening. They may be more emotionally reactive in nonthreatening situations, feel angry or scared more often, and be less able to regulate these uncomfortable emotions (McLaughlin & Lambert, 2017). Further, they may be more likely to struggle with sustaining attention during tasks in school (Whiting, Wass, Green, & Thomas, 2021). These students may seem like they are always in a state of fight, flight, freeze, or fawn (acting helpless) where aggressive, withdrawn, or avoidant patterns of behavior are likely (Barlow, 2002; Cannon, 1927; Walker, 2013). Students who are withdrawn may quietly disengage from activity (for example, stare out the window or put their heads down on their desks), while students who are avoidant may also disengage but may do it in a more externalized manner (yelling or leaving the room, for example).

Let's break this down further to truly understand how adversity can affect the brain, endocrine, and even immune systems of a student, which will then influence his or her behavior. First, consider how stress and anxiety affect the human body. You can think of stress as a disruption of homeostasis, or stability (Whiting et al., 2021). Imagine that an experience causes a student to experience fear or anxiety. The brain, specifically the amygdala, processes this emotion and alerts the hypothalamus that there is danger. The hypothalamus in turn signals the release of hormones such as adrenaline, which results in increased heart rate, sweaty palms, and other physical manifestations of stress. The hypothalamic-pituitary-adrenal axis, a set of complicated interactions between systems, is also activated and is responsible for ensuring the release of cortisol from the adrenal glands during these periods of stress. Cortisol provides added energy to enable someone to fight, flee, freeze, or fawn (Harvard Health Publishing, 2020).

These are natural systems, and when there is limited stress in a student's life, these systems will return to a state of homeostasis once the stress is over. Experiencing feelings of stress or anxiety from time to time can help students learn, perform, and achieve. Studies have also found that when students experience too much stress and too much cortisol in an ongoing way, their physical and mental health may be impacted. For example, such students may experience limited problem-solving skills and cognitive rigidity, which are symptoms of anxiety (Lee, Jamieson, Miu, Josephs, & Yeager, 2018). Too much cortisol may weaken one's immune system and increase feelings of anxiety, for example (Whiting et al., 2021).

Imagine a six-year-old student, Natalia, who has repeatedly witnessed domestic violence at home. This student also lives in a community where violence is a norm, and she does not have any supportive adults to whom she feels connected. Imagine the child was born with a more reactive temperament and has never been able to self-soothe very well. In this scenario, she has experienced multiple ACEs and consequently experiences *toxic stress* in which her body's stress response system is on overload. The student might be prone to anger and feel threatened much of the time. When she is at school and the teacher gives her critical feedback on her homework, she may rip up the paper or express extreme anger in what most would consider a fairly typical learning situation. Without protective mechanisms or preventative measures to buffer the exposure to ACEs, Natalia will likely continue to struggle with misperceptions of threat in her environment. This will influence her relationships with others and her ability to attend to her learning.

Not all children will experience the number of ACEs that a student like Natalia does. Her example is an extreme case. An adolescent boy, Mike, who has grown up with a mother who has experienced episodes of major depression, represents a less extreme example of an adverse childhood experience. His mother has what one may call a *flat affect*, in which her emotions rarely seem to vary. At times when she is feeling severely depressed, she retreats to her room and sleeps a lot. In this scenario, this child is growing up with an adult model who experiences limited joy or optimism and whose go-to coping strategy is sleep. Given the research on the relationship between depressed mothers and their children, he may experience behavioral concerns or depressive symptoms himself as he develops (Netsi et al., 2018). It should further be noted that not all children who have been exposed to ACEs, such as this young girl and adolescent boy, will experience negative outcomes. Some children may be resilient, due to their exposure to protective factors.

## Protective Factors

As researchers have become more knowledgeable about how risk factors influence a child's development, they have also pursued studies on the concept of resilience—the ability of some individuals to succeed in the face of adversity. Protective factors buffer some individuals from poor outcomes (Sharma, Mustanski, Dick, Bolland, & Kertes,

2019). For example, children who have access to at least one supportive relationship with an adult may be more likely to experience a healthier path in life (Doll & Lyon, 1998; Sharma et al., 2019). Research even indicates how the brain can be different for children experiencing such a protective mechanism: Children who have experienced trauma may perceive less threat in their environment if they have had a supportive relationship with their mother (McLaughlin & Lambert, 2017). Other protective factors include involvement with prosocial community organizations, such as recreational sports and clubs, and individual characteristics such as an easygoing temperament, high IQ, strong language skills, well-developed self-regulation skills, good social skills, or a generally optimistic attitude (Doll & Lyon, 1998; Kim, Oesterle, Hawkins, & Shapiro, 2015).

Schools can play a major role in creating protective environments for students. Protective factors in schools include practices that provide students with opportunities for consistency, connection, and compassion. These elements occur in practices, for example, where teachers and staff clearly define expectations for behavior (consistency), reinforce a growth mindset, meaning intelligence can be changed and enhanced (compassion; Yeager et al., 2019), and model healthy social and emotional behaviors and relationships (connection; Bear, 2010). Here, students can learn about building healthy relationships through their experiences with others, such as teachers and peers. Further, schools can be a place where students learn necessary skills for social and emotional development through explicit instruction. Such skills—social and self-awareness, self-management, relationship skills, and responsible decision making—support resilience and are associated with competencies defined by CASEL (2020).

Finally, schools can be environments that demonstrate reflection and compassion. When adults respond to each other and to students with an understanding of why they may be behaving in certain ways, it is more likely that they will respond with compassion. If a teacher who has a relationship with Natalia, for example, sees her rip up her paper in frustration, that teacher may be more likely to reflect on how to maintain high expectations for Natalia and to differentiate critical feedback delivery for better results next time.

## The School Day Experience

Now that we have learned about the biological, psychological, and social factors that contribute to children's development, let's take a moment to read the following case scenarios to better understand how these factors may interact and what they may look like when students and teachers interact in the classroom. We will return to the classrooms of Ms. Vogt and Mr. Matheson. Remember, these are teachers that have worked diligently to create classrooms based on consistency, connection, and compassion. Within these classrooms, we would like you to read about two students who come to school each day with a multitude of strengths as well as exposure to a number of risks.

## Natalia and Ms. Vogt

Let's continue with our reflection with Natalia and consider what a school day might be like for her. As noted before, Natalia is a young student, a first grader in an urban school setting. Natalia has a long history of witnessing domestic violence at home. Her father frequently is physically violent with her mother. He often leaves for days at a time, comes back and apologizes, and then is easily angered once again. Natalia lives in a neighborhood where poverty and gang violence are the norm, so she is not often allowed to play outside or have playdates with peers. As a baby, Natalia cried often, was not easily soothed, and her mother experienced ongoing depression. Due to her depression, Natalia's mother was often home but not often available to meet Natalia's social and emotional needs. As Natalia grew, she was hypervigilant and often experienced feelings of fear and anger while in her home environment. She did not receive positive attention very often and had learned that she could get attention when she was upset. When she has limited time with her mother during the day or wants something she can't have, she often gets so upset that she destroys items in her room or in her house. During these episodes, Natalia's mother either yells or gives Natalia what she wants so that she quiets down. Given the complexity of her home life and the interactions she has observed between her parents over time, Natalia also is afraid of making a mistake, particularly when her father is around. When her father corrects her behavior or yells, she feels afraid and confused.

Given the numerous ACEs that Natalia has already experienced in her short life, let's imagine what a day in first grade might be like for her. Consider that Natalia is not used to a predictable environment, positive adult attention, or exposure to peer relationships. Consider further that Natalia may be lagging in her social and emotional skill development and that she may experience frustration and sometimes fear while navigating a new and unfamiliar environment at school.

Let's imagine that Natalia has Ms. Vogt for a teacher. As noted earlier in the chapter, Ms. Vogt has given a great deal of thought to how to develop a classroom based on consistency, connection, and compassion. After morning circle, students transition to independent work, which most often relates to the minilesson objectives. Since the first day of school, Natalia has loved Ms. Vogt. She is kind, warm, and gives her positive attention that she has not experienced very often in her life. She likes her so much that she would like to sit next to her whenever she can during morning meeting, raise her hand and answer all of the questions Ms. Vogt asks the class, and do the best independent work all of the time so that her teacher is very proud of her.

With the school year underway, Natalia often struggles. Sometimes, other students get a chance to sit next to Ms. Vogt during morning circle. Sometimes, Ms. Vogt does not call on Natalia, even when she raises her hand. And sometimes, Ms. Vogt tells Natalia to fix some of her letters on her writing paper. When these situations happen, Natalia feels very upset. She mostly cries, and sometimes she can't stop until Ms. Vogt takes her aside to talk with her. When Ms. Vogt corrects her writing, Natalia usually feels upset and very mad, and sometimes can't help it and rips her paper into pieces. Ms. Vogt also seems upset when Natalia does this, which is a little scary for Natalia, but Ms. Vogt always does the same thing, which Natalia actually finds quite comforting. (Imagine the patience and self-regulation Ms. Vogt needs to do the same thing each time!) She directs Natalia to the cooldown area in the classroom, where Natalia can calm her body. The cooldown area is a quiet space or desk away from the bustle of the classroom where students can disengage, gather their thoughts, and not be distracted by the classroom. Natalia sits in the cooldown area and looks at the pictures there, with cartoons of children sitting comfortably and breathing deeply, and these remind her to take deep breaths. When Natalia calms down, Ms. Vogt usually comes over and tells her to clean up the paper that she tore up and reminds Natalia that it is OK to make mistakes and to ask for help if she needs it during writing time.

In addition to emerging problems in the classroom, Natalia also seems to have a hard time in less-structured situations, such as lunch and recess. Having not grown up with siblings and having limited opportunities for play with peers at home, Natalia finds lunch and recess to be overwhelming. She often feels like students do not like her or are maybe even angry with her. During recess, she often stands by the recess monitor, Ms. Lombard. Ms. Lombard is nice and sometimes plays catch with Natalia. Natalia wants to join some of the other games that the students are playing, but she is afraid to ask. She also feels too nervous to ask someone to play with her. While Natalia has developed a connection with Ms. Lombard, she likely needs help, or further intervention, to develop the skills to engage in peer interactions at recess time. Though Ms. Vogt has come to understand Natalia's behavior and has developed a relationship with her, Ms. Lombard may not know her as well or be as attuned to her needs on the playground.

In this scenario, it is clear that Natalia has endured some challenges in her life-time. It is also clear that Ms. Vogt and Ms. Lombard have provided her with positive connections and a consistent environment. Ms. Vogt has been compassionate and understanding toward Natalia, and she has maintained high expectations for her. In other words, Natalia's exposure to adverse experiences does not limit her opportunities to flourish within a positive classroom environment.

### Mike and Mr. Matheson

Turning our attention to Mike, let's recall that he is a ninth-grade student who has been exposed to adverse experiences, but fewer than those Natalia has endured. His mother suffers from a major depressive disorder, and Mike has grown up in a household in which a range of emotions is rarely expressed. Those around him have typically shown a fairly pessimistic glass-half-empty mindset. Mike lives with both his mother and father and has an older brother in college. They are a middle-class family, living in a house near the school.

Mike is a freshman this year, and he seems to be doing OK transitioning to high school. He is averaging Cs in his classes. He seems capable of the workload, but he often does not turn in homework. His favorite class is English. He likes that his teacher, Mr. Matheson, is animated, interested in the students, and enthusiastic about the books they read (connection). Even though English is his favorite class, Mike sometimes wonders why he should bother turning in the work—it is not like anything he turns in will be that good. Mike has a few good friends at school, but he is also among the quieter of the students with whom he spends time.

As we learned earlier, Mr. Matheson runs a tight ship and has clear instructional objectives and routines for each class period (consistency). He also has recently instituted a mood check at the beginning of class, and he likes to make a point of connecting with each student throughout the year (connection, compassion). He often takes time at the end of class to informally chat with students and find out about their sporting events, interests, and other aspects of their lives.

Recently, Mr. M. has been a little concerned about Mike. Mike generally produces work of adequate quality, but there have been times when he has not turned in homework. Mike is quiet, and during mood checks, when asked how he's doing, rarely varies from responding "OK" or "Tired." Although Mr. Matheson communicates very clear expectations for class discussions, group work, and homework, Mike just seems a little withdrawn and doesn't always perform up to what Mr. M thinks is his potential. Mr. Matheson realizes that many might just think of Mike as lazy, but he wants to dig a little deeper with a one-to-one mood check to understand why

Mike seems withdrawn and if there is anything he can do to support him in class (compassion). He also decides to help Mike set some goals to improve the quality and timeliness of his work.

Again, in this scenario, we can see that Mike has experienced hardship and may even be presenting with symptoms of depression. In this example, Mr. Matheson is another teacher who has purposefully used strategies that provide consistency and structure in the classroom and practices that ensure ongoing positive and compassionate connections with students.

## ····▶ Key Points

In this chapter, we delved into biological, psychological, and social factors that foster resilience—for example, positive relationships with parents or teachers, positive affect—and those that do not—for example, inconsistent environments and harsh adult-child interactions. We featured a discussion of risk and protective factors that interact with one another to create a profile for students that show up in our classrooms. We introduced two students and their teachers and the perspectives and experiences that they may bring to the school environment. These examples provided an opportunity to understand some of the simple practices teachers may institute to foster consistency, connection, and compassion as well as the complexity of current student social, emotional, and behavioral needs.

As we delve into the following chapters, we encourage you to reflect on your own practices as well as the student needs present in your classrooms. Do these scenarios resonate with you? To what extent do you feel like you understand why children behave in the ways that they do? To what extent have you explicitly thought through strategies that offer consistency, connection, and compassion?

# CHAPTER 2

# Using Universal Practices to Promote Consistency

This chapter's purpose is to provide teachers with universal strategies to design a consistent classroom environment that can serve as a protective factor and promote resilience for all students. These universal strategies are best practices that form the foundation for consistency in the classroom. Here, *universal* simply refers to practices that all students are exposed to.

Without structure and consistency in a classroom environment, there is ambiguity. Ambiguity often leads to confusion, and this confusion may devolve into problematic student behavior or anxiety. By providing consistency and eliminating any ambiguity, the classroom becomes more predictable and thus classrooms feel safer for students (CESE, 2020; Pickens & Tschopp, 2017; Simonsen et al., 2015; Thapa, Cohen, Guffey, & Higgins-D'Alessandro, 2013). This is particularly important for students with trauma or adverse childhood experiences, as they may view unstructured or unpredictable environments as anxiety-provoking or threatening (Cummings et al., 2017).

Researchers have identified a number of evidence-based strategies that promote consistency in the classroom (for example, CESE, 2020; Greenberg, Putman, & Walsh 2014; Simonsen et al., 2008; Simonsen & Myers, 2015). These strategies ensure predictability and consistency, thus laying the foundation of a safe and secure environment that supports resilience (Durlak et al., 2011; Jennings & Greenberg, 2009; Pickens & Tschopp, 2017; Simonsen et al., 2008; Taylor et al., 2017). In the upcoming sections, we outline strategies that start with arranging the physical environment of the classroom. We then discuss teaching classroom routines to students as a means to create structure. We build on that structure by then discussing teaching prosocial skills to students, particularly classroom expectations and specific SEL competencies. We also discuss how to prompt students and provide ongoing teaching to ensure students incorporate the skills into their repertoire. (Feedback is also critical to ensuring students learn prosocial skills, but we discuss that topic in chapter 3, page 65, because teachers can use feedback-driven reinforcement to also build connection among students.)

## Be Mindful of Classroom Arrangement

One way that we can create unambiguous environments is to focus on the physical arrangement of the classroom environment. Although it may sound odd—how does physical space bolster resilience in students?—the idea is to create predictability with movement in the classroom and to decrease any environmental factors that may lead to conflicts or issues in the classroom (Trussell, 2008; Wong, Wong, Jondahl, & Ferguson, 2018). For example, crowded areas may lead students to bump into each other or to inadvertently violate personal space, which could be stressful for some students. Predictability and order with the layout increase students' security and comfort because they know where things are physically located and how movement occurs in the classroom (Cummings et al., 2017).

It's important to consider traffic flow in the classroom, starting with student seating. Psychology scholar Natalie Marie Robichaux (2016) presents evidence to suggest that traditional seating arrangements, such as having desks in rows, are most likely to decrease disruptive behavior in the classroom. However, teachers may need configurations in which students can collaborate more readily, such as placing desks in pairs or small groups. Whichever way you decide to seat students, you can reduce the possibility of unwanted behavior by considering how easily students are able to move about based on the seating arrangement. You can also limit problematic behaviors with clear expectations for behavior in any particular part of the classroom. (For help with that, see Creating Consistency, page 6, and Teach Prosocial Skills, page 40.)

There is also the consideration of arranging the classroom to support students' ages, or one's teaching style or methods. In preschool and elementary classrooms, teachers will probably have a rug area, an in-class library to organize, or additional tables or centers to arrange. Ensuring easy movement back and forth to these areas, including visual cues to support movement and indicate how many students are allowed in an area, is important to consider. Secondary classrooms may have independent seats for whole-group instruction, as well as a group table for small groups or cooperative learning approaches.

These are other considerations, such as the following.

- Place frequently used materials in areas so as to prevent congestion or traffic jams. For example, keep the pencil sharpener, wastebasket, or computers away from students' desks to avoid distraction or a chance for students to disrupt each other (Harlacher, 2015; Trussell, 2008).

- Create an area to allow students to have time to decompress or process away from the action of the classroom. For example, a rug area with pillows or a desk set aside from the bustle and flow of the day. This gives students a space to access throughout the day to manage their emotions, use coping skills, or simply take a quiet break away from others (Minahan, 2019; Norris, 2003). In elementary classrooms, the cooldown area may be a space with a comfortable chair and posters with prompts for stopping and breathing. For secondary classrooms, it may simply be a table at the back of the room where students can work if they need space from peers or their regular seating arrangement.

In figure 2.1 (page 36), we offer an example of a classroom arrangement that supports resilience. As you can see, the desks are arranged to support easy movement throughout the classroom, including an easy view of the board for all students. Students can reach high-traffic areas, such as the sink, shelving, or closet, without interrupting other students. The small-group table is away from students' seats, which allows the teacher to view all students while they are seated at the small-group table. There are designated areas for students to do cooperative group work.

Also note, there is a designated cooldown area with a desk and carpet that students can use when processing emotions or practicing a coping skill. The cooldown area is an important part of a classroom that supports resilience, as it allows a private space for a student to process and regulate their emotions. The teacher, no matter where he or she is in the room, can see a student using this area. This is an area that the teacher can prompt a student to visit if the student is struggling to manage a strong

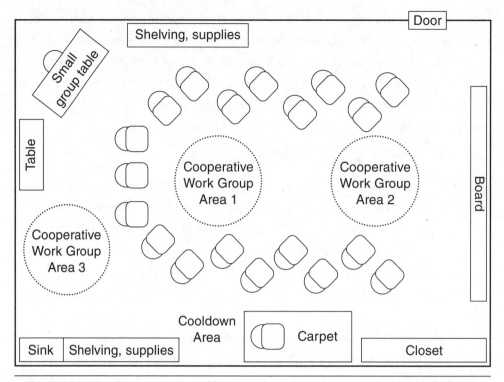

**FIGURE 2.1:** Example of a classroom arrangement that supports resilience.

emotion, or that a student can indicate the need to visit (Minahan, 2019). Teachers should communicate explicit expectations for how students should use such a spot, to ensure that they access it appropriately. These expectations might include language from the classroom expectations.

See the reproducible "Checklist for a Classroom's Physical Space" (page 64) for help creating a classroom arrangement that supports student resilience.

## Establish Routines

Creating routines can help teachers manage the day's flow and prevent students constantly asking them for certain things, but it can also lessen the anxiety a student may have about how to navigate the classroom (Cummings et al., 2017; Minahan, 2019; Pickens & Tschopp, 2017). By outlining routines and then teaching them to students, teachers increase consistency. Routines also reinforce predictability. In addition to clarity in the physical space, predictability in how the day unfolds is helpful for all students, but particularly for students dealing with trauma or mental health concerns (Minahan, 2019; Pickens & Tschopp, 2017). The following list provides strategies for creating predictable schedules—routines—that help students develop resilience by ensuring predictability and consistency.

- Provide a schedule of events on a whiteboard or on a small piece of paper for students and be sure to notify them of any changes well in advance. Offer necessary coping skills, such as positive self-talk or relaxation techniques, or processing time for students who have difficulty with changes in schedules.

- Break longer instructional periods into smaller, manageable chunks (Fonollosa, Neftci, & Rabinovich, 2015).

- Schedule less-desirable tasks before more-desirable tasks, such as independent work before peer or group work to provide incentive for completing the former task (Alberto & Troutman, 2013).

- Consider brain breaks throughout the day to ensure engagement and energy. Energy levels dip in the afternoon (Katznelson, n.d.), and using brain breaks and movement can offset those dips.

In addition to setting up the environment, teachers can also outline specific routines for students to follow to get their needs met (Harlacher, 2015; Simonsen et al., 2008; Stronge, Ward, & Grant, 2011) or to complete tasks (Harlacher, 2015; Simonsen & Myers, 2015). For example, students will need routines for requesting a pass to use the restroom, asking for help during independent work, using the cooldown area, and responding when processing emotions with classmates.

To identify routines, teachers can think about a needed routine (such as lining up at the end of class) and then the goal (lining up quickly and keeping hands and feet to themselves). From there, they can outline a series of steps to reach that goal. The more concrete, the better. Once the teacher has outlined the steps, then he or she can move to teaching the routines to students.

We suggest adapting the tried-and-true model of gradual release of responsibility to teach routines (Fisher & Frey, 2008, 2014, 2021), which is described in table 2.1 (page 38).

**Table 2.1: Gradual Release of Responsibility Process for Teaching Routines**

| Teaching Step | Description | Example |
|---|---|---|
| Model | The teacher explicitly shares and models the routine for students. | The teacher models the routine for using the cooldown area, outlining each step, such as (1) ask to use the area, (2) select a coping skill to use (for example, sit quietly, journal feelings, draw, and so on), (3) set a timer for five minutes, and (4) use the coping skill until the timer runs out. The teacher models what each step of the routine looks like. |
| Lead | The teacher asks students to perform the routine and ensures accuracy with each step. The teacher corrects any mistakes and has students perform the step correctly. | Students independently demonstrate each step of the routine, and the teacher has them redo any mistakes the correct way. For example, the teacher has students demonstrate that they can set the timer and then stop using the cooldown area when the timer alarms. |
| Test | Students perform the routine independently and without errors. | Students perform all steps of the routine without errors. For example, students select a coping skill and use it accurately without prompting or guidance. |

*Source: Adapted from Fisher & Frey, 2021.*

Transitions are important classroom routines that can be used to further build consistency. The overall goal of a transition is for students to wrap up the current activity and to quickly move on to the next activity with the required materials ready. Transitions can be trigger points for students who are resistant to changes in their schedule or when students must shift from a certain activity to one that may be less desirable (Minahan, 2019; Pickens & Tschopp, 2017). Any teacher can attest to the behavioral concerns that arise when students don't know how to transition from one activity to another, as they will certainly find ways to entertain themselves or fill their time when they're unsure what to do next. The use of transitions contributes to the predictability in environments that benefits all students (Harlacher & Rodriguez, 2018) but particularly those with social, emotional, and behavioral needs (Ingram, n.d.; Minahan, 2019; Pickens & Tschopp, 2017).

It's important to teach transitions in a way that's efficient and not stress inducing for students. We outline the general steps for transitioning here.

1. The teacher provides a signal that cues students to clean up their area and put away materials and supplies for the current activity or task.

2. Students move to the next activity in an organized manner. For example, they put away their mathematics books and homework, and then move to the area in the room for literacy instruction.

3. Students get out any necessary materials or supplies needed for the next activity.

4. Students indicate that they are individually ready by sitting quietly with eyes on the teacher or offering a verbal cue that is previously agreed on, such as saying, "Ready!" out loud.

Further, we offer some tips to ensure smooth transitions.

- Provide students with visual cues or advanced notice before a transition so they are not caught off-guard. This can be a couple of minutes prior or more time based on individual student needs (Pierce, Spriggs, Gast, & Luscre, 2013).

- Practice transitions until they take one to three minutes to complete, depending on the activities transitioning from and transitioning to. Transitions over more than a few minutes are associated with increased rates of problematic behavior (Buck, 1999; Mercurio, Schmitt, Loftus-Rattan, & McCallum, 2021; Yarbrough, Skinner, Lee, & Lemmons, 2004).

- Consider activities for students to do, such as prereading instructions for an activity or writing an answer to a prompt, while they wait for others to transition.

- Play music in the background to create a soothing environment that can reduce any stress some students may feel in connection to transitioning from a preferred activity to a less than preferred activity.

- Use reinforcement, such as verbal praise or tokens within a token economy, as a means to ensure quick transitions (we discuss reinforcement more in the next chapter).

- Use fun and engaging signals or cues for transition times, such as providing the start of a music lyric that students finish or a rhythmic clap.

Routines are an important part of creating consistency to ensure students know how to navigate the classroom and to provide them with predictability and consistency.

## Teach Prosocial Skills

Prosocial skills are foundational to creating a consistent classroom, as they provide structure for how students should engage with each other and clarify what is expected of them. As a general term, *prosocial skills* describe a set of skills that are associated with healthy social and emotional functioning (Gresham, 2002). These skills and the resulting behaviors benefit both the person and the larger society as a whole (Dunlap et al., 2009; George et al., 2009; Harlacher & Rodriguez, 2018). That teaching begins with initial instruction and then moves to providing multiple opportunities to practice the prosocial skills.

### Initial Instruction

For a classroom built on resilience, *prosocial skills* refer to two things: (1) classroom expectations and (2) CASEL's (2020) SEL competencies, as initially outlined in table I.3 (page 7). Figure 2.2 illustrates this relationship.

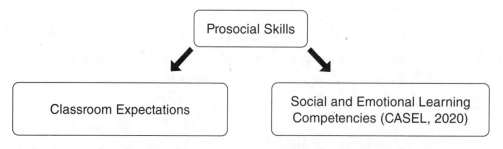

**FIGURE 2.2:** Prosocial skills map for *consistency*.

Classroom expectations form the culture and identity of the classroom and are general descriptions of expected behaviors or skills for success in the classroom (Harlacher, 2015; Simonsen & Myers, 2015). Although the expectations cover a wide range of skills and behaviors, they may not cover all of the needed prosocial skills to bolster resilience. Further, classroom expectations are critical for a consistent and predictable classroom, but teachers may find the need to target the specific teaching of certain prosocial skills that support resilience, such as self-management of one's emotions or recognizing emotions in others.

To that end, teachers can supplement the expectations by also teaching specific SEL competencies. For example, a high school may have classroom expectations that are *respect yourself, respect others,* and *respect your surroundings.* These are good expectations that create a positive environment, and they clearly outline behaviors that contribute to a positive environment. However, a teacher may find that they also need to teach students more explicit skills related to social awareness or self-awareness. (You'll recall social awareness and self-awareness are two of the five SEL competencies.) Consequently, this teacher would supplement the expectations by also teaching lessons on social awareness and self-awareness. Together, the teacher creates a consistent structure in the classroom with clear classroom expectations and then also supplements needed skills in students by directly teaching SEL competencies. We discuss teaching classroom expectations before teaching SEL competencies.

## Classroom Expectations

Students come to school with a variety of experiences and backgrounds, and their perception of what is acceptable in a classroom may differ from yours (Harlacher, 2015; Simonsen & Myers, 2015). Explicitly teaching what behavior is expected in the classroom creates consistency and predictability in the classroom, helping students learn how to be successful. In turn, this leads to a safer environment, providing security for all students (Harlacher, 2015; Pickens & Tschopp, 2017; Simonsen & Myers, 2015). In particular, students with adverse childhood experiences may experience anxiety in new environments, so creating security and predictability can reduce anxiety and allow them to be more ready to learn (Minahan, 2019; Pickens & Tschopp, 2017). We've also heard the argument that teaching expectations is important for elementary students but that middle and high school students should already know what is expected of them. Although secondary students will hopefully have had more exposure to behavioral expectations in previous classes, consider the feelings of safety, security, and clarity that you would hope to experience when you enter a new job or a new committee. Despite your experience and years working, having expectations defined for this new setting helps. In fact, research is pretty clear on this point: all people feel better and perform better when expectations are defined and communicated well (Meyer & Bartels, 2017).

A common group of classroom expectations is *be safe, be respectful,* and *be responsible* (McKevitt & Braaksma, 2008), as these largely cover any behavior or skill needed in a classroom. We offer other examples of classroom expectations in table 2.2 (page 42). In the table, notice that teachers can phrase expectations in the form of an

**Table 2.2: Examples of Classroom Expectations**

| School Level | Examples |
|---|---|
| Preschool | Be Safe, Be Kind |
| Elementary | Respect Ourselves, Respect Others, Respect Property<br>PRIDE: Prepared, Respectful, Include Others, Be Dedicated, Be Engaged |
| Middle | PAWS: Be Prepared, Act Responsibly, Work Hard, and Show Respect<br>High Five: Respectful, Responsible, Follow Directions, Hands and Feet to Yourself, Be There and Be Ready<br>ROAR: Respect, Organization, Attentiveness, Responsibility |
| High | POWER: Perseverance, Ownership, Working Together, Engagement, Respect<br>PRIDE: Preparation, Respect, Integrity, Diligence, Etiquette<br>Safety, Respect, Responsibility |

acronym (such as PAWS) or word them in a way that makes it easy to remember by raising one's hand (as with High Five).

Generally speaking, we believe the following about expectations (George et al., 2009; Harlacher, 2015; Simonsen & Myers, 2015).

- They should empower students by being positively worded (tell students what to do, not what not to do, for example, "Be productive," versus, "Don't waste time").
- They should reflect the desired character in the classroom.
- They should be limited to five total (more than five is hard to remember) and be culturally and developmentally sensitive.
- They should apply to all settings and routines in the classroom.

Once there are a few positively stated expectations, students need them defined across the various activities and contexts in the classroom. As seen in figure 2.3, each expectation can be defined for each context, thus creating a classroom matrix in which the expectations are translated into rules (George et al., 2009; Harlacher, 2015; McKevitt & Braaksma, 2008). This matrix visually depicts the range of the expectations. For instance, *responsibility* during seat work might look like staying focused on one's work and putting your cell phone in a designated spot so that you

| Expectation | Class Meeting (Whole Group) | Team Work (Small Group) | Seat Work (Individual) | Cooldown Space | Transitions |
|---|---|---|---|---|---|
| **Be respectful.** | • Listen to others who are speaking.<br>• Raise your hand to speak. | • Take turns talking.<br>• Listen to everyone's ideas.<br>• Do your share of the work. | • Focus on your work.<br>• Ask for help if you don't understand.<br>• Keep your voice low so others can work. | • Use the space when you need it.<br>• Follow instructions on the cooldown poster.<br>• Be considerate of others who need the space. | • Move on to the next activity or location on time.<br>• Listen for instructions.<br>• Leave your area clean. |
| **Be safe.** | • Stay in your space. | • Pay attention to personal space.<br>• Share materials appropriately and carefully. | • Stay in your work space.<br>• Keep your materials organized.<br>• Clean up when you are finished. | • Gently use the cooldown materials.<br>• Keep other items at your desk. | • Walk.<br>• Give others space to move. |
| **Be kind.** | • Pay attention to how others might think or feel by noticing their body language.<br>• Notice others' good ideas by paraphrasing what you hear. | • Pay attention to how others might think or feel.<br>• Notice others' good ideas.<br>• Try your best to learn from mistakes. | • Pat yourself on the back for working hard.<br>• Try your best to learn from your mistakes. | • Give yourself a moment to calm your body. | • Help others who need it. |

Source: Adapted from George et al., 2009; Harlacher, 2015; McKevitt & Braaksma, 2008.

**FIGURE 2.3:** Example of a classroom expectations matrix.

Visit *MarzanoResources.com/reproducibles for a free reproducible version of this figure.*

can't use it during that time. By defining what each expectation looks like across the different activities or contexts in the classroom, students know what responsibility looks like and sounds like concretely. Further, the routines that we discussed earlier can be referenced on the matrix itself. For example, the routine for entering the classroom can be a column within the matrix or certain routines, such as asking for help (where, under responsibility for seat work, the teacher can indicate "This matrix is then printed or created as a poster, flyer, or other visual tool for both students and the teacher to access").

## Choosing Expectations

Many schools may have schoolwide expectations. If yours does, we strongly recommend adopting those expectations for the classroom. This creates consistency between the school and the classroom, thus avoiding any confusion for students (Harlacher, 2015; Harlacher & Rodriguez, 2018). In the absence of schoolwide expectations, there are various ways to create clear expectations for the classroom. Teachers can develop a list of expectations on their own, using data to identify them (George et al., 2009). For example, teachers can review referrals or review their list of behavior concerns in their classroom to identify a skill they could teach to counter those concerns.

Another way to develop expectations is to think about what skills students need to be successful not only in the classroom but also beyond (George et al., 2009; Harlacher, 2015). A teacher can generate a list of adjectives or descriptors, such as *punctual, kind, invites others to join them,* and *able to keep track of assignments or homework,* and then combine them into three to five expectations that represent the values of the school and community, such as *considerate* and *responsible.* Teachers can also interview or talk with students and families about what values are important to them and then incorporate those values into the expectations.

Teachers can include students in the discussion of expectations, which helps create ownership of classroom norms (Harlacher, 2015). They can ask students, "What are three words that describe how you want to be treated in this classroom?" Have students write each of their three words on a separate sticky note and then post them on the wall. Sort the words together in ways that are similar. In our experience, the same types of words tend to be suggested (such as *respect, safe, kindness,* and *responsibility*). This way, you have systematically narrowed down a few key expectations with the support of students.

*Teaching Expectations*

After having selected expectations and defined them across routines and contexts within their teaching matrix (figure 2.3), teachers can then turn their attention to explicitly teaching them to students. This begins with creating lesson plans for each expectation. In figure 2.4, we offer a template for expectations, with example text italicized. The lesson consists of several steps, beginning with the name of the expectation and the rationale for why it's important. Examples and nonexamples are next, as they illustrate the boundaries and explicitness of the expectation.

| Step 1: Identify the expectation or expected behavior. | |
|---|---|
| Identified expectation: *Compassion* | |
| Step 2: Provide a rationale for teaching the expectation. | |
| Rationale: *It is important for us to have compassion because compassion shows we can understand what others feel and honor their needs. We can respect what others feel and create a classroom that is emotionally and personally safe.* | |
| Step 3: Define a range of examples. | |
| **Examples** | **Nonexamples** |
| 1. *A classmate shares during morning meeting that she had a rough night. You show compassion by making eye contact and paraphrasing her shared feelings.*<br>2. *A classmate accidentally bumps into you during transition time. You show compassion by seeing that he was in a hurry and bumping you was an accident. You ask if he's OK instead of being angry with him.*<br>3. *You see a mean post about a classmate on social media. You ask the poster to delete it, saying it's not kind to spread mean rumors about people.* | 1. *A classmate shares a personal story, and you smirk and laugh. You ask, "Why didn't you just shrug it off?"*<br>2. *A classmate bumps into you while gathering his things after class and getting out of his seat. You yell, "What's your problem?" instead of asking if he needs help.*<br>3. *You see a rumor about your teacher on social media. You laugh and share it with other classmates.* |

**FIGURE 2.4:** Example of a lesson plan to teach classroom expectations.          continued →

| Step 4: Describe activities or role playing for practice of expectation. |
| --- |
| Practice activities:<br>• Working in small groups, students create a video to teach others about compassion.<br>• Each Friday, students journal one way they followed the expectation that week. |
| Step 5: List methods to prompt or remind about the expectation. |
| Expectation reminder:<br>• Before class begins, have one or two students share how to show compassion during class. |
| Step 6: Describe how you will assess student progress. |
| Assessment criterion:<br>• Have a running log of instances when you witness compassion. At the end of the week, tally up the total and share with students. |

*Source: Adapted from Langland, Lewis-Palmer, & Sugai, 1998.*
*Visit **MarzanoResources.com/reproducibles** for a free reproducible version of this figure.*

With the examples, the teacher can outline the expectation across different routines. Teachers can develop some really creative "right way, wrong way" videos to help draw attention to the differences between examples and nonexamples of the expected behavior. Online resources such as those found at the Center on Positive Behavioral Interventions and Supports (www.pbis.org) and special education scholar Michael Kennedy's Homegrown SW-PBIS Videos (https://vimeo.com/groups/pbisvideos) provide good examples for creating such videos. The idea with use of examples and nonexamples within the lesson plan is to be as concrete and explicit as possible. Depending on the grade level, producing these explanatory videos can even be part of the lesson, with students forming production teams to create videos illustrating a specific expectation, as assigned by the teacher. This engages students in both creating and teaching the expectations.

Additionally, the lesson plan includes space for an engagement activity so that students can practice or apply the expectation to their own behavior. This step is critical for students to begin incorporating the skill into their repertoire (Frey, Elliott, & Miller, 2014; Gresham, 2002). You don't learn skills by talking about them alone, so practice and application are important here. Students can try the following in addition to producing videos.

- Role-play or write stories on characters demonstrating the expectations.
- Write letters to family members or community members about how students can display expectations.

- Design an app or video game to teach students the expectations.

- Read stories and look for expectations in the characters.

- Draw posters or create infographics of the expectations.

- Discuss the expectations and how they change across settings.

- Create a skit or school play to demonstrate the expectations.

It is best to have students only practice the "right way" to do the expectations, as you don't want them practicing errors or learning how not to meet the expectation. When having students practice the expectations, be sure to end with a positive example of meeting the expectation so that students have that as the last thing they see!

Steps 5 and 6 of the lesson plan are for the teacher to monitor and do. In step 5, teachers outline how they themselves will prompt the expectation moving forward. In step 6, they determine which data they'll use to monitor students' use of that expectation. We discuss prompting later in this chapter, and we discuss using data in depth in chapter 7 (page 153).

### Providing Follow-Up Instruction

Starting a school year by defining and teaching clear expectations for student behavior is important. However, teaching expectations just once on the first day of school is likely not enough for students to learn, remember, and follow new routines (Simonsen & Myers, 2015; Wong & Wong, 2018). After all, students need to hear new information at least eight times before they internalize it, and they need to hear it twenty-three times if it requires unlearning old, problematic behaviors (Wong & Wong, 2018).

Teach expectations and routines and have students practice them at the beginning of the year, but also think about other times and methods for teaching and practicing. Consider scheduling reminder lessons after students have had a break from school (such as winter break and spring break) or think about using data to guide reminder lessons for certain problematic behaviors, routines, or times of day (George et al., 2009; Harlacher & Rodriguez, 2018). For example, if students are receiving an increased amount of office referrals or peer complaints about certain behaviors, consider reteaching expectations.

---

**Practice in Action:** Teaching Respect

Mrs. Boyd had a middle school classroom where it was tough to teach. Students frequently interrupted each other (and her) and said rude things to each other. She decided to teach them two expectations: (1) respect toward staff and (2) respect toward others (Langland et al., 1998). She crafted two fifteen-minute lessons that included the skill name, examples and nonexamples, an activity such as role playing, and using precorrection and praise for the skill after teaching. Mrs. Boyd taught students one lesson on Monday and then spent ten minutes reviewing that lesson on Wednesday and Friday. The review lesson consisted of a group discussion with students in which they shared examples of respect they had seen the past few days and ways they showed respect themselves. She then taught the second lesson the following week. She then taught the second lesson the following week. After two weeks, Mrs. Boyd cut the rate of disrespectful behavior by half.

---

## SEL Competencies

Social and emotional learning is a set of competencies that enable people to navigate the social and emotional aspects of their life. As pointed out in this book's introduction, the five competencies outlined by CASEL (2020) are (1) self-awareness, (2) self-management, (3) social awareness, (4) relationship skills, and (5) responsible decision making. Students are more likely to develop resilience in structured classrooms with clear expectations and predictable routines (Skiba, Ormiston, Martinez, & Cummings, 2016). However, we encourage the active and explicit teaching of SEL skills to further nurture and bolster students' resilience (CASEL, 2020; Dusenbury et al., 2015; Gueldner, Feuerborn, Merrell, & Weissberg, 2020; Jennings & Greenberg, 2009; Norris, 2003). Teachers may find that teaching the classroom expectations may not be sufficient for meeting the needs of their students. For example, a teacher may find that their high school students are generally compliant and respectful in class and that they follow the classroom expectations, but they may need additional teaching of emotion regulation to navigate daily stressors from high school. Consequently, the teacher can provide lessons on SEL to their students to supplement the classroom expectations. In fact, students benefit more in classrooms that incorporate explicit instruction and practice opportunities in SEL competencies (Clarke et al., 2021; Durlak et al., 2011; Taylor et al., 2017).

Teaching SEL to students can contribute to equity within the classroom. Specifically, creating a classroom that has consistency and teaches SEL can result in a nurturing, safe environment that respects the diverse backgrounds of students. Additionally, teaching SEL and discussing emotional growth with students encourage authentic connection and relationships (Leverson et al., 2021; Schlund, Jagers, & Schlinger, 2020).

Incorporating the teaching of SEL into a classroom doesn't have to be daunting. In fact, it is tough to teach classroom expectations without also teaching SEL competencies! As we noted in the introduction (page 1), if your classroom expectations are *be safe*, *be respectful*, and *be responsible*, teaching those will inevitably overlap with the SEL competencies outlined by CASEL (2020) that are responsible decision making (be responsible), social awareness (be safe), and relationship skills (be respectful).

A straightforward way to teach SEL skills is to include them within the classroom matrix (Barrett, Eber, McIntosh, Perales, & Romer, 2018). Teachers can call attention to specific skills related to SEL for a given setting, such as "pause and identify my feelings before responding" for discussions or online settings or "invite others to join" for group work settings (Barrett et al., 2018; see figure 2.3, page 43). Teachers can then include examples and nonexamples of those skills as part of the teaching within that lesson. For example, when teaching safety as an expectation, an example may be, "During class online, a classmate makes a critique of your assignment that you shared with class. You take a deep breath and notice you feel tense from that comment before responding to your classmate," versus the nonexample of, "During class online, a classmate makes a critique of your assignment that you shared with class. You respond defensively by saying they're not smart enough to critique you."

Teachers can also embed certain routines related to SEL into the matrix and provide instruction on that routine to help students further learn and practice prosocial skills. For example, a teacher may teach self-management in the context of a certain setting; for example, when using the cooldown area in the classroom, students can use a relaxation technique to learn self-management of their emotions. The teacher then provides teaching and practice of that relaxation technique. Here, the teacher can outline the steps of the technique—(1) pause and ask yourself how you feel, (2) take a deep breath and clear your mind by saying "Shhh" to yourself or by picturing a pleasant image, and (3) take three deep breaths and focus on inhaling and exhaling—and provide some teaching and practice to students on how to use the relaxation technique.

Teachers can develop their own lessons to teach SEL, but there is a wide range of social and emotional curricula available that are developmentally appropriate, developed according to a research base, empirically tested, and meant to be delivered classwide. CASEL (n.d.) developed a protocol for vetting the highest quality curricula; visit https://pg.casel.org/review-programs for a list of curricula. These programs follow the research on effective instructional practices which are referred to as *SAFE*, so readers can have confidence they are following best practices (Jones et al., 2018; Payton et al., 2008).

- **Sequenced:** Sequenced instruction often includes a series of lessons or implementation of a curriculum with a clearly defined scope and progression.

- **Active:** Active practices include opportunities for student engagement and practice in social and emotional skills and strategies.

- **Focused:** Focused time should be allotted for instruction.

- **Explicit:** The instruction is for specific social and emotional skills.

If a teacher opts to make their own lessons on SEL competencies, they can use the lesson plan in figure 2.4 (page 45). In creating their own lessons, teachers can identify a given expectation and then teach skills related to that lesson. For example, if the classroom expectation is empathy, then they can also teach further skills related to empathy, such as compassion and cooperation. As another example, for the expectation *be safe*, teachers can teach more concrete skills, such as being on time and expressing one's emotions assertively and safely (Harlacher & Rodriguez, 2018).

In figure 2.5, we provide examples of expectations for a middle school classroom, the SEL curriculum a teacher has developed for two school months, and an example lesson plan. You can see the expectations of kindness and safety listed at the top row and then the specific skills the teacher will focus on each week. Each of the skills taught falls under one of the five SEL competencies. For example, *diversity acceptance* and *being neighborly and building community* fall under the SEL competency of relationship skills, while *patience and grace* and *active listening* fall under the SEL competency of social awareness. With this approach to creating an SEL curriculum, teachers can tailor their lessons each week or month to address specific skills in which their students need additional instruction.

| | Expectation: **Kindness** | Expectation: **Safety** |
|---|---|---|
| Week 1 | Diversity acceptance | Emotional safety |
| Week 2 | Being neighborly and building community | Creating a safe environment |
| Week 3 | Patience and grace | Active listening |
| Week 4 | (Review of lessons) | (Review of lessons) |

| Step 1: Identify the expectation or expected behavior. | |
|---|---|
| Identified expectation: Emotional safety | |
| Step 2: Provide a rationale for teaching the expectation. | |
| Rationale: Part of being safe includes not just physical safety, but emotional safety. We allow others to state their feelings without shame, ridicule, or being made fun of. We create a safe space for everyone to share their emotions. | |
| Step 3: Define a range of examples. | |
| **Examples** | **Nonexamples** |
| 1. Your classmate tells you that a comment made in class bothered him. You respond by saying, "That statement made you feel sad" to show that you understand his feelings.<br><br>2. You ask a friend how she's feeling, and you listen and repeat back what she says.<br><br>3. A classmate posts something mean on a social media platform. You message her privately and ask her to delete it because it would make others not want to log in to the platform. | 1. Your classmate tells you that a comment made in class bothered him. You laugh and tell him to not worry about it.<br><br>2. When your friend shares how she feels, you interrupt her to tell her about your day rather than listening and waiting until she's done.<br><br>3. A classmate posts something mean about someone online. Classmates reply and agree, which makes the targeted classmate feel teased and bullied. |

**FIGURE 2.5:** Example of a lesson plan for social and emotional competencies.

continued →

| Step 4: Describe activities or role playing for practice of expectation. |
| --- |
| Practice activities:<br>• Practice paraphrasing what others say in groups.<br>• Take a story the class is reading and identify the feelings that the characters have and if they feel safe or unsafe sharing them. |
| Step 5: List methods to prompt or remind about the expectation. |
| Expectation reminder:<br>• Remind students of ensuring people feel emotionally safe. Ask them to identify one thing they can do today to make others feel emotionally safe. |
| Step 6: Describe how you will assess student progress. |
| Assessment criterion:<br>• Have students self-report instances where they saw others feel emotionally safe each week. Document the occurrences and keep a running tally each week. |

*Source: Adapted from Langland et al., 1998.*

One strategy to help students develop resilience and build their own emotional awareness, and for teachers to understand students' triggers, is to provide students a brief lesson on emotional responses. For this lesson, teachers can select an emotion, such as anxiety, and discuss how anxiety affects one's thoughts, feelings, and behaviors (Gueldner et al., 2020). Students can then identify their own thoughts, feelings, and behaviors associated with that emotion by drawing them, selecting items from a checklist, or writing a summary of what they identified. From there, the teacher (and other students) can learn what to expect or see when students are feeling agitated or anxious.

Teachers can extend this lesson with a follow-up on identifying specific triggers for those emotions, thus helping both teachers and classmates understand students' triggers. We caution that if teachers ask students to discuss or identify triggers that they also give students time to process any emotions that may be stirred up by discussing triggers. We offer a brief summary of a lesson to use for this emotional awareness strategy in figure 2.6.

| Component | Description |
|---|---|
| **Introduction** | Introduce the lesson by telling students that they will identify anxiety and discuss how it is comprised of thoughts, feelings, and behaviors. |
| **Rationale** | Discuss the importance of knowing one's emotions and reactions so that one can fully understand and manage them. |
| **Content** | Share examples of thoughts, feelings, and behaviors associated with anxiety. For example, share your own thoughts, feelings, and behaviors or give a general description. Thoughts can include, "It's overwhelming" or "I can't do anything." Feelings can be panic or fear. Behavior can include both observable behaviors (not sitting still, wanting to pace) and physiological responses (heart racing, sweating, shortened breath). |
| **Engagement Activity** | Have students identify their own thoughts, feelings, and behaviors for anxiety. Ask students to share one by one or by volunteer. Then introduce an engagement or extension activity. For example, students can draw their behaviors on an outline of a person and add thought bubbles for their thoughts. They can write out a paragraph for thoughts, feelings, and behaviors. It's helpful to have students share a few things with the class or with the teacher so that others can be aware of how their emotions display themselves. |

**FIGURE 2.6:** Lesson plan on emotional awareness.

## Multiple Opportunities to Practice Prosocial Skills

Students who are taught prosocial skills through explicit lessons will not necessarily use those skills unless they have multiple opportunities across time and contexts to practice (Alberto & Troutman, 2013; Daly et al., 1996; Gresham, 2002). This is why social skills groups (for instance, small psychoeducational groups designed to teach students social skills) that happen outside of the classroom have not been found to be very effective in changing student behavior (Frey et al., 2014; Gresham, Sugai, & Horner, 2001).

Without linking lesson content to relevant, real-time practice opportunities, the time spent on such lessons is an inefficient use of resources. In the following section, we describe a few ways that classroom teachers can effectively offer ongoing teaching and practice opportunities for students. Specifically, teachers can have embedded practice opportunities, use explicit prompting, take advantage of spontaneous moments, and embed the skills into academic content.

### Embedded Practice Opportunities

Teachers can embed use of prosocial skills throughout the day and offer practice opportunities for students. Teachers might consider building in classroom routines that encourage daily practice of prosocial skills they have taught. For example, teachers may build in a daily emotion or mood check to help students build fluency in self-awareness. This emotion check also functions as an opportunity for teachers to take an emotion check of students as they start their day.

For elementary students, an emotion check might include each student choosing a laminated face with a basic emotion (happy, sad, angry, surprised, scared, or disgusted) each morning and placing it in a pocket chart on his or her desk, or on a visual graph that provides an anonymous depiction of how the class is feeling. Secondary students might benefit from plotting their current feeling across two dimensions on a mood meter, which ranges from unpleasant to pleasant emotions and high and low energy levels (Brackett, 2020), as shown in figure 2.7.

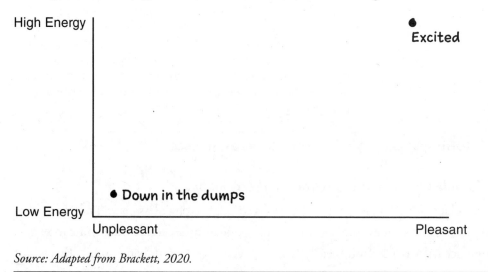

*Source: Adapted from Brackett, 2020.*

**FIGURE 2.7:** Simple mood meter example.

Students can record their moods on the mood meter on paper or a classroom poster, or they can download and track their moods over time on a software application on their phones. Mood Meter (http://moodmeterapp.com) is an example of such an app. Use of such a strategy may increase students' ability to recognize and name their emotions, and teachers may help to prompt students to understand why they might be feeling a certain way and offer a helpful way to manage and move forward. In table 2.3, we offer additional examples of embedding various prosocial skills throughout the day.

**Table 2.3: Examples of Embedded Practice Opportunities**

| Prosocial Skill | Example |
|---|---|
| Responsibility | Have students identify when they are being responsible as they use a daily planner or write down assignments for the day. |
| Self-management | Teach students how to use a cooldown area where they can go to manage a strong emotion. |
| Responsible decision making | Prompt students to use an area in the classroom to practice conflict resolution skills. |
| Social awareness | Use a morning meeting or circle time for students to practice reflecting emotions they hear in others and using active listening skills. |
| Safety and self-awareness | Have students identify their own emotions using *I feel* . . . statements either verbally in a group setting or in a journal. |
| Social awareness | When using cooperative learning or work groups, embed practice of the expectations or a specific SEL competency (such as active listening or perspective-taking) into the activity. |

## Explicit Prompting for Prosocial Skills

Prompts are powerful instructional tools because they allow teachers to proactively cue the behavior or skill use in students, as well as shift from a reactive approach to discipline to a preventative one (Alberto & Troutman, 2013; Darch & Kame'enui, 2003; Payton et al., 2008). The teacher can set up the classroom to frequently prompt students, through a variety of means, to use the prosocial skills taught to them. We categorize prompts into three types: (1) auditory, (2) visual, and (3) physical.

- *Auditory prompts* are, as they imply, sounds or spoken reminders to students to use a skill (Colvin, Sugai, & Patching, 1993; Harlacher, 2015; Haydon et al., 2010). For example, a teacher may prompt self-awareness while reminding about behavioral expectations by saying, "OK class, let's line up, but remember to keep hands and feet to yourselves to ensure we all feel safe." A teacher may also ask students to name the skill they just learned and then remind them to use that skill before an activity. A teacher may say, "Yesterday we learned a new skill about being safe. What was the skill we learned?" The students reply, "Keeping our hands and feet to ourselves." To both support the students' recall of the skill and prompt its use, the teacher responds, "Yes, that's it. So when you do your partner work, I want to see each of you paraphrasing and listening before you respond." A teacher may also use music or other sounds (for example, a bell ringing) to cue students to use certain skills or to follow routines (for example, a preschool teacher hums while prompting students to clean up; a high school teacher could play a movie quote or a chime to prompt students to transition to their next activity).

- *Visual prompts* are displays with words, icons, or images to remind students about a behavior or skill use (Colvin et al., 1993; Harlacher, 2015). We see visual prompts every day in the real world: the sign that tells you the speed limit, the arrow to indicate where to stand to order your food, or a crosswalk to indicate where to cross a street. Typically, classroom expectations are placed on a poster or banner and then displayed within the classroom. A middle school teacher can create cartoon faces that illustrate emotions with the label underneath it, for example (see figure 2.8).

**FIGURE 2.8:** Example of emotions to assist students with identifying emotions.

Further, visual prompts can include modifying the environment to prompt use of certain skills. For example, if you've ever turned off the lights to remind students as they enter a room to lower their voices, that is a visual prompt. (However, if you turned off the lights in response to loud noise, then it's corrective feedback!) Other examples of physical prompts include taping off areas in a classroom to remind students of physical space or color-coding a carpet area used for class meetings to remind students to responsibly identify their feelings during that time.

In the classroom, posters that represent specific SEL competencies or expectations can be helpful, as they remind students to practice skills as the need arises. For example, if a student is feeling angry, the teacher might direct the student to look at a "Stop, Count, Breathe In, Breathe Out" poster on the wall to calm the anger. This exemplifies a teacher directing a student's attention to a visual prompt, but sometimes visual prompts are in the background and serve as more of a passive prompt (that is, a prompt that students recognize on their own versus a teacher calling their attention to it, such as the poster). To avoid visual prompts falling into the visual wasteland where students ignore them, teachers can change their visual prompts every so often by creating new posters, changing the color of lettering and sizes of signs, or moving placement of visual prompts around to keep them new and fresh.

- *Physical prompts* are ones that use physical guidance to prompt certain behaviors. If you've ever placed your hand on a student's shoulder to guide them to their seat, that's likely a physical prompt. However, we don't advocate physically touching students and would instead reserve such prompting for situations where parental or guardian permission is given. We consider nonverbal prompts, such as the use of gestures or other nonverbal communication, part of the physical prompt family as well. Such prompts include modeling or mimicking of a skill. For example, a teacher could say, "Watch me" and then model the skill prior to students starting an activity that uses that skill. In table 2.4 (page 58), we offer more examples of prompts.

**Table 2.4: Examples of Prompts**

| Type | Example |
|------|---------|
| Auditory | • The teacher greets students as they enter the classroom and reminds them to start their bell work.<br>• The teacher reminds students to write down their homework assignments in their planner before leaving class (which reminds them to demonstrate the SEL competency of being responsible).<br>• The teacher sings the first line of a lyric, and the class responds with the rest of the line. The teacher then gives students a verbal direction. |
| Visual | • The teacher hangs a poster listing class expectations in a prominent location.<br>• The teacher reminds students to be responsible by raising their hands or using kind words by a sign on their desks.<br>• The teacher posts reminders of the expectations in a chat box during an online learning session.<br>• The teacher color codes bins for supplies (such as red for literacy, green for mathematics, and blue for geography) so students know what bins to grab supplies from based on a subject.<br>• The teacher uses a corner of the whiteboard to emphasize a given expectation or SEL skill each week. The teacher writes a previously taught skill in the corner and frequently points to it. |
| Physical | • The teacher uses a gesture (that is, placing a hand over his or her heart) to remind students to pause and engage in a relaxation technique to regulate their emotions.<br>• The teacher hands a student a talking stick (an object that signifies a student's turn to speak) during a classroom circle. |

Instead of waiting for the misbehavior to occur, the teacher can prompt the desired skill and decrease the chances of misbehavior altogether (Harlacher, 2015; Simonsen et al., 2008). Thus, teachers can focus on building prosocial skills in students rather than solely managing and correcting high rates of unwanted behavior. This isn't to say that unwanted behavior won't happen, but there may be a dramatic shift from teachers being on alert for such behaviors to focusing their attention on creating a more positive climate. Imagine a day where a teacher spends more time looking for desired skills rather than unwanted behavior. For example, teachers can prompt students to plan out their independent work time during class so that they devote enough time to complete their work before class ends (rather than students being off task and not completing their work). After the prompt, the teacher can then move about and praise and recognize students who planned out their work and are on task.

One key point is that prompts come before the behavior or skill use—they are *antecedents* (that is, triggers to elicit a certain behavior or skill) and are not reactionary tools or things that happen after a behavior occurs (Alberto & Troutman, 2013; Wolery, Bailey, & Sugai, 1988). For instance, if a teacher prompts students to raise their hands before an activity or engagement in a task, then that is a prompt. However, if a student then calls out without raising his hand, causing the teacher to remind him, "Oh, we don't call out in class; be sure to raise your hand," it is not considered a prompt. Instead, it's corrective feedback or error correction because the student's error is pointed out and he is asked to correct it by demonstrating a certain skill: in this case, raising his hand (Hollingsworth & Ybarra, 2017; Kame'enui & Simmons, 1990; Watkins & Slocum, 2004).

---

## Practice in Action: Ongoing Practice of Prosocial Skills

To help with transitioning into class and to practice prosocial skills, Mr. Coleson uses class starters each day with his eighth-grade class. He stands at his doorway to greet each student, offering a high five or fist bump as they enter the classroom. He then gives the class starter, which includes a personal icebreaker, a review of a prosocial skill, and a brief task to get started on the content for the day. Here are examples of Mr. Coleson's class starters.

- Write your responses to these questions as you wait for class to begin: (1) What song did you listen to today? (2) Where did you see a classmate show responsible decision making this week? and (3) Reflect on the passage we read yesterday. Do you think the main character acted honorably? Why or why not?

- Write your responses to these questions as you wait for class to begin: (1) What was a highlight from yesterday for you? (2) How have you shown emotional self-awareness today? and (3) Complete the equation below.

Mr. Coleson then spends a few minutes having some of the students share their responses to the first two questions. He then starts the day's lesson by discussing students' responses to question three. In using these class starters, Mr. Coleson provides students with a predictable routine to follow each day, as well as discussion or reinforcement of a prosocial skill prior to doing work related to the class content.

Another way to approach prompting is to first anticipate challenging behavioral patterns or routines in the classroom and then prompt students to practice their skills in advance of that challenging behavior actually happening. For example, we (Sara A. Whitcomb and a doctoral student) worked with Head Start teachers to identify a routine that students were still developing fluency with. Then, we had the teachers remind students to use particular social and emotional skills that they had previously learned through the Second Step program (www.secondstep.org) prior to that routine each day. Results of this study were promising, with teachers increasing their prompting during teachable moments and some classrooms decreasing the amount of challenging classroom behaviors as well (Kemp, 2020).

## Spontaneous Teaching Moments

In addition to embedded practice opportunities and prompting, teachers may also capitalize on teachable moments. *Teachable moments* are those spontaneous opportunities when a real-life situation arises in which students can practice some of the skills they have previously learned (Jones & Bouffard, 2012). For example, if a student is sad, a teacher might name what she sees to support emotion recognition and prompt a coping strategy: "I see that you may be feeling frustrated or sad. There is a tear in your eye and your face is a little red. Would you like to talk to me about why you feel that way? Maybe spending a few moments taking some breaths in the cooldown corner will help." As another example, imagine walking into a room and a student blurts out "Hello," causing a disruption. It would be easy to tell the student yelling is not OK, but taking the time to model the appropriate skill, such as waving quietly or whispering hello, for the student and then having him or her repeat the skill quickly turn that moment into a teachable one.

## Integration With Academic Content

Teachers can also integrate opportunities for students to learn and practice prosocial skills in academic content. Carol S. Dweck (2006, 2015) has widely influenced the field of education with her description of a *growth mindset*, which suggests that individuals can learn and make positive changes if they work hard and learn from mistakes. Her work is influential in helping students and teachers view learning as a process; one needs to practice an academic skill (rather than be perfect or master the skill after being taught it or practicing it once). Similarly, teachers can foster this mindset with respect to prosocial skills, as teachers can help all students see themselves as productive learners by setting high expectations (Yeager et al., 2014), providing constructive feedback, and framing errors as a normal part of the learning process.

Teachers can prioritize prosocial skills by also aligning students' learning of key competencies with academic objectives and by engaging in interactive pedagogy. For example, as teachers create an academic lesson plan, it may be helpful to regularly consider the classroom expectations or SEL competencies that students will need to meet academic objectives (CASEL, 2021). If students are working collaboratively on a science lab, for instance, they will likely need to communicate with one another, listen to each other, contribute ideas, and divide and conquer specific tasks. As such, it becomes clear that the lab is not just about the science objective, so teachers may also choose to teach and give feedback related to how groups are collaborating. CASEL (2021) notes that teachers may take different approaches to teaching students the prosocial skills they need to meet academic objectives. For example, teachers may model the skills, they may ask students what skills they may need to complete the academic assignment, or they may ask students to reflect on the skills used following the academic lesson. To align prosocial skills with academic lessons, we suggest the following.

1. Identifying the key objectives or standards of the lesson (for example, to write a rough draft of an essay)

2. Identifying the related prosocial skills needed to assist with the objective (for example, responsible decision making is needed to plan how to approach writing the essay)

3. Modeling or assisting students with using the prosocial skill in relation to the academic objective (for example, "Class, when you're planning out writing your draft, think about the three big steps you'll need to take to complete the draft during class time")

In addition to the preceding science example, another common way for teachers to integrate prosocial skills with academics is by engaging students in interactive discussions about characters in books, historical events, or other curricular content. Through such discussion, students can ponder the emotions and perspectives of others, such as why literary characters or historical figures made the decisions they did, and how students might have come to a different decision. Such opportunities encourage students to be reflective and to deepen their understanding of prosocial skills that have been explicitly taught.

---

**Practice in Action:** Recognizing Emotions
in Literary Characters

---

Mrs. Leeds is an eighth-grade English teacher, and she is a big believer in integrating SEL instruction with her academic lessons. Mrs. Leeds is purposeful about this approach and plans discussion questions about the chapters students are reading in books in advance of their daily book chats. Book chats are opportunities for students to pair up and share their understanding of the reading. For example, this week her questions and directions focus on social awareness (an SEL competency) and specifically on recognizing the emotions of others (which is the SEL competency of self-awareness). Students are reading *The Diary of a Young Girl* by Anne Frank (1952; 1993), and Mrs. Leeds's points for discussion focus on Anne's experience living in a small attic space with her family during the Holocaust. Ideas that she is asking students to respond to include, "Find an example in the chapter in which a character expresses fear. How about joy? Surprise?" Such questions will enable students to take the perspective of others and begin to understand how characters may feel in different contexts. Teachers may also extend such lines of questioning and ask students to identify times in their lives when they have seen others experience fear, joy, or surprise.

## Corrective Feedback and Reinforcement

Following a practice opportunity, whether it is from embedded practice, a prompt, or a spontaneous moment, there is an opportunity to provide students with corrective feedback or reinforcement for use of the prosocial skill. Corrective feedback is instructional and entails asking a student to perform the correct skill when he or she has made an error. For example, a teacher asks a student to walk down a hallway rather than run. For prosocial skills, a teacher may ask a student to rephrase a statement that made another student feel uncomfortable. (For example, "Jeremy, when you commented about John's phone, it felt like you were not demonstrating kindness toward others. Can you rephrase what you said to support our expectation of kindness?") Corrective feedback should be brief and provide the student an opportunity to demonstrate the prosocial skill, and then the school day continues.

Teachers can provide verbal praise when the student performs the correct skill, using reinforcement to strengthen the skill (Alberto & Troutman, 2013; Daly et al., 1996). They can also provide gestures (a thumbs-up), tokens (as part of a token economy), or a simple smile to acknowledge students' using certain skills. We expand on reinforcement in the next chapter and share strategies for ensuring students master the taught skills. We then discuss corrective feedback or error correction in chapter 5 (page 101).

## ····▶ Key Points

In this chapter, we provided a structure for consistency in a classroom. We discussed organizing the classroom from a physical perspective, including seating arrangements and facilitation of cooperative learning, to support resilience. Teaching prosocial skills is a critical aspect of consistency, as it establishes the norms, values, and expectations for how students engage with each other, the teacher, and the environment. We provided a lesson-plan template to teach prosocial skills, as well as ways to ensure ongoing teaching of those skills through embedding practice opportunities, prompting, spontaneous teaching, and integrating prosocial skills instruction into academic content.

# Checklist for a Classroom's Physical Space

| Factor | Yes | No |
|---|---|---|
| Are high-traffic areas free of congestion? | | |
| Can the teacher see all students and vice versa? | | |
| Are frequently used materials easily accessible? | | |
| Can all students easily see whole-class presentations, such as those on the projector or whiteboard? | | |
| Do students have ample room around their desks and seats? | | |
| Are desks organized in a way that facilitates teaching, whether in circles for group work or individual seats for independent work? | | |
| During small-group instruction, can the teacher still see all students? | | |
| Does the layout accommodate students with special needs? | | |
| Is there space available for students who need a quieter work environment or time to wind down? | | |

Source: Harlacher, J. E. (2015). Designing effective classroom management. *Bloomington, IN: Marzano Resources, p. 46.*

# CHAPTER 3

# Giving Feedback to Support Consistency and Build Connection

In the previous chapter, we discussed ways to create consistency in the classroom by arranging the physical space of the classroom and by teaching routines and prosocial skills to students. Here we expand on consistency by discussing how to use high rates of feedback or reinforcement to support students not only in mastering the prosocial skills but also to build rapport and connection with students.

Building a classroom that supports resilience includes an environment in which teachers provide more feedback to students on things they're doing well relative to feedback on corrections or mistakes that they make. Such an environment creates a safe, supportive space in which students can take risks, feel vulnerable, and learn new skills (CESE, 2020; Jones et al., 2018; National School Climate Center [NSCC], n.d.; Pickens & Tschopp, 2017; Simonsen et al., 2015). We know that classrooms that have a five-to-one ratio of praise to corrective feedback experience more academically engaged students and display fewer disruptive behaviors (Kern, White, & Gresham, 2007; Reinke, Herman, & Stormont, 2013). And this ratio isn't limited to just students. In fact, research has shown that married couples who give each other more positive feedback versus corrections have a lower rate of divorce

(Gottman, 1994), and business teams with more positive than negative statements are more productive (Losada & Heaphy, 2004; Zenger & Folkman, 2013).

We discuss using high rates of feedback in this chapter primarily as an instructional tool to reinforce skills. Further, having a supportive environment with a lot of positive feedback can help teachers build rapport with students, while also building students' connection to the classroom community and classmates (Gest, Madill, Zadzora, Miller, & Rodkin, 2014; Jennings & Greenberg, 2009; Pisacreta, Tincani, Connell, & Axelrod, 2011). When teachers create this kind of environment, students feel secure to express their emotional, intellectual, and personal needs, therein bolstering their resilience (NSCC, n.d.).

In this chapter, we use the term *reinforcement* interchangeably with *feedback* and *acknowledgment*, as all of those terms refer to feedback teachers give students with the intention of strengthening a previously taught skill (Floress, Beschta, Meyer, & Reinke, 2017; Simonsen et al., 2008). The term *reinforcement* may conjure up images of stickers and prizes, but reinforcement is not about making students feel better about themselves, though that can be a nice bonus to the use of reinforcement! Rather, we view reinforcement in the frame of changing behavior, as it can be a powerful instructional tool (Alberto & Troutman, 2013; Darch & Kame'enui, 2003; Oliver, Lambert, & Mason, 2019). Reinforcement refers to things or events that happen after a behavior that make the behavior *more* likely to occur again in the future (Alberto & Troutman, 2013; Baer, Wolf, & Risley, 1968; Wolery et al., 1988). With that idea, teachers can use reinforcement strategically to strengthen a variety of skills they teach in the classroom. Reinforcement is designed to communicate to students that the skill they're displaying is accurate, which in turn can lead to further, refined use of the skill (Oliver et al., 2019; Simonsen et al., 2008). You'll see in this chapter that reinforcement, especially when paired with prompting, can assist teachers in ensuring that students develop and learn the prosocial skills that were discussed in the previous chapter.

## Dispel the Positive Reinforcement–Low Motivation Myth

Historically in education, some educators expressed concern that the use of reinforcement may harm students' intrinsic motivation (Cameron, Banko, & Pierce, 2001; Ledford, Gerhart, & Fang, 2013). You can rest easy though, as the use of reinforcement is not linked to any detrimental effects related to effort or intrinsic motivation (Akin-Little, Eckert, Lovett, & Little, 2004; Cameron & Pierce, 1994; Ledford et al., 2013). In actuality, reinforcement—positive feedback—is effective in strengthening skills in students from preschool (Anhalt, McNeil, & Bahl, 1998; Hardy & McLeod, 2020) to the elementary level (Dufrene, Lestremau, & Zoder-Martell, 2014; Oliver et al., 2019; Simonsen et al., 2008) to the secondary level (Pisacreta et al., 2011). Of course, reinforcement is not magical; it can be less effective when it is not tied to a level of performance, such as when teachers give reinforcement when it's not contingent on a behavior; for example, five students are given access to a social media website after completing an assignment, but a sixth student is given access to the website despite not completing the assignment. Reinforcement is also less effective when teachers provide students with reinforcement for coming close, but not reaching, the established criterion, such as when a student still earns reinforcement when scoring 80 percent on a test, even though the criterion is 90 percent (Bowen, Jenson, & Clark, 2004). When used strategically, reinforcement is a powerful tool for teachers (Alberto & Troutman, 2013; Simonsen & Myers, 2015). In fact, when reinforcement is contingent on performance of a behavior, accessible (the standard to receive reinforcement isn't so high that's it's unattainable), varied (the teacher uses a mix of verbal and tangible reinforcement), and valued (students prefer or desire the reinforcement), it can be quite effective (Alberto & Troutman, 2013). In this chapter, we show you ways to use reinforcement well.

## Reinforce Prosocial Skills

The practices and guidance we offer for building connection and providing feedback are meant to send one simple message to students: you matter. Even students with complicated lives, who are juggling stressors and relationships and receiving messages elsewhere that they are not important, can come into your classroom and see that they have value by the type of verbal, nonverbal, and written feedback you provide. If you are unfamiliar with it, view the viral video (https://sbsk.org/story) where Chris Ulmer, a former special education teacher and founder of Special Books by Special Kids (https://sbsk.org), started each day by complimenting and praising each of his students. This effort is the essence of creating connection (and ultimately, of this book).

As illustrated in the video, Ulmer shows positive regard for his students when he compliments and praises them. We view *positive regard*, defined as caring and accepting students for who they are (Venet, 2021), as telling students they matter, making choices that show respect for their being (and you), and ensuring safety and structure in your classroom. Here, we summarize a few ways of showing positive regard from our own experience.

- Be consistent in your responses to students' acts of kindness and acts of unwanted behavior; predictability is safety.

- Be aware of your body language and nonverbals when students are sharing their experiences. Certain facial expressions or a closed-off body posture (for example, arms crossed) can inadvertently communicate judgment or disapproval to students.

- Communicate positive regard by acknowledging and reflecting on students' experiences (for example, "I hear you saying it's been frustrating this week").

- Create time and space for students to share their personal experience, even if it's a meme, a one-minute video, or a longer story.

- Determine the best way to offer feedback for individual students, such as whether a student prefers public or private praise or written or verbal praise. You can learn this as you get to know the students, or you can simply ask them to share their preference during a conversation or in response to a brief, confidential question.

- Acknowledge mistakes and let students understand making mistakes is normal (Berger, Rugen, & Woodfin, 2014; Dweck, 2006). Doing this can create a space where they feel safe being vulnerable (Pickens & Tschopp, 2017). Further, teachers can be transparent with their mistakes to further normalize errors.

- Create a judgment-free classroom and space for students to express who they are as individuals. Students are often figuring out who they are, so it is important to help them determine ways of expressing themselves that respect other people's dignity.

Here we offer ways to create high rates of feedback, an important part of helping students transfer skills they are learning into their normal repertoire of skills. After initial teaching, reinforcement helps students build fluency and sustain their use of the skill (Kern et al., 2007; Reinke et al., 2013; Simonsen et al., 2008). To ensure students have sufficient reinforcement of prosocial skills, teachers can use behavior-specific praise on a daily, immediate basis, but they can also provide long-term reinforcement. We cover these forms of reinforcement in the following sections.

## Behavior-Specific Praise

One of the most powerful tools a classroom teacher has for building and strengthening skills in a student is behavior-specific praise (Gage, Grasley-Boy, & MacSuga-Gage, 2018). Teachers can directly praise and acknowledge students' use of prosocial skills, therein strengthening their ability to navigate stressors and bolster their resilience. *Behavior-specific praise* (BSP) is a manner of feedback in which teachers praise students for the use of a discrete skill. It consists of identifying a skill or behavior a student performed and then providing clear feedback that indicates to the student what was beneficial or accurate in the performance.

To provide behavior-specific praise, teachers can identify a skill they want to strengthen in a student, notice when the student uses that skill, and provide verbal praise of use of that skill. Behavior-specific praise is different than *general praise*, which does not actually communicate to students what they did well (Cook et al., 2014; Jenkins, Floress, & Reinke, 2015; Lewis, Hudson, Richter, & Johnson, 2004; Simonsen & Myers, 2015; Sutherland, Wehby, & Copeland, 2000). See table 3.1 for examples of behavior-specific versus general praise.

**Table 3.1: Behavior-Specific Praise Versus General Praise**

| Behavior-Specific Praise | General Praise |
|---|---|
| "Lane, you were very respectful when others were sharing their thoughts in the morning meeting. Thank you." | "Nicely done, Lane!" |
| (Looking at student) "I liked how you were honest about your feelings and used the cooldown area to take a moment before you started working." | "This is awesome. You're all doing great!" (Looks at student briefly) |
| "Tyron, thank you for arriving to class on time and starting your work while your classmates arrived. That shows me you're being responsible." (Provides Tyron a token) | "Excellent!" (Hands token to Tyron) |
| A teacher privately types in a chat box to a student, "I see your camera is on, you're looking at the screen, and completing the work. Thank you for being engaged and responsible!" | "You're doing great!" (Posted to everyone in the online learning session) |

Whereas general praise contributes to a more affirming environment and communicates positivity to students, behavior-specific praise contributes to individual skill acquisition in students (Floress et al., 2017; Sutherland et al., 2000). Teachers can intentionally use behavior-specific praise to ensure students learn the skills taught in a classroom. By receiving direct feedback on the skill, students know that they are accurately using the skill and that it's valued by the teacher and the overall classroom community. In fact, behavior-specific praise is associated with a variety of outcomes, including increased on-task behavior, increased engagement, increased response accuracy during instruction, and decreased disruptive behaviors (Allday et al., 2012; Hawkins & Heflin, 2011; Pisacreta et al., 2011; Rathel, Drasgow, Brown, & Marshall, 2014; Sutherland & Wehby, 2001; Sutherland et al., 2000). When students receive frequent feedback on the skills they're using, teachers can use behavior-specific praise to shape students' initial use of the skill and then refine skill use. For example, they can provide feedback such as, "I like how you're listening to others by making eye contact. Could you work on summarizing what you hear them say to show them you understand?" There isn't a magic pill in education, but behavior-specific praise comes awfully close when we consider all of the positive outcomes associated with it. And it's quick and free, making it an easy and affordable strategy to use with students.

## Knowing How Much Behavior-Specific Praise Students Need

In a positive classroom climate, teachers provide students with praise at a ratio of at least five praise statements to one redirect or piece of corrective feedback (Reinke et al., 2013; Simonsen & Myers, 2015). Though it can take time to build a ratio that high, one can take solace that even increasing to a two- or three-to-one ratio can lead to beneficial outcomes for students (Floress et al., 2017; Pisacreta et al., 2011). For building resilience, students need a high rate of behavior-specific praise related to the classroom expectations and the SEL competencies being taught to them (Barrett et al., 2018; Jones, Jones, & Vermette, 2009; Yoder & Gurke, 2017).

There are a variety of ways teachers can ensure they provide a high rate of behavior-specific praise, including tangible reminders. For example, a teacher can place five coins in one pocket. Each time she reaches into her pocket and feels a coin, she can provide praise and then move the coin to her other pocket. Once she moves all five coins to the other pocket, she then moves them back to the first pocket one by one. Instead of coins, a teacher could also place five pieces of tape on the corner of her desk or projector. Then, each time she sees the tape, she moves one piece to the perpendicular corner and provides praise to a student for a given skill. In lieu of tangible reminders, a teacher could also set a random timer on her phone or use a phone application that provides a random vibration or alarm to prompt the teacher to provide praise (George, 2009; Harlacher, 2015).

Teachers can also track their own rate of reinforcement by recording themselves. A teacher can set up a ten-minute recording (even audio only) during instruction a few times a week or a few times in a day. We recommend selecting a time to do this when you can use reinforcement strategically to strengthen a prosocial skill or expectation. After the recording, you can listen to it and count the number of praise statements versus corrective statements. Then simply calculate the ratio by dividing praise statements by corrective statements. For example, if a teacher tallied fifteen praise statements and three corrections, fifteen divided by three equals five; thus, that teacher has a five-to-one ratio for the recorded time period (Harlacher, 2015; Musti-Rao & Haydon, 2011). Alternatively, a teacher could have a colleague observe for a short period of time and keep track of praise versus corrections (Harlacher, 2015).

By tracking their own praise statements, teachers can increase their rate simply by the process of seeing data on their use of praise (Gage et al., 2018; Reinke, Lewis-Palmer, & Martin, 2007). If gathering and viewing the data each day don't lead to a substantial increase, then teachers can set goals and reward themselves for reaching that goal. They can also partner with a colleague and support each other in their use of praise much like you might enlist the support of a friend to make sure you stick to your exercise routine.

One strategy that supports high rates of feedback as well as builds relationships among classmates is positive peer reporting (Burns, Riley-Tillman, & Rathvon, 2017; Moroz & Jones, 2002). This strategy has students praise specific groups of peers or a target peer on specified days. Positive peer reporting is helpful for students who enjoy peer attention, particularly if those students display unwanted behavior for peer attention. To use this strategy, the teacher explains how students can praise their peers, which consists of the following steps. Teachers may wish to teach students how to handle receiving praise, such as simply saying "Thank you" to the person who offers it (Burns et al., 2017; Murphy & Zlomke, 2014).

1. Looking at the person to praise

2. Making eye contact and smiling (if appropriate)

3. Describing what they did well (this is the specific description needed for behavior-specific praise)

4. Providing a compliment or saying, "Nice work" or "Good job!"

Once students know how to give a compliment, the teacher can randomly choose a peer or group of peers each day for the class to acknowledge and praise. Students can earn points and a reward for praising each other, if need be, though this may run the risk of making the praise disingenuous. We recommend this tactic more for younger students and on a temporary basis to have students practice initially praising or recognizing others. Additionally, the teacher should ensure students learn to praise effort and behaviors that reinforce the expectations rather than personal appearance, possessions, or socioeconomic status. Finally, positive peer reinforcement does not have to be an all-day event; instead, it can take short periods of time, such as ten to thirty minutes (Nimocks, 2011). For example, the teacher can remind students to look for learned prosocial skills in each other and to acknowledge them during a given activity in class. Secondary students may just need a reminder for this, but elementary students may need more structure and guidance (that is, "Between now and lunch, which is about three hours from now, I want you all to try to notice at least one nice thing someone does today and tell them what you noticed").

---

## Practice in Action: Students Acknowledge Each Other

Mrs. Gomez wanted her students to acknowledge and support each other. She decided to provide a bobblehead to them. She would praise a student for using an expectation and then place a bobblehead on his or her desk. That student could display the bobblehead on his or her desk for as long or as short as he or she wanted, but in twenty-four hours, the student had to acknowledge another student for a prosocial skill and then give that student the bobblehead for his or her desk. Throughout the week, the bobblehead would move around the classroom from one desk to another, serving as a visual prompt to use the prosocial skills.

### Pairing Behavior-Specific Praise With a Token

Some students may benefit solely from the social reinforcement that comes with BSP, but others may need something more tangible. To that end, behavior-specific praise can be paired with a tangible token, such as a paper ticket, stamp, or signature (George et al., 2009; Simonsen & Myers, 2015). The token serves as a physical reminder that the student displayed a skill accurately. Teachers can fade out use of tokens over time as students display the skill, thereafter using social or verbal praise to maintain the skill rather than the tangible reinforcement (Harlacher, 2015). Consequently, behavior-specific praise is a *temporary tool* to build a skill. Once a student is fluent with the skill and is able to maintain it over time, teachers can taper off using behavior-specific praise on that particular skill and transfer it to a new skill they are teaching (George, 2009). Thus, the praise is used intentionally and to a clear end, such as sustained use of a skill.

## Reinforcement

Whereas behavior-specific praise and tokens provide immediate, daily feedback, teachers can use long-term reinforcement to further strengthen students' use of a skill by providing reinforcement that is more challenging for students to obtain, such as saving up tokens to earn a free period (Alberto & Troutman, 2013; Simonsen et al., 2008). Long-term reinforcement allows teachers to raise a skill's criterion or standard, since it requires students to maintain the skill over time and use it more frequently or with more precision to earn reinforcement (Harlacher & Rodriguez, 2018).

Long-term reinforcement is often connected to high-frequency reinforcement (Harlacher & Rodriguez, 2018; Simonsen et al., 2008). For example, if students earn tokens or tickets, they can use them to purchase items at a classroom store. A ticket can be worth one dollar, for example, and the items students may purchase can vary in value and size with corresponding prices. Figure 3.1 illustrates a classroom menu of items available for students to purchase (note that not all items are tangible and include social items as well).

| Item | Cost |
| --- | --- |
| High five from teacher | One ticket |
| High five from classmate | One ticket |
| Small item from store | Five tickets |
| Round of applause from class | Five tickets |
| Magazine | Fifteen tickets |
| Fifteen minutes of screen time | Thirty tickets |
| Lunch with classroom teacher | Fifty tickets |
| Lunch or thirty minutes with teacher of choice | Seventy-five tickets |

**FIGURE 3.1:** Sample store menu for a classroom.

Aside from purchasing items from a classroom store, students can use tickets for a raffle. Students who earn a ticket can be entered in a monthly or weekly drawing for a prize. Each week, a student could win student of the day and sit in a special chair, wear a certain hat, or have access to certain items or activities. A student could earn first place in line for lunch as well, or a homework help or homework skip pass. For other prizes, a student could earn a seat at the front of the class (for the extroverts) or a more private seat (for the introverts). Students could win large prizes as well, such as a sweatshirt with classroom expectations on it or other items (these can often be donated by local vendors). The idea is to provide varied prizes that are highly desired, thus providing motivation for display and maintenance of desired skills (George, 2009; Harlacher & Rodriguez, 2018).

## Group Contingencies

When used strategically, group contingencies can lead to improved morale and camaraderie among students because they encourage students to support each other (Alberto & Troutman, 2013; Marzano, 2003; Stage & Quiroz, 1997). Group contingencies can also provide another angle for reinforcing students' skill usage. Consider the pros and cons of each in table 3.2 before choosing which to use. In addition to long-term rewards, you can provide students reinforcement through the group contingencies in table 3.2 (Alberto & Troutman, 2013; Simonsen et al., 2008).

Given all these types of reinforcement—behavior-specific praise, long-term reinforcement, group contingencies—teachers can organize reinforcements using the structure in table 3.3 (page 76). Doing so can ensure a comprehensive and varied reinforcement plan for given skills. We included a row for *noncontingent reinforcement*, which isn't tied to any criterion or behavior. For example, noncontingent reinforcement can include offering time for students to relax and talk about their interests with each other, playing a game as a class, participating in outdoor field activities or a class party, or providing time for students to share something fun or interesting about their culture or home life. Teachers can provide this type of reinforcement to build rapport and relationships with students, as well as to build the classroom's climate and culture (Jennings & Greenberg, 2009; Norris, 2003; Thapa et al., 2013).

## Table 3.2: Group Contingencies

| Type | Example | Pros | Cons |
|---|---|---|---|
| Independent contingency | The reward is available to any student who reaches the criterion. An example is the school store: any student who earns enough "money" to buy an item may do so. | This contingency allows students to earn a reward regardless of a peer's behavior. | This contingency may not build group cohesion. |
| Interdependent contingency | The reward is available only when the entire class reaches the criterion. For example, all students must score a 70 percent on a test to earn a reward. Or, all students earn tokens that the teacher places into a basket; when students reach a certain number of tokens, the class earns the reward. | This contingency builds group cohesion and clarifies social norms. | Students need instruction to not blame classmates when they do not collectively earn the reward. (The class can role-play not earning a reward to be sure they're kind to each other when this occurs.) |
| Dependent contingency | The reward is available based on only one student's performance or a group's performance. For example, one student must earn ten tickets in a week so that all students can have a popcorn party or fifteen minutes of screen time. | This contingency can help students who are ostracized or socially isolated build better social relationships. Keep the bar low for the students at first so they earn the reward, then raise the criterion as they meet it. | Students need instruction for how to handle not earning the reward, such as saying, "Oh well. We can try again tomorrow." |

*Source: Adapted from Alberto & Troutman, 2013.*

**Table 3.3: Comprehensive Reinforcement Plan**

| Reinforcement | Description | Example |
|---|---|---|
| Immediate, short-term reinforcement | The teacher provides acknowledgment on a high-frequency basis. | Praise students' use of classroom expectations an average of five times per hour and provide a token with that praise. |
| Long-term reinforcement | The teacher provides acknowledgment contingent on students displaying skills over time or accumulating a set number of short-term reinforcements. | Students save their tokens to purchase items in a class store. |
| Group contingency | The teacher provides acknowledgment for prosocial behavior using group contingencies. | When the class earns a set number of tokens, students vote on a larger prize, such as fifteen minutes of social time, a popcorn party, and so on. |
| Non-contingent reinforcement | The teacher provides acknowledgment that is not contingent on performance of a skill or behavior. The teacher designs activities to promote group cohesion and student-to-student relationships. | Each Monday, a student is the student of the week and shares information about his or her culture and family. Students also have regular connection circles two days a week to celebrate their successes in school and at home. |

*Visit **MarzanoResources.com/reproducibles** for a free reproducible version of this table.*

---

## Practice in Action: Tunnel Cheer

One way to reinforce students' skill use and build connection among them is to provide public praise and acknowledgment. A free and easy method is to take a few minutes every other Friday to have your students line up facing each other to form a tunnel. Have one student stand at the front and announce an accomplishment he or she did related to the classroom expectations or a prosocial skill, such as

"I invited a classmate to eat lunch with me" or "I worked hard on my history essay." Then, everyone cheers, and the student runs through the tunnel, getting high fives and cheers from classmates. (Picture a sports team tunnel!) You can select one student each time you do this or have a few students at a time.

## Employ Best Practice for Feedback

Now that we have covered ways to use high rates of feedback to reinforce the teaching of skills, we shift to the hardest part of doing so: sticking to it! The techniques we describe in this chapter are not difficult to learn or do. In fact, we're certain that most of our readers know these methods and use them to some degree already. However, where things become likely to fall apart is when there isn't an efficient or effective system to support the teacher in using the aforementioned methods (Simonsen & Myers, 2015; Sugai & Horner, 2006). It's easy to try a new skill or method for a couple of days, but over time the method may fade away because it hasn't taken hold and old habits take over (Kratochwill, Elliott, & Callan-Stoiber, 2002; Noell, Duhon, Gatti, & Connell, 2002; Wolery, 2011). Have you ever tried a New Year's resolution? You're pumped and motivated for the first few weeks of the new year, but it's easy to revert to old habits by February! To avoid this, we offer a few tips to make implementation go smoother.

- Focus on one skill at a time.
- Use reinforcement for a short period of time.
- Encourage students to give feedback.

### One Skill at a Time

When providing reinforcement for skills, we recommend focusing on one skill for a week or two at a time. This can make things more manageable for teachers and allow them to focus on getting students fluent in a skill before focusing on another one (Daly et al., 1996; Frey et al., 2014; Gresham, 2002). For example, a teacher may have taught an SEL lesson on Monday on demonstrating empathy toward others and identifying others' feelings. Then, over the course of the week, the teacher prompts herself to reinforce that skill by using behavior-specific praise targeted to that skill (she can use one of the strategies we mentioned earlier in this chapter). At the end of the week, the teacher sets aside a ten-minute review session in which students share how they used that skill and where they saw other students using it. The students can then identify a goal for using that skill in the coming week (Langland et al., 1998). The teacher has thus created a structured time to focus on and acknowledge that skill and make the skill more sustainable over time. Once students have shown they are fluent with the skill, the teacher can shift to another prosocial skill or expectation (Harlacher, 2015; Jones & Bouffard, 2012; Langland et al., 1998).

## Brief Moments of Time

Another way to make use of reinforcement more manageable is to initially use short periods of time to reinforce students rather than using reinforcement all day, each day (Anhalt et al., 1998). Various researchers and educators use this approach, so we offer a general summary of the steps here (Anhalt et al., 1998; Bowen et al., 2004; Oliver et al., 2019; Theodore, Bray, Kehle, & Jensen, 2001). To begin, teachers identify a given skill for students to learn, such as actively listening with peers or showing empathy when others are sharing their perspective. Students first learn the skill using the guidelines and the lesson plan covered in chapter 2 (page 33). Then, during a brief set time (anywhere from ten to forty-five minutes), such as cooperative groups for mathematics work, the teacher can announce that he or she wants students to use the target skill. During that time, the teacher monitors the room and provides behavior-specific praise for all students using the skill. The teacher also prompts students not using the skill when they should, and briefly corrects errors for students who misuse the skill.

Additionally, the teacher can make use of the skill a game and provide points for students or teams. These games can vary in several ways, including a random reward that is unknown to students until they earn it, such as mystery motivator (Waguespack, Moore, Wickstrom, Witt, & Gaydos, 1994), or they can include a response-cost option in which students can lose points or rewards for displaying unwanted behavior, such as the good behavior game (Barrish, Saunders, & Wolf, 1969). The teacher can use tally marks, stickers, or other icons on a poster or board to visually display the points students earn.

The following steps (Harlacher, 2015) describe a general approach that teachers can modify to meet each classroom's needs.

1.  Identify a skill that students or an individual student needs practice using. This can be anything from raising one's hand instead of calling out or paraphrasing what others say before responding or giving one's own thoughts.

2.  Select a criterion to earn a reward. For example, perhaps the teacher wants at least ten instances of the skill during a group discussion or that each student should display the skill at least once throughout the day.

3.  Divide the class into teams. The teacher can make two teams by dividing the class in half or use natural clusters in the class for teams (such as, students sitting at a table are one team). Teams are not necessary, as each student can be his or her own team. However, teams can create social norms and expectations, thus reinforcing community in the classroom.

4.  Teach or remind students of the skill that will be the focus for the time being. This teaching can take place right before the use of the game or even earlier, such as the day before.

5.  Create a visual system for each team or student to record the praise earned for displaying the skill. This can be tally marks on the board or a sticky note for each student or stickers on a team poster. Elementary teachers might use a symbol, such as a star. When students display the taught skill, the teacher gives a tally mark or other symbol, indicating that the team or student displayed the skill and earned a point in the game.

6.  Announce to the class that you'll be playing the game (you can give the game a name or simply say you'll be looking for the skill identified in step 1 during the upcoming time period). Throughout the specified time period, acknowledge and recognize the skill using behavior-specific praise and mark each instance of the skill on the visual system.

7.  At the end of the time period, provide a reward based on the predetermined criterion. These rewards can be simple, such as having students act like their favorite animals for twenty seconds, or more substantial, such as the winners earning first place in line for lunch or a homework skip pass.

Whether we are considering young children, adolescents, or even adults, reinforcement is a way in which we learn. Positive feedback most often increases the chances that we will engage in newly learned behaviors again. Up until this point, we have written about general properties for reinforcement as they apply to all students; however, we thought it would be important to include a particular note on reinforcement with adolescent students. Many might assume that adolescents care more about what their peers think and less about what adults think. Researchers surveyed middle and high school students to get a clearer sense of adolescent preferences for reinforcement (Fefer, DeMagistris, & Shuttleton, 2016). Findings indicated that students care more about teachers' opinions of their work than the opinions of their parents or peers. Additionally, adolescents were more likely to prefer quieter, less public forms of praise such as gestures like a thumbs-up or a fist bump, but other forms of public or tangible reinforcement were acceptable, too.

### Student Ownership

The teacher doesn't have to be the only one providing reinforcement and contributing to a positive climate. Students can also reinforce each other and give feedback for using the prosocial skills taught. For example, students can learn how to use praise by stating a peer's name and thanking that peer for using a designated skill. It might sound like, "Hey, Brooke. I just wanted to say thank you for being inclusive and inviting me to sit with you at lunch" or "Cole, I appreciated you listening to others and asking Greyson to talk more about his frustrations during group work time." Students can also reinforce one another using tangible rewards. For example, teachers can give students perforated tickets, with the top part being a reward for the student. The student can then tear off the bottom part of the ticket and give it to a classmate (George, 2009; Harlacher, 2015). Students can also share examples of when classmates use a given skill during a classroom meeting or during a share time.

Additionally, students can self-monitor their behavior (Hawken, Crone, Bundock, & Horner, 2021; Todd, Horner, & Sugai, 1999). Once the teacher is confident that students are using a skill, they can self-monitor with a sheet such as the reproducible "Self-Monitoring Form" (page 82), although some students may require a more structured gradual release process that we describe in chapter 2 (page 33). Students can learn how to track themselves and monitor their data, though teachers will need to spend time teaching them how to do this. At specified times, students can share instances over the past week where they used or displayed the skill. Teachers can also give students the form on Monday, with students then identifying a goal for the week of what they'll do to use the skill, and then sharing on Friday how they met that goal.

## ⋯▶ Key Points

In this chapter, we outlined the importance of high rates of feedback for reinforcement of prosocial skills. We discussed use of behavior-specific praise and long-term reinforcement, as teachers will want to build a comprehensive reinforcement plan as part of their teaching of prosocial skills. Teachers can use behavior-specific praise, reinforcement, group contingencies, and noncontingent reinforcement to have a robust and comprehensive way to acknowledge and provide feedback to students. Not only can this reinforcement strengthen skills, it can also build connection and rapport because teachers are spending their time acknowledging students and creating an overall positive climate. We also outlined ways to make reinforcement work and be a natural part of the school day.

# Self-Monitoring Form

| Name: | Key:<br>1 = Still work to do<br>2 = Improving<br>3 = Excellent |
|---|---|
| Date: | |
| Goal: | |

| Expectation | My Rating | | |
|---|---|---|---|
| | 1 | 2 | 3 |
| | 1 | 2 | 3 |
| | 1 | 2 | 3 |
| | 1 | 2 | 3 |
| | 1 | 2 | 3 |

# CHAPTER 4

# Creating Classrooms That Support Connection

In the previous chapter, you learned how to use reinforcement and feedback to strengthen prosocial skills in students. In this chapter, we outline ways to intentionally develop relationships between teachers and students, among students, and with families.

In addition to creating a consistent and predictable environment in which students receive high rates of feedback, it is critically important that teachers think strategically about supporting development of healthy relationships. Because we are social beings, it's not surprising relationships are so important. Just watch any group of middle schoolers and you'll see the budding need for social relationships as they clamor for each other's time and attention (Yeager, 2017). Relationships are more than just a social need, however. They're an immensely important protective factor. In fact, a student who has just one healthy attachment to an adult in school is likely to experience higher levels of social engagement and engage in less risky behavior (Anderson et al., 2004; Decker et al., 2007; Zolkoski, 2019). Better teacher-student relationships are also associated with improved academic performance (Decker et al., 2007; Rucinski, Brown, & Downer, 2018). Additionally, adolescents who feel respected by their teachers have fewer suspensions and manage their emotions better than those who do not feel respected (Yeager, 2017).

We're not just focused on teacher-to-student relationships, though. Having strong student-to-student relationships in which they respect and support each other contributes to a positive climate and provides a safe, predictable environment (Gest et al., 2014; Jones & Kahn, 2017; Yoder & Gurke, 2017). This is particularly important for students dealing with trauma, as an environment's predictability can ease their stress response and anxiety (Pickens & Tschopp, 2017). Strong relationships among students also actively break down stereotypes and cliques, as students don't see "us versus them" and instead see the entire classroom as "us" (Aronson & Patnoe, 2011; Aronson, Stephan, Sikes, Blaney, & Snapp, 1978). Students should feel welcomed and safe to be themselves and to express their intellectual, emotional, and personal needs. This doesn't mean that everyone must be close friends, but rather, everyone should feel supported and valued as a member of the classroom community (NSSC, n.d.).

Finally, building connections with families is critical, as teachers are able to learn about students from their caregivers and gain insight about what strategies might work best for them. Further, caregivers can also learn from strategies that teachers implement in the classroom and try them at home.

## Build Positive Teacher-Student Relationships

Developing warm teacher-student relationships is foundational for building a healthy classroom climate, reducing problematic behaviors, and ensuring students' academic success (Bergin & Bergin, 2009). For some teachers, building relationships comes quite naturally, but for others, this may be more challenging. Further, teachers are pulled in multiple directions each day, which may make it difficult to develop meaningful relationships with students. Teachers are tasked with designing and delivering high-quality instruction, managing behavior, keeping up with administrative and organizational tasks that keep a classroom system functioning, and many other responsibilities. Additionally, while teachers often learn in their training programs about the importance of warm teacher-student relationships, they may have little exposure to specific strategies and practice opportunities that facilitate the development of such relationships in the context of a busy school day (Schonert-Reichl, Hanson-Peterson, & Hymel, 2015). In this section, we provide you with a number of such strategies and opportunities so that you may effectively build positive relationships with your students.

### Greeting Students

You can establish relationships with students from the beginning of the year by greeting them individually on the first day, introducing yourself, and then pointing them toward available (or assigned) seats as they enter the classroom. This makes a personal connection, but it also establishes clear boundaries and expectations that you can build on for classroom management. By personally greeting students, the teacher communicates (outright or subtly) that the adult in the room cares about them. You can ask students how they want to be greeted as a way of respecting their boundaries. This allows students choice and voice if they want a verbal greeting, visual greeting, or physical greeting, if they have a certain nickname, and so on. They can also use a signal or say "No, thank you" if they don't want to be greeted on a particular day, allowing them to identify and set appropriate boundaries. This is a great example of embedding instruction on self-management and is important for students who are having a rough day, need space, or are dealing with social, emotional, or behavioral concerns.

It might seem like a given, but an important strategy is for teachers to focus on learning the names and accurate pronunciation of student names (Glenz, 2014). Students want to know that their teachers care enough to say their names or nicknames correctly. For example, a colleague of ours spent the entire school year mispronouncing a student's name. Every day, he would take attendance and say the student's name, pronouncing it "Pee-yo-bee." The student was too kind to correct our colleague, but it turns out her name was *Phoebe*, pronounced "Fee-bee." Imagine being this student and what was going through her mind each day at attendance. Although the students found this situation amusing, it highlights the importance of learning people's names and the importance of using a person's name for building equity and relationships (Khan-Baker, 2016).

After that first day, teachers can continue to greet students at the door prior to them entering the classroom. To do so, teachers can stand at their door and personally greet each student in a manner that is appropriate and respectful to both the teacher and the student. A teacher can develop a handshake for each student, a simple fist bump or elbow tap, a verbal question (even as simple as, "Good morning, how are you?"), or a side hug.

Researchers Clayton R. Cook and colleagues (2018b) expand this idea with their positive-greeting-at-the-door strategy. Cook and colleagues (2018b) find that middle school classrooms increased the amount of time students were academically engaged and decreased disruptive behavior when they included the following four components.

1.  Connecting with students at the start of class with a positive verbal or nonverbal interaction

2. Providing precorrection that reminds students of expectations as they enter the room

3. Providing private statements to students who may have had difficulties the day prior

4. Providing behavior-specific praise to students to reinforce the expectations of certain desired behaviors

By greeting students at the door, the teacher can also gauge the extent to which students are in a good or bad mood. A teacher can assess students' levels of emotion and attention and then plan accordingly, such as by allowing for a brief cooldown, a brief talk with the teacher, or journaling prior to asking the student to begin the classwork.

### Checking in About Emotions

In chapter 2 (page 33), we briefly touched on the idea of mood checks (Brackett, 2020)—times in the class period when students can check in on their current emotional state. Morning meetings are a common example of this strategy. This is an excellent strategy for students of all ages and can be implemented in a variety of ways. Lower-elementary students can point to faces that match how they feel, or they can place a card naming an emotion in a pocket chart; teachers may then choose to have students graph how the class feels. Adolescents can access the mood meter app we discussed in chapter 2 and track their moods and energy levels.

While these strategies are excellent for students to build self-awareness and social awareness, they can also be useful for teachers working to build relationships with their students. Teachers can use emotional check data as a guide for how their students are feeling overall, which students might need extra attention or comfort, and other concerns. For example, if a teacher notices that most students identify feeling stressed, the teacher may take a moment to help them identify the source of their anxiety (an upcoming test) and practice a stress-reduction strategy (a mindful moment or deep breathing).

### Relational Contact

Besides greetings at the start of the day, teachers can consider other brief pockets of time throughout the day to provide students with *noncontingent positive attention*, or attention that is given freely rather than in response to meeting an expectation. This strategy entails teachers engaging in conversation to get to know students. Teachers follow students' lead in this scenario, ask questions, and show interest. For example, in one classroom, a high school teacher regularly took a few minutes at the beginning of class to check in on weekend events or special occasions with students. Many of her students were celebrating their quinceañeras that year, a special milestone when young Latinas turn fifteen years old. The students seemed to enjoy sharing these moments important to their culture with their teacher. Thinking ahead and planning for relational contact in a busy class schedule can be really helpful.

To plan for relational contact, teachers may consider particular times during the day, week, or class period when they can build in time to get to know students. They might start with a prompt such as, "What was the highlight of your weekend?" or, "What's one thing you're looking forward to doing after school?" Often, it can feel hard to give up instructional time, but brief pockets saved for relationship building can demonstrate that you care and may make instructional time more productive.

## Embedded Academic Activities

There are additional strategies that enable teachers to establish relationships with students early in the school year. For example, one commonly used strategy is from the Responsive Classroom (www.responsiveclassroom.org) approach, which asks students to write or illustrate their hopes and dreams for the school year. Another strategy, often used with older students, is composing "who I am" poems, modeled after the works of famous poets, such as Walt Whitman and Maya Angelou, where students have the opportunity to share the identities that define them. Teachers may also choose to have students set personal goals for their academic year and revisit the goals periodically throughout the year. Of course, teachers can also use numerous icebreakers early in the school year, such as having students stand up or sit down if they hear certain descriptors about their likes or dislikes called out, to get to know their students. All of these activities allow students to share a bit about themselves, and teachers can join in some of the activities so that students can get to know them, too. The key message here is that teachers make time in their schedules for these opportunities, which is key to relationship development; it is part and parcel of building resilience in the classroom.

## Active Supervision

One way to build relationships (while also strengthening skills in students) is through active supervision—the intentional focus on a desired behavior, with the teacher moving about the classroom, scanning for desired behavior, and then interacting with students by providing feedback on the behavior (De Pry & Sugai,

2002; Haydon & Kroeger, 2016). This is an excellent time for teachers to provide behavior-specific praise related to desired behaviors, positively interact with students, and correct undesired behaviors that emerge. When the teacher identifies unwanted behavior, he or she can provide brief, private error correction and have students demonstrate the appropriate skill or behavior. (We'll discuss error correction more in chapter 5, page 101.) Active supervision is a useful tool for actively monitoring and reinforcing skills, and teachers can also use this time to record or document data on use of classroom expectations or other forms of data.

To use active supervision, follow these steps.

1. Identify a skill that students need to have reinforced or highlighted. This can be a skill all students need reinforced or a skill that one or a few students do. If you choose a skill for just a few students, you'll still praise all students for the skill.

2. Move about the classroom to have close proximity with students.

3. Scan the room and look for instances of the identified skill.

4. Provide praise and feedback to students on use of the skill.

5. Continue to move about the room and interact with students in a positive manner, providing behavior-specific praise for the skills being reinforced. Provide brief error corrections if necessary.

## Efforts With All Students

Teachers may want to think strategically about establishing and maintaining relationships with students that they find particularly difficult to relate to for one reason or another. For example, students that engage in challenging (and potentially attention-seeking) behavior may benefit from strategic relational contact. Teachers can think ahead about when and how to connect best with such students. It might be that certain students respond best to humor, pop culture references, or a simple compliment or question that indicates interest in their lives. Additionally, some students may not wish to have public attention from adults, and it is worthwhile to think about how to quietly connect with such students through a quick note, quiet thumbs-up, or other unobtrusive effort.

A researched example of a similar strategy is called *banking time*, in which teachers set aside ten to fifteen minutes a few times per week to connect with a student (Driscoll & Pianta, 2010). This is an opportunity for teachers to follow a student's lead and spend time focusing on the individual student. This might include inviting the student to eat lunch together; attending a student's extracurricular activity, such as a play or sporting event; or playing a game. Teachers may need to think ahead so that they can schedule such opportunities to bank time during lunch, recess, before class, at the end of class, or after school.

Despite these efforts and intentions, conflict will happen in a classroom between a teacher and one or more students. Such conflict might occur when a teacher perceives a student or group of students as not following directions or meeting classroom expectations, disrupting instruction, or avoiding tasks. Teachers might handle such matters by redirecting students back to expected behaviors, but sometimes teachers may feel frustrated and react in ways that are unhelpful to student learning, such as giving harsh reprimands. If teachers are overly stressed or tired, they may be more likely to be reactive in response to students (McIntosh, 2020). Similarly, when students come to class deprived of or satiated from attention, the learning environment, or teacher or peer interactions, they may be more likely to be reactive and engage in problematic behaviors. In either case, whether or not teachers respond effectively to student behaviors, it is important that teachers make efforts to restore the relationship. This might involve circling back to the student and doing one of the following (Kincade, Cook, & Goerdt, 2020).

- Providing praise for engaging in expected or other positive behavior
- Apologizing for a harsh reprimand
- Engaging in a problem-solving discussion
- Attempting to understand the student's perspective by asking what they were experiencing or what they were telling themselves
- Showing kindness to the student by pointing out something positive they're doing or using their name and asking them to engage in a class activity (for example, pass out papers or organize materials)
- Sharing your experience with the situation ("I was feeling frustrated"), stating you want to support them ("I'm not sure how to support you, but I want to"), and asking them what would help you to help them in the future ("What can I do to help you if we find ourselves in the same situation?")
- Asking for a do-over

## Nurture Positive Student-Student Relationships

Teachers can also facilitate relationship building among students. In this section, we explore activities designed to build relationships between students and celebrate a sense of community in the classroom, thereby providing all students access to positive experiences with each other. Positive teacher-student relationships, in addition to positive peer relationships, are important to nurture as they are linked to students' increased self-concept, connectedness to school, and decreased emotional symptoms, such as anxiety (Wang, Hatzigianni, Shahaeian, Murray, & Harrison, 2016).

Certainly, the morning meeting can help establish relationships among students (Abry, Rimm-Kaufman, & Curby, 2017; Bondy & Ketts, 2001). Teaching students how to respond when their peers share in the circle is an important part of this strategy's success (Abry et al., 2017; Kriete & Davis, 2014; Norris, 2003). We advocate for teaching students to listen first before responding or reacting. A simple rule can be for students to paraphrase or repeat back what their peer said before they offer a new thought or how they feel. For example, a student may express that she feels frustrated with her peers talking or being disruptive during work time. Students can learn to first hear the peer ("You're saying you feel frustrated when others are disruptive") before they share their own thoughts or feelings ("I feel frustrated, too, because it's hard to do my work"). This establishes a norm of active listening prior to offering one's own thoughts. This can be particularly helpful for students to build resilience, as it provides practice positively navigating conflict or emotionally charged conversations. Further, the morning meetings can bolster resilience by providing students an environment to identify their feelings, express their thoughts, and engage in building healthy relationship skills (Abry et al., 2017; Edutopia, 2015; Kriete & Davis, 2014; Minahan, 2019).

Additional examples of ways to nurture positive student-student relationships follow.

- Provide students each week with a forum, such as a designated space in the classroom, where they share or visually display information about their personal lives and culture.
- Throw classroom parties or celebrations, such as an ice cream social or popcorn party, where students have an opportunity to positively interact with each other.

- Blend opportunities for students to share information about themselves, their families, or home environments into assignments. For example, in an English or history class, students can write an essay about themselves or their families' history, and research and share their family's genealogy. If teachers choose such an assignment, it is important to offer choices or options in such assignments since not all students live with their biological families. In music class, students may be asked to select and play a song that is important to them or their families.

Teachers can also directly teach relationship skills to students as part of their classroom expectations or SEL instruction (Dusenbury et al., 2015; Jennings & Greenberg, 2009; Yoder & Nolan, 2018). We touched on this in chapter 2, but teachers can plan academic lessons around social awareness, empathy, and understanding others' emotions using the template in figure 2.4 (page 45). Teachers can then plan activities to practice the relationship skills after students learn them, such as using cooperative learning, jigsaws (where groups of about four each are responsible for a piece of research and then come together to teach each other), or assigning students who don't know each other as partners for an assignment and providing structured procedures for them to follow. Structured procedures, such as classwide peer tutoring methods, giving specific roles to students, or providing questions to ask each other can reduce students' anxiety about what to say or how to engage with classmates they don't know.

Additionally, teachers can provide icebreakers or getting-to-know-you activities for their students that include structured opportunities to respond. Prompts for such activities can include asking students, "Who is your favorite musician?" "What would be the best food for lunch?" or "What kind of car would you love to have?" By having students share details with each other, they begin to see each other as rounded individuals with depth and complexity rather than a stereotype, cliché, or part of a clique (Aronson & Patnoe, 2011). That said, it's important that any prompts are culturally sensitive and won't lead to triggering conversations for students who have experienced trauma. Keeping the conversations on lighter topics (sports, weather, music, entertainers, and so on) before asking more personal questions ("How many siblings do you have?" "Who do you live with?") is a safer approach. Teachers can also intentionally pair up students who may not know each other or students with varying social status to break down barriers and reduce social isolation among students in the classroom (Gest et al., 2014).

---

### Practice in Action: Mentor Team

Create a mentor team that supports new students or students with fewer relationships in class. Students may volunteer to participate on such a team, or teachers may select students they have observed to be kind, helpful, and friendly. This can be applicable in K–12 settings, but the activities that mentors engage in will look different based on the students' developmental level. For example, in elementary settings, the team can have a friendship bench or support corner in which they befriend students during unstructured times, lunch, or recess (depending on the age of the students). Mentors and students who are looking for a friend can sit on the bench, and mentors can invite the others to play, eat, and so on. In middle and high school, mentor students may be assigned to new, incoming students. Mentors can sit with their incoming students at lunch, show them where to find classrooms, and serve as someone that new students can approach with questions. The team can provide support for several days or a few weeks for a new student or provide support once a week for students who have fewer classroom relationships (Labrie, 2014).

---

## Create Family Connections

Building relationships with families is also critical to student resilience (Patrikakou, 2016). After all, families have important information to share about their students and they are jointly responsible, in collaboration with teachers, for supporting student social, emotional, behavioral, and academic growth. To promote healthy student learning, teachers can partner with parents and caregivers in three primary ways, according to psychology researchers Michelle I. Albright, Roger P. Weissberg, and Linda A. Dusenbury (2011): (1) two-way communication efforts, (2) family involvement at home, and (3) family involvement at school.

### Two-Way Communication Efforts

First, teachers can establish simple strategies for two-way communication with families. Each week, a teacher can write to the families of half of the students (and the other half the next); alternatively, a teacher can write a paper note, email, or text message to a quarter of the families each week, respectively, for four weeks. Some teachers use downloadable software applications such as Remind (www.remind.com/apps) to send these communications. The content can be simply one or two sentences describing an area of *glow* (where the student did well) and an area of *grow* (an area to improve on). This note could be divided into sections, with one section for teacher comments and one section for family members' responses or comments. By inviting family comments, teachers can open lines of communication throughout the school year.

These techniques for grades preK–12 are evidence based and can be structured to focus on certain prosocial skills that students are learning (Jurbergs, Palcic, & Kelley, 2007; Sheridan, Smith, Kim, Beretvas, & Park, 2019; Smith, Sheridan, Kim, Park, & Beretvas, 2020). For example, one month a teacher might focus notes on self-awareness, while another month targets self-regulation or social awareness. Some schools with whom we work have also established routines, such as Wonderful Wednesdays, to connect weekly with the family of one or two students who have worked to perform particular targeted prosocial skills. Such notes might sound something like, "It is a Wonderful Wednesday, and I just wanted to let you know that Javier has consistently shown social awareness and kindness to others in the classroom. I have seen him help others with cleanup tasks, share his snack with a friend who forgot theirs, and invite others to play during indoor recess."

Of course, in addition to communication centered on individual student performance, it also helps families for teachers to communicate overall classwide happenings via email, weekly newsletters, or other formats, and provide regular updates about what specific prosocial skills students are learning. In fact, some SEL curricula include family newsletters to send home. Such communication may define the skill, what it looks like and sounds like, what parents and caregivers can do to remind the student to practice or reinforce the skill, and relevant children's or youth literature that families can share and discuss at home. Such communication boosts social and emotional competence and mental health (Sheridan et al., 2019). The example completed template in figure 4.1 is one that teachers can send home with students.

| Classroom Expectation | Inclusiveness |
| --- | --- |
| Description | Showing value for each other and treating others with dignity, which builds community and healthy relationship skills |
| What it looks like in my classroom | Listening to one another, helping one another, asking questions about each other's interest without judgment, accepting others |

**FIGURE 4.1:** Prosocial skills template.

continued →

| What it sounds like in my classroom | Kind words, one voice at a time during group discussions, inviting others to join groups or activities |
| --- | --- |
| What to do at home | Ask your child to share what he or she saw students do that was inclusive of others or a way he or she feels included by others at school. |
| Text | To Kill a Mockingbird (Lee, 1960). Read and share ways that the characters did and did not show inclusion or acceptance for others. |

Visit **MarzanoResources.com/reproducibles** for a free reproducible version of this figure.

## Family Involvement at Home

In addition to communication efforts, teachers can also involve families in student learning. Teachers can send home optional assignments for students to complete with parents or caregivers if they have time. This homework might include a word search or crossword with key social and emotional vocabulary or classroom expectations. Joint activities such as these might help to spark discussion between students and their parents or caregivers, where students can share all they have been learning.

Another strategy that Albright and colleagues (2011) suggest is teachers creating a skill chart focused on specific social, emotional, and behavioral skills that students are learning and what they may look like at home. Families can use this guidance to build awareness of what students are learning at school and to practice these skills at home. We provide an example in figure 4.2 in which family members can anticipate and remind students to use particular skills and acknowledge them for doing so; we also provide a customizable reproducible "Classroom Skill Chart" (page 98).

Similarly, teachers might encourage families to create a matrix, much like the class-wide matrix in chapter 2 (page 33), but with expectations across home routines, including remote learning, before school, mealtimes, play time, homework time, and bed time (Center on Positive Behavioral Interventions and Supports, & Center for Parent Information and Resources, 2020). Figure 4.3 (page 96) provides an example of a matrix for expectations in home settings, and the reproducible "Skill Chart for Home" (page 99) can go home with students.

| Skill | Anticipate | Teach or Prompt | Acknowledge |
|---|---|---|---|
| Self-Awareness | | Help child to identify feelings he or she may experience. For example, you may say, "Remember, on the first day of school you might feel both nervous and excited." | Praise child for naming emotion or recognizing certain characteristics about him- or herself. For example, you may say, "Nice job recognizing your emotion. I appreciate that you can talk about emotions." |
| Social Awareness | Consider your child's ability to notice others' emotions or experiences. | Remind your child to consider others' experiences. For example, you may say, "Remember, other students are probably nervous on the first day of school too." | Praise child for noticing others or indicating the perspectives of others. |
| Self-Management | Consider how your child manages strong emotions or intense situations. | Remind your child about the expectations for the environment and strategies for coping with strong feelings. For example, you may say, "Remember, if you are feeling nervous, you still need to go to school, but you can practice taking deep breaths and telling yourself, 'It will be OK!'" | Praise your child for managing strong emotions such as extreme fear, anxiety, or excitement. |
| Responsible Decision Making | Consider how your child makes decisions about his or her behavior when experiencing strong feelings. | Remind your child about strategies for remembering responsible behaviors. For example, you may say, "Remember, when you are feeling angry, you have a choice. You can say or do hurtful things, or you can cool down first before you do anything you might regret." | Praise your child for managing challenging situations and making responsible decisions. For example, you may say, "I really appreciate how you were able to stop and think when your friend said something mean to you. That shows such responsible behavior!" |
| Relationship Skills | Consider how your child connects with other individuals. Think about how he or she initiates and maintains relationships and navigates conflict, and other social behaviors. | Remind your child that relationships can be challenging and what it takes to have healthy friendships and relationships, such as being kind, being honest, and reaching out. | Praise your child for navigating relationships positively. For example, you may say, "It sounds like your friend said unkind things. I really appreciate that you advocated for yourself without being unkind." |

**FIGURE 4.2:** Example skill chart.

| Expectation | Virtual Learning | Social Media Use | Before School |
|---|---|---|---|
| Respect | Keep background noise low. Use chat box to ask questions. | Engage in conversation using kind words. | Be polite when waking up. Get ready quickly so others can use the bathroom. |
| Responsibility | Complete assignments on time. Show your best effort. | Keep your password secret. Log out when done. | Check that you have all your materials. |

**FIGURE 4.3:** Example matrix for home setting.

Parents or caregivers can create these matrices by attending a family night in which they learn how this matrix works, then adding what the skills may look like in the home environment. Another option is for teachers to provide students with a blank matrix so students can work with their parents to complete their matrix. A teacher could also record a minilesson on how to complete or use the matrix to share with families as well. Families can also learn, with support from the classroom teacher, to teach the expectations to their children (such as discussing examples and nonexamples of the expectations), remind them to follow the expectations, and provide positive feedback when students follow the expectations (Center on Positive Behavioral Interventions and Supports, & Center for Parent Information and Resources, 2020).

## Family Involvement at School

Parents and caregivers should feel encouraged to practice skills with students at home, and they may be more motivated to practice if they also feel welcome in the classroom environment. Albright and colleagues (2011) recommend that teachers invite families to engage in the school setting to the extent that they are able and offer strategies to facilitate this. In one strategy, teachers invite parents and caregivers to visit the school and observe the class during an SEL lesson or morning circle time. In some schools, parents and caregivers are even encouraged to participate or co-lead SEL lessons.

If parents and caregivers are unable to participate during the school day, they may be able to attend a family night that focuses on SEL efforts at school. Such evenings can be organized like a workshop, where parents and caregivers learn about overall strategies for supporting student development or specific strategies for working with individual students' social and emotional behaviors. During these family nights, families and teachers can discuss the importance of SEL and how both the school and the home are places for teaching and reinforcing those competencies. Together, these discussions can lead to more alignment and agreement on methods or ways to build SEL competencies in students. During parent or caregiver-teacher conferences, teachers can also structure collaborative conversations that include discussion of students' social, emotional, and behavioral development. For example, the teacher may define key competencies (self-awareness, self-management, social awareness, responsible decision making, relationship development) for the caregiver and offer examples of student strengths and challenges in each of these areas. The teacher may then invite the caregiver to respond with observations of each competency in the home environment.

## ····▶ Key Points

Relationships are at the foundation of universal classroom practices. Classrooms that emphasize both consistency and connection are places where students are more likely to feel secure and open to learning. In this chapter, we illuminated ways in which teachers can strategically build connections with students and families while simultaneously teaching prosocial skills. We offered strategies for teachers to intentionally build relationships with students while also creating opportunities for students to build self-awareness and social awareness. Some of these strategies (such as greeting students at the door, engaging in brief emotional check-ins, and actively supervising all students) are simple acts that can provide large benefits. We gave examples, such as mentor teams, to foster student-student relationships. We also offered structures for encouraging positive relationships with families, focusing on building feasible two-way communication opportunities and strategies for sharing in student social and emotional learning across home and school contexts.

# Classroom Skill Chart

| Skill | Anticipate | Teach or Prompt | Acknowledge |
|-------|-----------|-----------------|-------------|
|       |           |                 |             |
|       |           |                 |             |
|       |           |                 |             |
|       |           |                 |             |
|       |           |                 |             |

# Skill Chart for Home

We are learning skills at school that also apply at home. The first row is an example. Please fill this out together with your child and talk about these expectations and how you both can show them.

| Expectation | During Meals | Social Media Use | Before School | After School | Bedtime |
|---|---|---|---|---|---|
| *Example:* Responsibility | Complete assignments on time. Show your best effort. | Keep your password secret. Log out when done. | Check that you have all your materials. | Check that you have all your materials. | Make sure materials are ready for next day. Brush teeth, use bathroom, wash hands. |
| | | | | | |
| | | | | | |
| | | | | | |

# CHAPTER 5

# Employing Discipline That Ensures Consistency

S o far in this book, we have covered some of the challenges many students face, how to create consistency by effectively teaching and reinforcing skills to support resilience, and how to develop connections by creating a classroom climate that encourages retention of skills. Now, we shift our focus to consistency as it relates to discipline in a classroom that bolsters resilience. We discuss a comprehensive discipline structure that promotes consistency, the supportive discipline framework.

We discussed the importance of consistency so that students know what's expected of them and how to engage with each other and the teacher in chapter 2 (page 33). Consistently employing discipline and responding to students' unwanted behavior can further create predictability and safety in the classroom (Jones & Kahn, 2017; Pickens & Tschopp, 2017). When teachers provide that consistency, students know the boundaries and there are no surprises, which is especially important to students who have experienced trauma, who may constantly search for signs of danger in an effort to protect themselves (Pickens & Tschopp, 2017). If teachers don't account for surprises, and they lack consistency in or awareness of what happens when a boundary is crossed, they can create stress in students (Minahan, 2019). When there is a consistent and transparent process, students know what to expect when someone breaks a rule. Additionally, students will see rules as fair, and teachers will avoid instances of "Why didn't *they* get in trouble?" when other students are disciplined for disobeying the same rule (Yeager, 2017).

## Know the Principles of Discipline

Here, we outline three key principles behind discipline in a classroom that promotes resilience: (1) discipline is built on teaching, (2) use of behavior theory ensures that teaching is function based, and (3) ensure flexibility by having a variety of strategies for managing behavior. Taking these three principles together, we want our readers to see that discipline is a teaching opportunity, not just punishment. We're not saying that certain aversive consequences or punishments aren't useful, but there is a mindset that discipline that focuses on teaching and reinforcing a skill prior to punishment bolsters resilience (Harlacher & Rodriguez, 2018; Horner, Sugai, Todd, & Lewis-Palmer, 2005). The goal with discipline is to ensure students are safe and that they start (or continue) using prosocial skills to manage their emotions and replace maladjusted skills.

### Understand That Discipline Is Built on Teaching

First and foremost, discipline is actually built on teaching prosocial skills, not just punishment of unwanted behaviors. For discipline, instead of focusing on what behavior to get rid of, teachers can ask what behavior (that is, prosocial skill) can replace the unwanted behavior the student is currently using (Crone et al., 2015; O'Neill, Albin, Storey, Horner, & Sprague, 2015). The teacher's discipline is then structured around strengthening or teaching a missing skill. In doing so, teachers actually can make the unwanted behavior *less useful* and therefore help the student replace the old behavior with a new, more socially beneficial skill (Crone et al., 2015; O'Neill et al., 2015).

For example, say a student is verbally aggressive toward peers. The teacher could choose to punish the behavior with an in-school suspension, but we know that behavior is functional and purposeful (Crone et al., 2015). That student's aggression served a purpose—perhaps leading peers to leave the student alone and give the space that student needs. If the teacher punishes the behavior with in-school suspension without providing the student with a more adaptive behavior to replace the aggression, sooner or later, the student will revert to using that aggression. Being asked to stop using a behavior without being provided a new behavior leaves only a matter of time before people use the previously learned behavior (Crone et al., 2015; Frey et al., 2014).

To avoid this, the teacher should center discipline around reinforcing a desired skill (O'Neill et al., 2015). In this example, the student is provided instruction on expressing emotions assertively, rather than being verbally aggressive, to get needs met. (The general skill taught was to *be safe*, which was defined as expressing emotions assertively and safely; in doing so, the student can ask for space rather than be verbally aggressive.)

### Consider Behavior Theory

To best teach students prosocial skills, we advocate for use of behavior theory (also referred to as *behaviorism*; Alberto & Troutman, 2013). Highly influenced by psychologist B. F. Skinner (1953, 1976) and John Watson (1913), behavior theory explains how to support students and how to intervene in many cases. Because of this, understanding behavior theory enables teachers to better support students. In this section, we describe some terminology before discussing how to use behavior theory.

*Behavior* is an observable and measurable act that happens in a context—not something that occurs in a vacuum. This is the *behavior chain*, depicted in figure 5.1, in which behavior is triggered by antecedents and then maintained by consequences in the environment (Alberto & Troutman, 2013; Dunlap, Harrower, & Fox, 2005; Wolery et al., 1988). An *antecedent* is an incident or moment that triggers a behavior. Following the behavior, some form of consequence occurs that either reinforces the behavior (making it *more* likely to occur again in the future) or punishes the behavior (making it *less* likely to occur again; Alberto & Troutman, 2013; Baer et al., 1968; Skinner, 1953, 1976; Watson, 1913; Wolery et al., 1988).

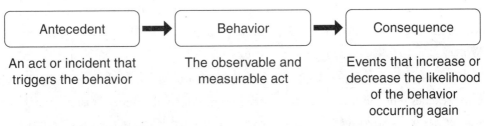

*Source: Adapted from Dunlap, Harrower, & Fox, 2005; Wolery et al., 1988.*

**FIGURE 5.1:** Behavior chain.

Hearing the seatbelt chime when you get into your car is a pretty immediate antecedent to getting someone to perform the behavior of buckling up. By buckling up, you then avoid the annoying sound and are therefore more likely to buckle up next time you get into the car (for this reason and many others). As a school example, consider a middle schooler in social studies class. When asked to participate in small-group work with peers (the antecedent), one student becomes very engaged and frequently asks his peers about the activity and their thoughts (the behavior). This leads to laughter and rapport with his classmates (the consequence, which is reinforcement in this case). This middle schooler has a behavior chain in which group work triggers engagement from him with his peers, which results in a lot of peer attention.

As you can see, *consequence* is neither a positive or negative term and simply refers to events that occur after a behavior. Often, reinforcing a desired skill can be sufficient to strengthen learning, though the addition of a mild punishment or aversive correction can support students using a new skill (Alberto & Troutman, 2013; Simonsen et al., 2008). Generally speaking, when supporting students to use a new behavior, teachers will use *teaching strategies* to teach the student the new skill. (We discussed teaching strategies in chapter 2, page 33, as part of the universal practices.) After instructing, teachers then use *prevention strategies* to prompt the newly taught behavior. They also use *response strategies* to reinforce the new skill and to provide any corrective consequences or action for use of the unwanted or old behavior (O'Neill et al., 2015). Knowing the consequences that most often occur after a behavior allows a teacher to make an educated guess about the purpose (that is, the function) of the student's behavior. In fact, behavior theory posits that all of our behaviors are purposeful and serve one of two functions: (1) trying to gain something or (2) trying to avoid or escape something (Alberto & Troutman, 2013; Skinner, 1953, 1976). What do people try to gain or try to avoid or escape? Behavior theory provides us three categories: (1) someone's attention, (2) something tangible, such as an item or activity, or (3) some sort of sensory need (Skinner, 1953, 1976). Thus, behavior theory says that all of our behavior can be understood as serving one of six functions, which are illustrated in figure 5.2 (Alberto & Troutman, 2013; Baer et al., 1968; Wolery et al., 1988).

As an example, imagine a student argues with his teacher to get out of work. What if the teacher sent the student to the office for arguing? That student just got what he wanted, as he is no longer doing the work and instead is talking with the administrator. However, if the teacher identified and then provided support in line with the function of the student's unwanted behavior, then the student could learn a new skill to replace the old skill. In this example, the teacher could allow the student to ask for a short break using a pass or signal; at the same time, the teacher would provide additional instruction for any academic skill gap the student has.

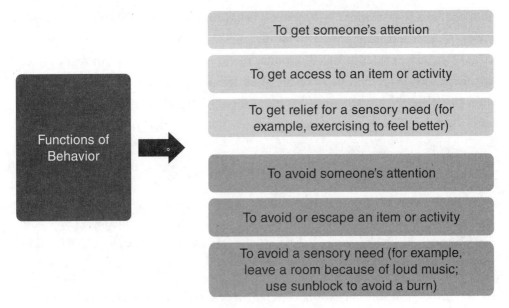

Source: Adapted from Alberto & Troutman, 2013; Skinner, 1953, 1976.

**FIGURE 5.2:** Functions of behavior.

Knowing the behavior chain and how behavior serves a function, teachers can assess what the triggers are for specific behaviors. Accordingly, teachers can put strategies into place and adjust the environment to minimize or avoid triggering the unwanted behavior (this chapter and chapter 6, page 133). Also, teachers can provide antecedents (for example, verbal reminders, visual posters) that prompt the desired behavior that the student can use to replace unwanted or unhelpful behaviors (Crone et al., 2015).

### Be Flexible by Having a Variety of Strategies

The third principle is to ensure you can be flexible by equipping yourself with a variety of strategies to manage behavior and de-escalate situations. Knowing that discipline is built on teaching and that behavior theory is the frame for how best to teach prosocial skills, teachers will need a variety of strategies to manage behavior. As teachers, you'll know your students individually and therefore can match a strategy to them. For example, some students may need a firm reminder and then space to follow a rule, whereas others may need humor to offset certain behavior. With a variety of strategies, you can adjust your approach accordingly.

However, be sure to match your response sensibly to the situation. Don't have a disproportionate response to a student, which can be difficult when dealing with the sometimes-powerful emotions felt in the moment of a difficult situation.

Too weak of a response may not correct a behavior, and too much of a response may lead to additional damage and harm for the student (Harlacher, 2015; Yoder & Nolan, 2018). There are evidence-based response methods we'll share later in this chapter, but we acknowledge that there's a bit of an art as to when and how to apply such strategies. (We give a framework for using these strategies later in the chapter.) For now, the point is not to use a wrecking ball when a fly swatter will do, and vice versa.

## Use the Supportive Discipline Framework

Before we describe our supportive discipline framework, please note that it is most appropriate for mild behaviors versus major behaviors that administrators may handle. Consider the breakdown of behavior types (Harlacher & Rodriguez, 2018; Todd, Horner, & Tobin, 2006).

- *Minor behaviors* or *classroom-managed behaviors* are behaviors that are relatively mild in nature and do not necessarily pose a danger or threat to others. Examples include being disruptive, not following directions, or talking back.

- *Major behaviors* or *office-managed behaviors* generally disrupt the learning environment and pose more than just a mild disturbance to the classroom. Examples include fighting, harassment, bullying, drug possession, and severe property damage. Administrators usually handle these.

- Then there are *crisis behaviors*, which pose a direct and immediate threat. These examples include weapon possession, assault, threatening self or others, or destroying the room.

If your school has a discipline plan or follows tenets of positive behavioral interventions and supports, it likely has designated which behaviors are minor, major, and crisis behaviors. However, even if your school doesn't have such guidance, we encourage you to identify a list of behaviors that are minor, major, and crisis and how to respond accordingly. For example, following guidance from PBIS Apps (www.pbisapps.org) in the absence of school classifications of behavior, teachers can determine which behaviors are under which categories. Doing so meets the principle of being clear and consistent—teachers know ahead of time which behaviors they'll manage, and the students know which behaviors are ones that get them sent to the office and those that do not.

This consistent structure can help relieve students' anxiety about ambiguity in the environment and thus bolster their resilience (Barrett et al., 2018; Eber et al., 2020). As a result, teachers will be less likely to send students to the office for minor behaviors, such as not having their homework or talking back, or keeping students in their classroom for behaviors that should be sent to the office, such as destruction of property or aggression (Bradshaw et al., 2012; Harlacher & Rodriguez, 2018; Taylor-Greene et al., 1997). By identifying what behaviors are classroom-managed and the strategies to use accordingly, then teachers can operate in that structure rather than escalating the response based on the behavior in the moment.

We use *supportive discipline framework* because the structure is centered on teaching and supporting students to use prosocial skills and improve their resilience. By using a discipline approach focused on teaching skills, teachers can concentrate on the prosocial skills students need that enhance their resilience. More so, teachers won't focus solely on rule violations and what punishment to administer; instead, they'll work with a supportive mindset to collaboratively help students gain the skills they need to navigate their lives. This shift in the classroom focus is important for many students who may experience school as a punishing experience. (Recall in chapter 1, page 17, our discussion that many students experience a lot of failure, rejection, and difficulty in school.) By acknowledging what students do well, building relationships (topics we discussed in chapters 3, page 65, and 4, page 83), and having a teaching-based discipline framework, you can make school a more positive experience for many (Crone et al., 2015; Darch & Kame'enui, 2003; O'Neill et al., 2015).

We outline three levels in the supportive discipline framework that correlate to a behavior's frequency or severity. Level one is for mild or infrequent behaviors, and level two is for behaviors that are either mild but repetitive or a bit more invasive than mild ones. Level three is for behaviors that are persistent or very disruptive or severe. We describe each level next and provide examples of strategies for each level. Figure 5.3 (page 108) illustrates the supportive discipline framework.

## Level One: Correcting Errors for Mild and Infrequent Behaviors

When handling behaviors that are minor or happen infrequently, such as talking out of turn or getting out of one's seat when not appropriate, your best course of action is brief error correction. Students have been taught the classwide expectations, and you have ongoing reinforcement to strengthen those expectations and skills. So, when a student makes a mistake, a simple reminder and correction may be all that are really needed.

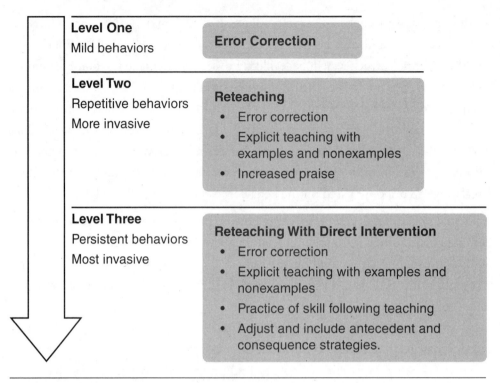

**FIGURE 5.3:** Supportive discipline framework.

*Visit **MarzanoResources.com/reproducibles** for a free reproducible version of this figure.*

To use error correction, follow these steps.

1. State the expectation the student isn't following: "That's not the way we ask for things we need in class."

2. Model the expectation briefly: "We show value for others by being kind, so we might say, 'May I please use the stapler?'"

3. Ask the student to use the expectation: "Now you try."

4. Acknowledge the student's use of the skill and then move on with the day: "Thank you for showing value for others and following our classroom expectations."

A long conversation, shaming the student, or expressing disappointment aren't needed. Instead, simply state the mistake, identify the expectation, have the student do it, and then you're done (Harlacher, 2015; Simonsen et al., 2008).

When students do not follow directions or comply with the error correction, we advise a planned interaction or script. Determining how to engage with a student who is being defiant or perhaps escalating a situation can be nerve-wracking in the moment. Consequently, it helps to have a plan ahead of time for what to say and what to do so that you can give the request and walk away. This allows a student time to process how to respond and removes emotion from the situation (Harlacher, 2015; Mackay, McLaughlin, Weber, & Derby, 2001). We offer an example in figure 5.4 of how to respond when students need reminders.

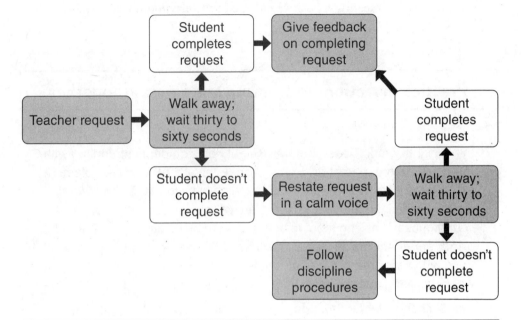

**FIGURE 5.4:** Flowchart of providing reminders to students.

*Visit **MarzanoResources.com/reproducibles** for a free reproducible version of this figure.*

Additionally, having phrases that place the choice on the student is important.

- **If . . . then:** For example, "If you choose to finish your work, then you may earn electronic screen time." Such a statement makes the situation about empowerment (the student has a choice), and it makes it about natural consequences (if X happens, then Y happens).

- **When . . . then:** This can be helpful for stopping students whose thinking is escalating and who may need suggestions for making a positive choice or managing their emotions. For example, perhaps a student is feeling anxious and unable to calm themselves in the moment. A teacher could say, "When you use the pause-and-reflect technique, then you'll be able to manage your anxiety and focus on the task at hand." For instances of disrespect or defiance, a teacher could say, "When you are calm and being respectful with your tone, then I can listen to your needs." This brings back the focus on a prosocial skill, such as the classroom expectations, and reminds students that you will listen to their needs once they make a given choice about their actions. This also emphasizes that the classroom expectations are not just rules students must abide that don't mean anything; instead, they are a way of creating a positive culture in the classroom (Norris, 2003; Simonsen & Myers, 2015).

---

## **Practice in Action:** Prompting and Praising Together

In his eighth-grade classroom, Mr. Knight helps students struggling with the classroom expectation *Show dignity toward others*. He selects a skill related to dignity toward others, which is including and welcoming others. He defined this skill as using active listening, inviting them to join your group, and asking them to contribute during discussions. Mr. Knight prints small sheets of paper (skill sheets) that list the expectation (dignity toward others), and the related skills students will practice that week (actively listening, inviting others, and asking others to contribute).

The skill sheets have a space for five checkmarks, like in figure 5.5. Mr. Knight places the sheets on each student's desk, and throughout the day and week, he praises students when he sees them use one of the skills listed on the skill sheet. Students then enter a checkmark or star on their skill sheet. After five checkmarks, students place the skill sheet in a bucket and get a new skill sheet for their desk. The sheets served as visual prompts for students—and Mr. Knight—for the given skill, and Mr. Knight continues to praise and acknowledge students using the skills. The skill sheets are tallied into the bucket, and when it reaches a certain level, students can receive a larger reinforcement (as we outlined in chapter 3, page 65).

> Expectation: Show dignity toward others.
>
> ☐   ☐   ☐   ☐   ☐
>
> - Actively listening
> - Inviting others to join your group
> - Asking others to contribute during discussions

**FIGURE 5.5:** Example of a skill sheet.

### Level Two: Reteaching for Mild but Repetitive Behaviors or More Invasive Behaviors

Even with error correction, students may continue to make mistakes or misbehave. A student may also display a behavior that is too invasive to only warrant an error correction, and therefore a level two response is needed. Here, the teacher provides error correction in the moment and then provides additional instruction later, be it the next free moment, later that day, the next day, or some other time. For example, imagine a student says something crude. The teacher provides error correction, such as, "Tom, saying that is not OK because it can make others feel unsafe. We use language that values others. Please state your needs another way." Following that error correction, the teacher can then reteach the student class expectations about safety at a later point. This reteaching can be brief, such as conferencing with the student for a few minutes to review examples and nonexamples of the expectation. After the reteaching, the teacher can spend the next few days increasing their praise to the student who is practicing the retaught skill. This supports students with a layered approach, combining the error correction of level one with the additional support at level two in the form of reteaching the expectation and reinforcing that skill.

The additional praise is an important piece, as it can help strengthen the retaught skill (Gage et al., 2018). The student wasn't able to integrate the skill into his or her repertoire with the first teaching of the classroom expectation that was done with the entire class (as we discussed in chapter 2, page 33), so additional reteaching and reinforcement are needed. To provide adequate reinforcement, teachers can mentally self-monitor and remind themselves to watch and praise the student that was retaught. However, this can be easy to forget with the pace of a school day. We suggest using strategies outlined in the previous chapter, such as setting a timer (the alarm on your phone, for instance), or using a visual reminder (such as a sticky note on your desk) or a tangible prompt (like coins in your pocket).

### Level Three: Reteaching With Direct Intervention for Continued Behaviors or Most Invasive Behaviors

For behaviors that persist or students that need continued support with certain behaviors, the next step is to reteach the expectation again with more explicit or extensive teaching (Alberto & Troutman, 2013; Harlacher, 2015). In addition, the teacher adjusts the environment or further supports the student with more direct intervention or strategies (O'Neill et al., 2015). For level three, the teacher reteaches the expectation to the student with examples and nonexamples, as well as an activity to practice the skill. From there, the teacher will need to adjust the environment so that the student receives more direct prompts or antecedents to use the desired skill and reinforcement after the student does use the desired skill (for example, a teacher may add visual prompts and then provide specific praise after a student uses the skill; Crone et al., 2015). This is where your bank of strategies will come in handy. We illustrate the teaching process for level three in figure 5.6 and then provide a list of strategies to consider next.

| Step | Example |
|------|---------|
| 1. Identify the unwanted or undesired behavior. What did the student do? | The student is talkative and off task when asked to do assignments (for instance, talks to peers, plays on phone during seat work). |
| 2. Identify the previously taught expectation that would replace or eliminate the unwanted behavior. | The expectation is being responsible. Instead of being off task, the student will stay engaged in work. |
| 3. Reteach the behavior or skill explicitly using examples and nonexamples. Tailor these examples and nonexamples to the student's situation. | Examples include keeping phone put away, reading the textbook and taking notes, and asking a peer a question related to the assignment. Nonexamples include playing on the phone, talking to peers about nonschool topics, and making noises to themselves. |
| 4. Provide the student a way to practice or actively engage in the retaught skill. | After a lesson on being responsible, the student is asked to write two ways he is being responsible. After a few days, the student is asked to share how he was responsible over the last few days. |
| 5. Identify a strategy that adjusts the environment to (1) prompt the taught skill and (2) reinforce the taught skill. | The teacher greets the student when he enters the room and reminds him to be responsible during class, particularly during seatwork. The student can document the percentage of work completed during the class period, which the teacher then reviews. The student can earn a pass to be first in the lunch line if he completes at least 80 percent of the work. |

**FIGURE 5.6:** Reteaching expectations in level three.

## Practice in Action: Expressing Feelings for Self-Management

One student had difficulty managing her emotions in Mrs. Lorraine's seventh-grade classroom. To help reteach processing and managing emotions, Mrs. Lorraine wanted to teach the student not to let her emotions build up so long before expressing them. She illustrated this concept of emotions spilling over by having a minilesson in which she talked about anger and other feelings being similar to a cup being filled with water. She then had the student hold the cup and would fill the cup with some water. Mrs. Lorraine then talked about the emotions adding up and then eventually, there's too many emotions (too much water) for the person (the cup). They would then spill out. She shook the cup to illustrate emotions spilling everywhere. Mrs. Lorraine told the student that instead of letting the water spill out, she could pour water out from time to time and keep the water level low. She told the student how she could pour water out by journaling, talking to someone, or meditating. Mrs. Lorraine had the student identify a way to talk about her emotions. The student chose journaling, so each day in class Mrs. Lorraine would prompt the student to use her journal as a way of managing her emotions. She would then praise and reinforce the student when she used her journal or when she identified and expressed her emotions in responsible and prosocial manners. In this situation, Mrs. Lorraine successfully used brief reteaching, prompting, and praise to bolster this student's social and emotional competency and bolster her resilience.

### Continuum of Responses

Here, we want to share a variety of low-intensity to higher-intensity strategies that teachers can use to encourage students to use the prosocial skills they have learned, particularly the classwide expectations. These strategies are helpful throughout the entire supportive discipline framework and thus offer flexibility with how and when you use and apply them. The Midwest PBIS Network (n.d.) provides a list of least invasive to more invasive and direct strategies as part of its Classroom Practices series. (See also Alberto & Troutman, 2013; Harlacher, 2015; Simonsen & Myers, 2015.) These interactions are listed from lowest intensity to highest.

- **Planned ignoring:** This is a decision to intentionally ignore certain behaviors, such as a student blurting out or making comments that are out of line. The notion is to ignore those behaviors, not the student, and to provide attention or acknowledgment for other desired skills or behaviors.

- **Physical proximity:** This is a method of moving closer to a student who is displaying an unwanted behavior because the closeness of an adult might deter the behavior.

- **Signal or nonverbal cue:** In this method, a teacher uses a signal to indicate to students that a behavior needs to stop. This signal can be flipping a card displayed at the front of the class, a hand gesture, or flashing the lights. The teacher should teach this signal beforehand, and students should understand that the signal indicates the need to self-check their current behavior.

- **Praise of the desired behavior in others (praise around):** Teachers praise and acknowledge those students displaying the appropriate or desired skill. The idea is that other students will witness the praise, remember that they can receive similar praise for the same behavior, and then adjust their current behavior.

- **Direct eye contact:** Here, the teacher uses direct eye contact to communicate to a student that a behavior needs to change. This can be accompanied with a signal as well (such as one finger over the mouth to indicate quieting down). Consider the students' age and the classroom context. Some students may view direct eye contact as a trigger, culturally inappropriate, or an aggressive stance, so be mindful of your student's history when using this method.

- **Redirection:** The teacher directly tells the student that what he or she is doing is not OK and gives a clear redirection; for example, "You are being disruptive. I need you to quiet down and focus on your work."

- **Support for a procedure or routine:** The teacher offers the student support for the behavior, and may or may not pair that support with a redirect. The teacher can say, "Here, it looks like you need some assistance with (current task). How can I help?" Or, the teacher may break down the current task into smaller steps and provide the directions one at a time to the student. For example, the teacher may say, "OK, Jennifer, let's get your book out first. OK, now let's open and start your computer."

- **Reteaching:** This refers to more direct reteaching of the desired skill. The teacher can provide in-the-moment reteaching or set up reteaching outside of the time that the student is engaging in unwanted behavior.

- **Choice provision:** In the moment, the teacher can offer choices that may be instructionally related, such as, "You can start on your homework or read quietly." The teacher may also offer choices that describe the reality of the situation by telling the student things such as, "You can either start your work and be a part of class today or move to the back of the room to do your work and not be a part of our discussion today" or, "You have two options right now: work quietly and earn screen time or continue to be disruptive and spend your lunchtime in here doing your work." The latter two choices lay out the natural consequences of following directions versus not following directions. We expand on this concept later.

- **A conference with the student:** The teacher calls a meeting with the student in a collaborative, cooperative sense. The conference is about understanding what the student needs and communicating why the current behavior is not helpful. It is a proactive meeting done prior to another occurrence of a potential issue, not a reactive one to punish the student after the behavior. The goal should be to have a mutually decided agreement between the student and the teacher to follow. The two could develop a more extensive plan, but the student and teacher can have an agreement that the student will make a conscious effort to use a chosen prosocial skill rather than continue to use the unwanted skill.

# Employ Discipline Strategies That Align With the Supportive Discipline Framework

In this section, we provide strategies that you can use throughout the supportive discipline framework, though we encourage you to use them primarily in level three because they are intensive strategies designed to address the quality of behaviors targeted at level three. These strategies center on an instructional approach that assumes the student has been retaught the desired skill. Following reteaching of a skill, the teacher then uses antecedent strategies to prompt the student's use of the skill and employs consequence strategies to reinforce the student's use of the skill. As part of the consequence strategies, teachers may also use corrective consequences to correct any unwanted behaviors.

To help you develop a bank of strategies to use, we have selected various evidence-based strategies and organized them into three categories: (1) antecedent strategies, (2) reinforcement strategies, and (3) corrective consequences. When selecting strategies, it's important to keep in mind a student's developmental level, their cultural background, and their personal preferences. The strategies should respect the student's dignity and value and be culturally appropriate (Leverson et al., 2021). Teachers can examine their own culture and biases as they select strategies and then consider if the chosen practices would be culturally inappropriate for students. They can also have discussions with their students to determine what is culturally appropriate when it comes to managing behavior with them.

### Prevention (Antecedent) Strategies

Antecedents occur before a behavior and prompt use of a skill (Alberto & Troutman, 2013; Wolery et al., 1988). In this case, prevention strategies are used to manage antecedents and typically are prompts to trigger or remind a student to use a taught skill.

### Precorrection

Precorrection is a great strategy that teachers can use for just about any skill that they wish students to learn. In precorrection, the teacher verbally prompts a student to recall a behavior prior to a situation to increase his or her use of that behavior while also preventing the use of an unwanted behavior (CESE, 2020; Colvin et al., 1993; Haydon & Kroeger, 2016; Simonsen et al., 2015).

For this strategy, the teacher can talk to the student briefly when he or she enters the classroom or prior to starting a given activity. The teacher greets the student and welcomes him or her to the room and then reminds or asks the student what skills to keep in mind during the upcoming activity. This check-in can be a brief conversation, or the teacher can make it a little more involved by having the student practice or act out the skill in question. Such an interaction can set the student up to have a positive experience, allows practicing the skill accurately, and creates a connection between the adult and student (Colvin et al., 1993; Cook et al., 2018b). In addition to the check-in, the teacher can provide the student with a visual or tangible prompt on his or her desk as a steady reminder of the targeted skill. For example, the teacher can make a sign for the student's desk or place written notes in his or her planner or textbook.

## High-Probability Requests

This strategy is particularly beneficial for students who are, shall we say, not exactly *eager* to follow directions (Bross, Common, & Oakes, 2018; Chambers, 2006; Davis, Brady, Williams, & Hamilton, 1992). *High-probability requests* are ones in which the teacher makes small, easy-to-comply requests of the student before making a more difficult request. To use this strategy, identify three easy things for the student to do, such as passing out papers, putting a book away, or giving someone a high-five. Present the student each of the three requests, either in a row or spaced out over a brief period of time, and provide praise after the completion of each request. Then make the more difficult request, which we call a *low-probability request.* By having the student do easy, fun, or successful requests first (the high-probability requests), teachers can build momentum in the student to continue to follow directions and display the desired expectation or skill (the low-probability request). A sequence may look like this.

1. Students enter the classroom and start the work written on the board. One student struggles to start his work and often talks or disrupts other students during this time. The student has been taught the skill of being responsible with his work and being respectful by not disrupting others.

2. The teacher greets the class: "Welcome, everyone! Please look at the board and begin your work." The teacher then individually addresses Johnny, the student in question: "Hey, Johnny, good to see you. How about a fist bump to start the day?" This is the teacher's first high-probability request.

3. After Johnny gives her a fist bump, the teacher responds, "Awesome, thank you. Can you take your seat?" This is the teacher's second high-probability request.

4. Johnny takes his seat, and the teacher continues: "Thank you. Everyone, I see you all quieting down and starting your work. That's very respectful. Johnny, can you read the bell work out loud to everyone?" This is the teacher's third high-probability request.

5. Johnny reads the work out loud, and the teacher gives him a head nod and thumbs-up before saying, "Now everyone can get started. Johnny, can you begin your bell work?" This represents the low-probability request because it's a request that Johnny has not previously completed when asked.

For this strategy, notice the additional strategies embedded throughout. There was the use of praise for the entire class for beginning their work (which provided a small break from requests for Johnny) and the use of relationship building with Johnny (the fist bump). One can see the layered approach of the strategies and how they build on each other to help with managing behavior.

## Instructional Choice

Instructional choice offers students options on tasks that they are being asked to complete (Dunlap et al., 1994; Hoffman & DuPaul, 2000; Lane, Menzies, Parks, Oakes, & Lane, 2018; Walker, 1979). Instructional choice is helpful for students who may not follow directions and are working on being responsible with their choices and schoolwork. For this strategy, the teacher gives the student a menu or list of two or more choices and asks the student which he or she would like to do. For example, the teacher can ask a student to choose an activity (for instance, "Would you like to work on comprehension questions or vocabulary right now?") or ask him or her to choose the preferred order of activities (for example, "Would you like to work on comprehension questions or vocabulary?"). The notion is that when provided a choice, a student who feels stressed or struggles with following directions will feel more empowered and safer by having a say in his or her day or activities (Pickens & Tschopp, 2017).

The strategies in this section are useful for prompting students to use the previously taught skills. Although we discussed them in relation to one student, they can certainly be strategies applied to several students or the entire class. For example, instructional choice can easily be offered to every student in the classroom at certain times rather than just one student. Next, we describe a few strategies to reinforce skills in students as part of the supportive discipline framework.

## *Reinforcement Strategies*

Reinforcement strategies are a type of response strategy used to strengthen skills in students (Alberto & Troutman, 2013; Wolery et al., 1988). They can be applied to one student, but it is usually better to apply them classwide for two reasons. First, you can protect the student who most needs the strategy by keeping him or her anonymous; there is no special attention or different circumstances that may alert the class that the student needs additional support. Second, the following strategies benefit all students, whether they have a skill that needs strengthening or not (Alberto & Troutman, 2013; Harlacher, Roberts, & Merrell, 2006).

## Motivation Dots

This is a simple strategy that is helpful for getting students to complete work that they may not want to and keeping students engaged in their work. In this strategy, students earn dots, which are stickers that they can place on their work in order to skip certain problems or items on an assignment (Doyle, Jenson, Clark, & Gates, 1999; Jenson, Rhode, Williams, & Reavis, 2020). To use this strategy, follow these steps.

1. Explain to students that they can earn dots for completing a certain amount of work. For example, if they complete three mathematics problems during their independent work time, they can earn one dot. Students can then place that dot next to a mathematics problem that they want to skip.

2. As students work on a given assignment, move about the room and provide dots to students who meet the agreed-on criterion.

3. Also provide behavior-specific praise for other skills or behaviors you see, along with recognizing students meeting the criterion.

The dots can vary in size, color, and shape. Additionally, the skipped problems for a student can serve as data for the teacher for reteaching or reviewing certain content. This strategy works well with mathematics problems, but you can adjust what the dot means to adapt this strategy for use in other content areas. For example, students who work quietly for ten minutes can earn a dot, which means they get a three- to five-minute technology break. For reading, earning a dot can allow students to ask a friend for help with pronouncing a word or answering a question on a task. The general idea is that by asking for some work completion, the student earns a break from other work. This strategy is particularly helpful for students who complete little to no work, as it can jumpstart work completion. Over time, the criteria can be raised (for example, instead of earning a dot after three mathematics problems, students must complete five mathematics problems now) to increase overall work completion in students.

## Break Pass

The break pass is a tool that allows a student to appropriately ask for a brief break from work. It is a great strategy for students who use disruptive behavior to avoid doing work (Collins et al., 2016; Cook et al., 2014). The break pass teaches the student to use a more socially acceptable behavior (in this case, pulling out the break pass) to earn escape from work rather than using procrastination, yelling, or arguing to avoid work (Crone et al., 2015). To use this strategy, create a small number of break passes for the student (we suggest making them the size of a credit card) and teach the student a routine for using the break pass. During a specified work period, give the student a set number of passes and allow the student to use his or her passes to ask for a brief break from work. The student can raise his or her hand and hold up the pass. The teacher acknowledges the pass, takes it, and provides a break of a few minutes to the student. During this break, the student can sit quietly, get a drink of water, use relaxation techniques, or do a nondisruptive activity, such as doodling or reading a book. After the time is up, the teacher checks in with the student and makes sure he or she is prepared to continue, and the student returns to work. If the student has any break passes left over at the end of the specified time period, those passes can be translated into some sort of reward (Cook et al., 2014).

## Differential Reinforcement

Differential reinforcement refers to reinforcing the desired behavior to reduce the occurrence of the unwanted behavior while not reinforcing the unwanted behavior (Alberto & Troutman, 2013). The teacher can set up a plan in which the student is rewarded for displaying lower rates of the unwanted behavior or using an alternative behavior.

With differential reinforcement, teachers can provide stepping-stones for students and remove reinforcement for an unwanted behavior, as it may be difficult for students to suddenly stop using an unwanted behavior and to start using a new behavior. Teachers can acknowledge students for incremental steps toward mastery of a new skill, and they can acknowledge students for reducing the use of an unwanted behavior.

- **Differential reinforcement of low rates of behavior:** A student earns reinforcement for using less of a behavior during a specified time; that is, a student is praised for making fewer than five negative self-talk statements during mathematics class. (In this example, a student often makes self-defeating statements, such as "I can't do this" or "I'll never get this.")

- **Differential reinforcement of other behavior:** A student earns reinforcement for a behavior, regardless of use of other behaviors during a specified time; for example, a student is praised for making positive self-talk statements during mathematics class ("I can learn this topic") regardless of how many negative self-talk statements the student makes.

- **Differential reinforcement of alternative behavior:** A student earns reinforcement only if the student uses a behavior that replaces an unwanted behavior during a specified time; for example, a student is praised for making positive self-talk statements while not making any negative self-talk statements during mathematics class.

- **Differential reinforcement of incompatible behavior:** A student earns reinforcement only if the student uses a specified incompatible behavior that replaces an unwanted behavior during a specified time. An incompatible behavior is one in which the unwanted behavior and desired behavior can't be performed at the same time; for example, a student is praised when the student sits down and uses a relaxation technique versus the unwanted behavior of pacing anxiously around the classroom.

We outline types of differential reinforcement in table 5.1.

**Table 5.1: Types of Differential Reinforcement**

| Type | Description and Example | Pros and Cons |
|---|---|---|
| Differential reinforcement of low rates of behavior | The student is reinforced for displaying a lower rate of an unwanted behavior. For example, the student is rewarded if he or she calls out fewer than five times during a period. | Can lead to a gradual reduction in behavior, but the student may still perform the unwanted behavior |
| Differential reinforcement of other behavior | The student is rewarded if he or she doesn't display the unwanted behavior during a given time. For example, the student earns a reward if he or she goes thirty minutes without calling out. | Encourages a cessation of one unwanted behavior, but the student may still perform other unwanted behaviors and still earn a reward |

continued →

| Type | Description and Example | Pros and Cons |
|---|---|---|
| Differential reinforcement of alternative behavior | The student is rewarded for using a behavior that replaces the unwanted behavior, such as raising his or her hand instead of calling out. | Focuses on a replacement behavior, but the student may still perform the unwanted behavior, along with the replacement behavior, and still earn a reward |
| Differential reinforcement of incompatible behavior | The student is rewarded for using a replacement for the unwanted behavior, but the replacement behavior is impossible to do while also performing the unwanted behavior. For example, a student is rewarded for walking instead of running down the hallway. (The student can't physically run and walk at the same time.) | Focuses on a replacement behavior, but it can be hard to identify an incompatible behavior |

## Chance Jars

This strategy is a whole-class method in which the reward and the criterion for the reward are varied each time it is used. This method is helpful for a variety of behaviors or skills, as the teacher can identify the skill to reinforce, reteach it to students, and then use chance jars as a way to reinforce the skill. For this strategy, follow these steps, which are slightly different from the original chance jar intervention (Burns et al., 2017; Theodore et al., 2001).

1. Find two jars and label one *Criteria*. To the Criteria jar, add slips of paper with the words *Whole Class*, *Highest*, and *Lowest*. Be sure to also include individual slips of paper with each student's name on them.

2. Label another jar *Reinforcement* and include several slips of paper that have a variety of reinforcers on them. These can be tailored to your class, but examples could include a popcorn party, no work for ten minutes, homework help pass, and fifteen-minute technology break.

3. Before class begins, select a skill for a student or students that needs strengthening. Teach the desired skill, including a discussion of the skill and modeling examples versus nonexamples of the skill (use the lesson plan outlined in chapter 2, page 33).

4. Indicate to the class that students can earn a reward if they reach a predetermined number of points. For example, students can earn the

reward if they earn ten points during the time period that you specify, depending on the name drawn out of the Criteria jar. You can use the chance jars for thirty minutes, a class period, or longer. We suggest selecting a time period that is natural or manageable, such as the length of a lesson or a class period.

5. During the time period, students can earn a point for displaying the desired behavior. If a student displays an unwanted behavior, he or she is given a warning and a chance to correct the behavior. If the student does not, you may choose to deduct a point, or you simply provide error correction and move on.

6. Track the number of points using a clipboard or some sort of electronic tracking software or application.

7. At the end of the time period, pull a slip of paper out of the Criteria jar.

   - If a student's name is drawn, all students can earn the reward if that student met the criterion. For example, if the student whose name was drawn earned five points, then all students get the reward.

   - For the slip labeled Whole Class, all students receive the reinforcement if every student met the criterion.

   - For the slip labeled Lowest, all students earn the reward if the student with the lowest number of points met the criterion. For Highest, all students earn the reward if the student with the highest number of points met the criterion. You can also add variations to the Criteria jar, such as class average or class median (which can also be instructive for mathematics classes).

8. If the criterion is met, then draw a slip from the Reinforcement jar; students receive whichever reward is written on the drawn slip. If students have not met the criterion, then there is no reward.

## Corrective Consequences

Corrective consequences are another type of response strategy that uses a direct approach to communicate to the student that a certain behavior is not useful in the current context. The consequences can be thought of as punishment in that they reduce certain behaviors, but they are not necessarily aversive or physically painful strategies for students (Alberto & Troutman, 2013; Harlacher, 2015).

Use these corrective consequences to correct misuse of a skill. In this section, we cover the following forms of corrective consequences with step-by-step instructions for implementation.

- Time-out from reinforcement

- Self-management of behavior

- Hairband or rubber band intervention

- Behavior contract

## Time-Out From Reinforcement

*Time-out* is a term most are familiar with, but we would venture to guess that it has been used incorrectly a lot of the time. To ensure safe and effective use—the extent to which time-outs can harm students has been a point of discussion (for example, Siegel & Bryson, 2016)—it's important that teachers understand a time-out is time out from *reinforcement*. It's not time out from the teacher or a chance for the teacher and students to ignore the student altogether. This time-out is simply a method to stop reinforcement if a student engages in unwanted behavior (Alberto & Troutman, 2013; Ryan, Sanders, Katsiyannis, & Yell, 2007). It's a brief break from the current situation to remove the reinforcer from the unwanted behavior, be it someone's attention or access to an activity. Further, reconnecting with the student after time-out and providing a positive connection can ensure that time-out is about the student's behavior and not the student (Martinelli, 2021).

Time-outs have various forms, and the degree to which the student is separated from the environment can vary. For instance, the teacher might not allow a student to participate in the current activity but let the student remain in the room or group; this is called a *nonseclusionary time-out*. Or, the teacher may ask the student to move away from the group or current activity but still allow the student to view and watch it; this is called a *contingent observation*. The teacher can also ask the student to leave the room and go into the hallway or another classroom—although we know that going into the hallway invites all sorts of attention from others. Having the student leave the room is an *exclusionary time-out*.

Exclusionary time-outs that involve sending the student to another room require the cooperation of both teachers. Here are steps to use that procedure (Burns et al., 2017; Nelson & Carr, 1996; Ryan et al., 2007).

1.  Teach the class the time-out procedure ahead of time. For exclusionary time-out, teach students to go to another teacher's classroom door and wait until they are given permission to enter the classroom. While they are in the second classroom, they sit in a designated area and complete a worksheet with the following questions.

    - What happened?

    - What behavior earned the time-out?

    - What will you do when you return to class?

2.  Once the form is complete, the student raises his or her hand, and the teacher checks that the questions are answered appropriately and then sends the student back to the original classroom.

3.  The student again waits at the door of the original classroom until the teacher permits the student to enter.

4.  Debrief with the student quickly and ensure that he or she understands what prompted the time-out and what to do differently moving forward. The debrief should not be lengthy or a shaming experience. Instead, it's meant to center the student on the desired skills to use and allow him or her to move on from that instance. Regardless of the type of time-out used, debriefing is the critical part of time-out because it is a teaching moment needed for effective discipline (Martinelli, 2021; Sugai & Colvin, 1997).

## Self-Management of Behavior

We discussed a straightforward method of self-monitoring for students in chapter 3 (page 65), but using self-management as part of level three is more involved and detailed. The form of self-management focuses on gradual ownership and awareness of a given skill for a student (Burns et al., 2017; Loftin, Gibb, & Skiba, 2005; Rafferty, 2010). After teaching the skill in level three, you can use this method to direct students' attention to mastering and using the skill over time, thus ensuring students can manage the skill with little to no prompting from the teacher. To use this strategy, follow these steps.

1.  Identify a classroom expectation or prosocial skill that would replace the unwanted behavior and explicitly teach it to the student (see figure 2.4, page 45).

2. Break that skill into three to five explicit parts.

- For example, if the skill is being responsible, the parts can have materials ready, work quietly during independent work time, clean up the work area, and take notes during class.

- If the skill is social awareness, the parts can be make eye contact when talking to others, say things that value or affirm others, and express understanding when possible by saying things like "I hear that" or "That seems frustrating."

3. Provide students with a card that lists the skill and its parts. Next to each skill, add two columns, one for the student and one for the teacher, along with a three-point rating scale that indicates the student's use of the skill as shown in figure 5.7.

| Rating scale: 1 = Didn't follow, 2 = Followed some of the time, 3 = Followed all of the time | | | |
|---|---|---|---|
| **Skill: Being Responsible** | **My Rating** | **Teacher Rating** | **Match?** |
| Have materials for class. | 1  2  3 | 1  2  3 | Yes   No |
| Complete work during class. | 1  2  3 | 1  2  3 | Yes   No |
| Clean up area when needed. | 1  2  3 | 1  2  3 | Yes   No |
| Write down assignments and homework. | 1  2  3 | 1  2  3 | Yes   No |
| **Totals** | ___ out of 12 | ___ out of 12 | ___ out of 4 |

**FIGURE 5.7:** Example of self-monitoring card for students.

*Visit MarzanoResources.com/reproducibles for a free reproducible version of this figure.*

4. Indicate to students that you want them to use the card to monitor their own use of the skills listed on the card. At specified times, prompt students to rate their behavior in the My Rating column. Following that, go to the individual student, rate the student's behavior in the Teacher Rating column, and then discuss any discrepancies. The goal is for students to understand the rating and match their ratings

to yours, not to provide punishment around what the rating actually is. (Your ratings will be more accurate than the students' initially, so the intention is to ensure accuracy of the students' ratings first.) For example, if a student's use of a skill only earns a 1 in your perspective, but the student has rated herself as being at level 3, then you will discuss why the student's rating does not match yours (rather than discuss what the student may do about earning a 1). In having this discussion, the student can learn the nuances of the ratings and learn how to accurately self-rate.

5. Provide a reward for the first few days for students if they match their ratings to yours, as your ratings will be the accurate measure of the students' skill. The reward is intended to motivate them to accurately rate their behavior. Once students accurately rate themselves and match the teacher's ratings, they are ready to self-monitor their behavior. The teacher can then stop rating the students. Students can then earn points for reaching a certain goal.

6. After students consistently reach their goals in a set time period—we suggest four out of five days of meeting their goals for two weeks (Hawken et al., 2021)—you can change the focus to a new skill and fade out your rating of the old skill.

## Hairband or Rubber Band Intervention

For this strategy, a student and teacher identify a behavior that is problematic for the student, such as talking out of turn, being disruptive, or making hurtful comments, and the teacher then asks the student to regulate that behavior (Intervention Central, n.d.b). In addition to identifying the target problem behavior, the teacher and student also identify a corresponding replacement behavior.

At the start of a given time period, the student receives up to six rubber bands, hair ties, or scrunchies to place on one wrist. The teacher then instructs the student to regulate the behavior and use the more prosocial skill. During the time period, if the student displays the unwanted behavior, he or she moves a band from one wrist to the other. If the student has at least one band left on the original wrist, he or she can earn a point or tally mark. When the student receives enough points or tally marks, he or she can earn a reward.

We suggest starting with short periods of time to give the student a chance to feel success. You may also modify the intervention by using tokens in a jar or removable stickers on a board on the student's desk rather than rubber bands. Over time, the teacher can reduce the number of rubber bands or lengthen the time that the student uses the rubber bands. Keep in mind that you can also give the student positive feedback and acknowledgment for displaying the prosocial skill.

## Behavior Contract

A behavior contract is a formal agreement between the student and the teacher that outlines expected behavior and consequences if a student adheres to it, including both reinforcement and any corrective action if the contract isn't followed (Burns et al., 2017; Lewis, 2019). To create a behavior contract, you can follow these steps.

1. Teacher meets with the student to discuss the student's behavior. The teacher discusses what the student does well, areas for improvement, and behaviors to do more of and ones they can do less of.

2. Together, the teacher and student set goals for increasing certain behaviors and any needed reductions in other behaviors, and discuss the data used to monitor the contract.

3. The teacher identifies what will happen if the student reaches the goal and if he or she doesn't reach the goal. (Does the student earn something?)

4. The two agree on a start date for the contract and a review date to check progress, and then sign the contract.

### *Repair Conversations*

In class, there will be times when students and the teacher may find themselves in in aversive interactions, such as a student being rude to others, yelling disrespectfully in response to a direction, or even getting angry and leaving class. Consequently, some harm may be done and students should be afforded opportunities to repair that harm by engaging in a repair conversation (Costello, Wachtel, & Wachtel, 2009; Maynard & Weinstein, 2020; McCammon, 2020).

1. The teacher first confirms that the student is ready for the conversation by checking that the student is mentally prepared to discuss the incident and agrees to do so.

2. The teacher expresses genuine care for the student, such as telling the student how he or she is enjoyable to have in class or that the teacher cares for the student's well-being.

3.  The teacher asks the student to share what happened, giving him or her a chance to talk about the incident calmly. Here, the teacher can help the student discuss his or her thoughts and feelings and how the incident developed by asking questions, thinking aloud, or describing what the teacher saw during the incident. The teacher listens, allowing the student to have his or her voice in the situation.

4.  The teacher can share how the incident impacted him or her and others, and the two then discuss what can be done to repair the harm. The teacher can remind the student of the expectations of the classroom, and the two can then make a plan for the student to be successful. Plans might include actions such as the student apologizing and agreeing to use a certain coping skill next time, or the student and teacher agreeing on a signal to use in future incidents when either one needs a pause rather than continuing the incident and creating an aversive interaction.

We provide a list of steps to use for repair conversations in figure 5.8.

| Step | Example |
|---|---|
| 1. Confirm that the student is willing and able to have a conversation. | "Can we talk for a few minutes about what happened yesterday?" |
| 2. Express genuine care for the student, such as reiterating the value he or she has in class or the student's contribution to the class. | "You are important to this class, and I really appreciate your perspective when we discuss history. You challenge others to really think about events in history and how they impact today." |
| 3. Ask the student to share what happened and how he or she felt. | "Can you tell me what happened when you got upset?" |
| 4. Ask the student who was impacted or what harm was done. | "How do you think you getting upset affected others?" |
| 5. Share the impact it had on you as the teacher. | "When you yelled, it made me feel like you didn't care about the class. I also felt disrespected." |
| 6. Discuss what to do to repair the harm and develop a plan. | "Do you have ideas on how to avoid this in the future? What can you do to fix the situation?" |

**FIGURE 5.8:** Questions to use for repair conversations.

*Visit **MarzanoResources.com/reproducibles** for a free reproducible version of this figure.*

The conversations can be brief and should leave the teacher and student feeling more capable and confident of handling situations better next time (Minahan, 2019). The overall intention is to express concern and care for students, allow them a chance to share their experience, and to then work together to create a plan to repair any harm done. These conversations can include particular students who have been impacted by the incident, particularly if part of bolstering the student's resilience is to improve the student's relationships or social awareness. We encourage teachers to reiterate the classroom expectations related to empathy or respect as students engage in those conversations; you might start by saying something like, "We want each of us to be heard in this conversation, so let's remember to be respectful when sharing our thoughts and to listen before we respond." The overall tone of the conversations should be one of taking responsibility for one's actions and feeling empowered to do well next time.

We offered a few strategies in this chapter, but a plethora of others are available. Visit any of the following websites for more ideas to add to your strategy list. Teachers can use the reproducible "Supportive Discipline Framework Template" (page 132) to customize their own supportive discipline framework.

- The Evidence Based Intervention Network (https://education.missouri .edu/ebi/interventions) offers interventions based on whether the student is initially learning the skill, working on becoming proficient in the skill, or needs help generalizing the skill to other settings.

- Intervention Central (www.interventioncentral.org/behavioral -intervention-modification) offers a wide range of evidence-based strategies.

- The National Center on Intensive Intervention's tools chart (https:// charts.intensiveintervention.org/bintervention) offers a summary of vetted behavioral interventions, including descriptions and evaluations of the studies examined.

## ····▶ Key Points

In this chapter, we described a framework that fosters consistency in the classroom. This supportive discipline framework centers on teaching and reinforcing desired skills. To that end, discipline should be instructional, teachers should have a variety of strategies for responding to unwanted behavior, and the approach to discipline should be clear and transparent. The supportive discipline framework consists of three levels: level one (error correction), level two (reteaching), and level three (reteaching with direct intervention). Overall, the goal of discipline is to ensure each student uses prosocial skills or a resilience-enhancing skill rather than repeat a skill or behavior that is detrimental to the student.

# Supportive Discipline Framework Template

| Level One<br><br>Brief Error Correction | Steps to follow:<br>1. State the expectation.<br>2. Model the expectation.<br>3. Ask the student to use the expectation.<br>4. Acknowledge the student's use. | |
|---|---|---|
| Level Two<br><br>Error Correction With Reteaching | Steps to follow:<br>1. Correct errors.<br>2. Reteach with examples and nonexamples.<br>3. Increase praise. | |
| Level Three<br><br>Reteaching With Direct Intervention | Steps to follow:<br>1. Correct errors.<br>2. Teach explicitly with examples and nonexamples.<br>3. Let students practice skills following teaching.<br>4. Adjust and include strategies (see below). | |
| Mark strategies to use:<br><br>*Antecedent strategies*<br>☐ Precorrection<br>☐ High-probability requests<br>☐ Instructional choice<br>☐ Other: | Mark strategies to use:<br><br>*Reinforcement strategies*<br>☐ Motivation dots<br>☐ Break pass<br>☐ Differential reinforcement<br>☐ Chance jars<br>☐ Other: | Mark strategies to use:<br><br>*Corrective consequences*<br>☐ Time-out from reinforcement<br>☐ Self-management of behavior<br>☐ Hairband or rubber band intervention<br>☐ Behavior contract<br>☐ Other: |

# CHAPTER 6

# Adjusting Discipline for Compassion

In the previous chapter, we outlined the supportive discipline framework for managing behavior while also supporting students' use of prosocial skills. Here, we offer ways to show compassion while ensuring that discipline is respectful of students' needs. We offer a compassionate response from a place of understanding. We believe it is necessary to first attempt to understand the complex chronic behaviors (including escalation patterns) of students and then proceed with direct intervention.

Managing student behavior is a challenge for many educators (Gonzalez, Brown, & Slate, 2008; Scholastic, & Bill & Melinda Gates Foundation, 2013), and when we add on the layer of students who have increased social, emotional, or behavioral (SEB) needs or who have experienced trauma, effective discipline can be tricky. Students dealing with such life stressors may escalate more quickly when facing discipline, so teachers have to manage challenging behavior tactfully (Pickens & Tschopp, 2017). To do so, teachers can build off the established structures for consistency and connection in their classroom and slightly adjust them for students with SEB needs. Based on students' specific needs or their current emotional state, teachers can adjust the strategies we've described so far throughout this book to meet their students' needs.

This isn't to say that teachers throw consistency out the window with some students. Rather, there is an art to working with real students and applying strategies.

By approaching discipline from a place of understanding, teachers can know when and how to apply the discipline structures they've created in their classroom (Eber et al., 2020). Further, they can create ways to develop connection with students and reinforce their use of prosocial skills (Jones et al., 2018).

We offer several strategies or considerations to keep in mind as teachers work with students who have SEB needs and who may be experiencing a heightened emotional state during school. We also share the escalation cycle, which is a particular pattern that some students with SEB needs may show. Our goal in this chapter is to share flexible methods that show compassion for students as you support them in bolstering their resilience.

## Make Strategy Adjustments for Students With Social, Emotional, and Behavioral Needs

We've described several principles and strategies throughout the book that are important for students with social, emotional, and behavioral needs or ongoing mental health needs, including teaching prosocial skills, creating a predictable environment, building authentic relationships, and using reinforcement to build classroom culture. When managing day-to-day interactions, students can become upset or triggered by various factors in the environment. If that happens, they may enter fight, flight, freeze, or fawn responses (Barlow, 2002; Cannon, 1927; Walker, 2013), making use of the aforementioned strategies in the previous chapter less effective (Goleman, 2005; Pickens & Tschopp, 2017).

Given that the strategies mentioned in the previous chapter will be helpful with all students, students who have experienced stressful events, have mental health needs, or are just having a rough day may need some additional considerations when you engage with them. By adjusting strategies based on a student's needs or responses, teachers can ensure they have a classroom that is compassionate. The following sections address ways to adjust strategies.

- Connect first.
- Describe instead of direct.
- Allow time to process.
- Use short, clear directions.
- Interrupt the heightened state.

- Use a neutralizing routine.
- Frame things positively.
- Be flexible.
- Anticipate and offset triggers.

## Connect First

When students escalate or are triggered, they are likely feeling unsafe and disconnected from their environment (Goleman, 2005; Ingram, n.d.; Knight, 2019; Pickens & Tschopp, 2017). Because of this, a good response is to first establish a connection. Ask the student if he or she feels safe or what he or she may need. For example, you can state, "I can see you're having a hard time and perhaps feeling unsafe or threatened" and then ask, "What do you need to feel safer?" Although your exact phrasing can differ, the goal is to convey empathy and understanding. Your response should focus on making the student feel safer and more in control than he or she currently feels. When doing so, be sure to use neutral nonverbal responses, such as keeping your distance from the student's personal space, relaxing your posture, and even getting to the student's eye level, if possible. If the student responds verbally, or gives a nonverbal cue like nodding, you can work on addressing his or her fear or need for safety.

Once the student is calmer and more engaged with you, then you can discuss whatever discipline is needed. If the student is not responsive, allow space, focus on others in the classroom, and then check back in a minute or a few minutes. Space and distance can allow emotions to come back down, whereas increasing interaction or trying to force compliance can escalate the situation (Goleman, 2005; Pickens & Tschopp, 2017).

## Describe Instead of Direct

Students may have moments throughout the school day in which they're experiencing anxiety or certain emotions attached to their past. This can express itself in various ways, such as being withdrawn, irritable, or sullen; pacing; or being unable to sit still. When students are experiencing heightened or anxious states or feeling elevated, they may not be experiencing things clearly or in a typical fashion. In fact, they may be experiencing what psychologist Daniel Goleman (2005) calls *emotional hijacking*, in that they are consumed by emotions and not aware of everything around them or actively processing input in a logical, coherent manner. Because of this, they need time to calm down and allow the flooding of emotions to recede (Ingram, n.d.). To help with that, teachers can describe or reflect the feelings they are seeing in the student rather than focusing on directions and compliance. Students who are dysregulated could benefit from someone scaffolding emotional awareness for them by describing what they see, using a statement such as, "I see you're very angry and perhaps hurt. I'm wondering if what Jim said earlier was hurtful to you." By reflecting the emotions and feelings seen in students, the teacher can help students process their emotions and de-escalate (Jennings & Greenberg, 2009; Minahan, 2019).

### Allow Time to Process

If reflecting on emotions and verbal discussion aren't helpful for students who appear escalated, or they simply need time to gather themselves, allow other ways for them to process and manage their emotions. Accordingly, allow time for them to process at their own pace and with mild, preferred activities, such as journaling, drawing, or simply sitting quietly and using meditation or relaxation techniques. Once students have reduced their agitation or anxiety, engage them in a debrief to help them understand that despite experiencing some uncomfortable emotions, they were able to process and return to a normal, less heightened state. Help them see the growth in this, as students with histories of trauma may have difficulty recognizing small moments of growth in emotion-regulation skills (Knight, 2019; Minahan, 2019).

### Use Short, Clear Directions

Students who are escalated or feel anxious may also have a hard time processing and understanding the situation they're in. Accordingly, simple and clear directions are better over multistep or complex directions. Provide direct, clear, and easy-to-do directions, one at a time, to students and wait for completion after each one. Giving multistep directions may escalate and confuse the student (Ingram, n.d.). For example, saying, "Why can't you just do your work?" is vague and doesn't communicate a direction—it hints at one, but it mostly communicates frustration (Forehand & McMahon, 1981). Also, saying, "I need you to sit down and stop arguing. Your paper isn't out, it should be on your desk, and you need to clean up your work from earlier. You need to complete your work and stop being disruptive," is an immense amount of information to give a student. The student will likely get lost weeding through all that information, so it's best to provide one clear direction at a time. Tell the student simple directions that won't be misinterpreted (Burns et al., 2017; Forehand & McMahon, 1981; Ingram, n.d.; Pickens & Tschopp, 2017).

### Interrupt the Heightened State

Another approach can be offering the student a coping skill to interrupt his or her heightened state (Norris, 2003; Pickens & Tschopp, 2017; Yoder & Nolan, 2018). In doing so, the teacher shifts the focus away from the student's anxious state or defiant behavior and onto de-escalating. This break from the escalation allows the student to self-regulate and bring down any elevated emotion (Goleman, 2005).

This technique involves setting a timer for a few minutes and asking the student to use relaxation techniques. The student can mold clay, doodle, listen to calming music, or count slowly as part of the relaxation techniques. The teacher can also direct the student to a cooldown area, where the student can do a low-grade activity to calm him- or herself, such as flipping through a magazine, putting a puzzle together, drawing or coloring, or journaling. The cooldown area should always include relaxation techniques, such as deep breathing or muscle-tension reducing exercises, or an emotion-processing worksheet like the reproducible "Cooldown Considerations" (page 151) in which students respond to statements such as, "I'm feeling____ because _____" "What I need is _____" and "What I can do is____."

Teachers should instruct all students in use of the cooldown area before they require someone to use it. When a student uses the cooldown area, the teacher sets a timer to ensure the student doesn't use the area to escape work. The student can use the area for ten minutes, after which the teacher checks to see if the student is ready to return to the work area or if he or she needs one more ten-minute break. After that ten-minute break, the student must return or the teacher determines if additional support, such as the supportive discipline framework, is needed. The cooldown technique is different from a time-out because time-out is about removing reinforcement from the student. Conversely, the cooldown area is about regulating emotions and using coping skills. Additionally, use of the cooldown area is a voluntary choice; never force a student to use it. By having students use and practice emotion regulation skills, teachers can assist them in bolstering their resilience.

As a technique for teaching students self-management of emotions and de-escalation, active response beads can help interrupt heightened emotional states (Grskovic et al., 2004). When a student is agitated or when behavior is escalating, the teacher can give the student a string of beads and instruct him or her to use them to calm down by sliding the beads back and forth. Specifically, students count a bead, slide it from one end of the string to the other, and exhale after each bead. If making a string of beads is not possible, the student can also receive a chart that has numbered dots on it. The student can count each dot and exhale after each one, moving from one to ten. This method stops the unwanted behavior and focuses the student on a task to allow his or her emotions to calm down. From there, the teacher can debrief and get the student back on track for the day.

## Use a Neutralizing Routine

Another effective approach when working with students who are agitated is to stop the escalation of the situation by using a neutralizing routine (McIntosh, 2020).

When interacting with students who find themselves feeling stressed or escalating, a teacher can offer a neutralizing routine to offset those emotions. A *neutralizing routine* is a response to unwanted behavior that is instructional rather than punitive or harsh. Where the previous section discussed a coping skill for the student to interrupt the heightened state, the neutralizing routine can be used by both student and teacher to offset emotions each is experiencing. For example, a teacher can recognize that he or she is agitated or not feeling very patient with a student. Instead of interacting in a manner that could inadvertently escalate things, the teacher can first recognize his or her vulnerable point and then use a neutralizing routine. For example, the teacher can say, "Let's talk at a break," rather than continuing to engage with the student; the teacher can tell the class they are feeling frustrated and lead them all in taking a few deep breaths to calm down. The routine allows time for emotions to cool by delaying a decision or lengthy interaction, and also stops the teacher and student from going down a previously predictable and unhealthy pattern, such as the teacher reprimanding the student, the student responding with further escalation, and the situation becoming bigger and more destructive.

Neutralizing routines are used as a means to reduce implicit bias (McIntosh, 2020), but we suggest it's an effective way to interact with students who present challenging behaviors that teachers may sometimes find difficult to address. Examples of neutralizing routines include asking to see the student after class, taking two deep breaths before intervening with the student, modeling a cooldown strategy aloud, such as, "I'm feeling stressed, so I'm going to count to five and take a deep breath," or asking the student to redo the situation in accordance with classroom expectations by saying something like, "Try that again in a way that's safe, respectful, and responsible."

---

## Practice in Action: Neutralizing Routine

Mrs. Ladino teaches history to sophomores. During teacher-led discussions, Janice often blurts out and makes comments unrelated to the topic. One day, Janice made a sarcastic comment that the class laughed at. "Please be appropriate in class, Janice," said Mrs. Ladino. Janice continued making off-task comments and jokes during the teacher-led discussion. Mrs. Ladino felt herself getting frustrated. ("Here we go again," she thought.) Rather than reacting in the moment and providing discipline by sending Janice out of the room, Mrs. Ladino used a few neutralizing routines amid her frustration. She first delayed responding by telling the students to turn to their neighbor and share what they'd learned so far from the discussion. With the class focused on talking to classmates, Mrs. Ladino took stock of her body and feelings and took two deep breaths to calm herself down. She then reframed the situation by thinking to herself, "OK, I'm frustrated because Janice appears to be seeking attention. Rather than be annoyed with her, let me understand it as Janice seeking connection. What connection does she need?" Mrs. Ladino then approached Janice and spoke to her privately: "You know I care about you and I want you to be connected in this class, but your comments are off task. Let's talk at the next break." Feeling calmer, Mrs. Ladino continued her discussion. After class, Mrs. Ladino was able to speak to Janice about how Janice's comments were disruptive, and Mrs. Ladino specifically asked the student what she needed so that she would feel more connected in class. They both understood each other's needs after the discussion; Janice understood why her comments were so disruptive, and Mrs. Ladino understood why Janice needed connection during those moments.

## Frame Things Positively

Students with SEB needs may have negative thinking or play negative loops in their head about themselves (Ingram, n.d.; Minahan, 2019). When they experience a mistake or an incident that is aversive, they may play this loop, thereby adding on to an already uncomfortable experience (Minahan, 2019). This places teachers in a delicate position, as they frequently address mistakes and can't avoid correcting students' errors or unwanted behavior. To manage this, a teacher can convey positive regard to a student, despite needing to address an error.

Keep in mind that the classroom should have a high ratio (five to one) of positive to negative feedback to create a supportive environment (Kern et al., 2007; Reinke et al., 2013). When addressing behavior, the teacher can frame feedback with positive intent. For example, saying, "I see you used the order of operations we discussed, but there's one mistake with addition here" instead of bluntly saying, "You made a mistake." Additionally, framing things positively and encouraging students to take power over their choices can benefit students in managing their emotions, using verbal encouragement such as, "Tomorrow is another chance to apply what you learned!" By framing things positively, students can learn emotion regulation and self-management, bolstering their resilience and ability to cope with situations (Knight, 2019; Minahan, 2019).

## Be Flexible

Some teachers may feel that they need to discipline students immediately when they break a rule or when they are confrontational. We don't believe this is necessarily the case, although we understand teachers may worry how other students perceive a lack of immediate action. A teacher can always come back to discipline and provide appropriate responses to handle students who are not following classroom expectations or rules. When students break rules, are defiant, or engage in other unwanted behaviors, it's important not to add fuel to the fire or to let the student push any more of your (or their classmates') buttons.

By focusing on de-escalation first in heated situations, you'll ensure everyone is safe and becoming more emotionally regulated rather than dysregulated (Ingram, n.d.). Discipline can come later, but you can't always de-escalate easily after you've escalated the situation. Students who are experiencing trauma or triggers in their environment may not respond calmly to further escalation or discipline in the moment; help them calm down, then come back to discipline and repair for any rule violations when the student is more receptive to listening (Ingram, n.d.; Pickens & Tschopp, 2017).

## Anticipate and Offset Triggers

Students with SEB needs may view the environment as a threatening place; in turn, they continuously scan their surroundings for signs of danger (Pickens & Tschopp, 2017). They may also have triggers or stimuli that they've associated with traumatic events (Minahan, 2019). Changes in routines, a lack of choice, sensory changes (such as an increase in noise level), or being unaware of surprises can provoke some students. To identify a student's trigger, teachers can ask students what makes them uncomfortable either one on one or as part of their methods to build relationships. Once teachers know students' triggers, they can offset them. For example, providing a schedule each morning to students who don't do well with changes can help them anticipate changes in their routines. Teachers can offer journaling or time for students to process their emotions if weekends or holidays are triggering.

In table 6.1, we indicate some common triggers and ways to offset them. As part of all these examples, we encourage teachers to have students use a coping skill or prosocial skill that they have learned. This allows the focus to be on healing and using adaptive reactions to triggers.

**Table 6.1: Examples of Triggers and Ways to Offset Them**

| Trigger | Example of Ways to Offset |
|---|---|
| Conflict with a peer | • Have students journal to process emotions or write down assertive responses.*<br>• Discuss with students about how they can handle the situation. |
| Holidays, family events | • Ask students about their emotions and allow space to process event.<br>• Have students journal or draw to process emotions. |
| Weekends or unstructured time | • Review schedule and structure upon return to school.<br>• Allow students to teach or practice a routine. |
| Changes in schedule or routine | • Notify students of upcoming changes as soon as possible.<br>• Offer a printed schedule on students' desks or write schedule on board.<br>• Remind or offer use of a coping skill to manage anxiety from schedule change. |
| Sensory changes (temperature, noise, and so on) | • Use coping skills such as headphones to cancel out noise, or meditation to offset the sensory change.<br>• Offer a short-term solution, such as headphones to block sound, or time in another room to offset temperature changes. |

From all these tips or adjustments, we hope readers see a common approach of ensuring safety for the student, offering a method to stop them from being emotionally dysregulated, and then supporting them in using a beneficial response to their current state of mind. Students with SEB needs are likely using an adaptive coping skill that worked for them in one setting but may prove unhelpful in different settings (Pickens & Tschopp, 2017).

As shown in figure 6.1 (page 142), when students experience a stressful event, they can become emotionally escalated and dysregulated and use a skill that, although adaptive previously, is now maladaptive. For example, they may have withdrawn in response to a stressor in the past, but now when they withdraw, it creates other consequences (such as poor relationships with others or an inability to resolve the stressor). As such, they need to learn a new pattern to navigate that event. The top row illustrates students' use of prior skills, which are reinforced over time as students use them (that is, the skill is successful at navigating the emotional arousal, despite it creating other issues; Goleman, 2005; Pickens & Tschopp, 2017).

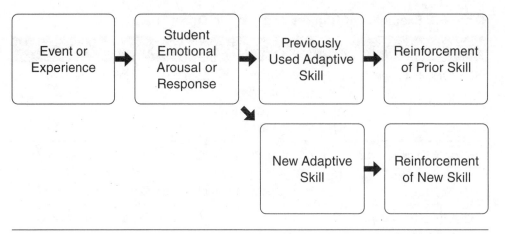

**FIGURE 6.1:** Model of intervening with students with trauma histories.

Recall that people use skills that are purposeful and functional. In contrast, we want students to use a new adaptive skill that can help them navigate the event without creating other adverse consequences (illustrated in the bottom row). Teachers can prompt and reinforce new skills that are more adaptive for the context; for example, a student who may withdraw in response to something stressful can be prompted to journal their emotions as a way to regulate them (Hawken et al., 2021; Jennings & Greenberg, 2009). That's not to say that teachers need to be counselors, but it is important that they are able to recognize when students are triggered so that they may prompt those students to use a more adaptive response. For many students, a pattern of escalation and previously used skills may be a more ingrained pattern that is reflective of the escalation cycle, which we discuss next.

## Know the Escalation Cycle for Earlier Prevention

Now that we have outlined ways to adjust strategies for students with SEB needs, we turn our attention to understanding students who may escalate quickly or are more volatile. Although a student's quick escalation, volatility, or violent responses can be stressful and frightening, these explosive displays do follow a predictable pattern (Colvin & Scott, 2015). By understanding the pattern, teachers can intervene in a proactive manner to de-escalate the situation.

Aggressive responses occur in seven phases: (1) calm, (2) trigger, (3) agitation, (4) acceleration, (5) peak, (6) de-escalation, and (7) recovery (Colvin & Scott, 2015). Each phase has distinct behaviors that students display. Accordingly, the teacher's response changes based on the stage the student is in, as shown in table 6.2. With table 6.2, we describe each stage, the educator's suggested response, and an example of a ninth grader, Kerry, whose behavior escalated into being argumentative, making rude comments, and tearing up paper.

**Table 6.2: Phases of the Acting-Out Cycle and Suggested Educator Responses**

| Phase | Typical Student Actions | Suggested Educator Response | Example |
|---|---|---|---|
| Calm | The student is compliant, cooperative, and follows routines and directions. | Rely on universal practices, including reinforcement and brief error correction. | Kerry was agreeable to directions and completed her work. The teacher praised and acknowledged her for being respectful and responsible. |
| Trigger | The student experiences an adverse conflict or situation. | Employ prevention strategies (page 116) to offset triggers or remind student of previously taught skills to manage triggers. | Kerry often experienced interpersonal conflict with her peers. She also was in counseling for substance abuse; she wanted to use drugs when she experienced conflict with peers. The teacher checked in at each start of class and asked Kerry to identify her mood. |
| Agitation | The student gets off task and becomes unfocused, anxious, or agitated. | Allow the student space to process his or her agitated state and encourage use of coping skills. | Kerry was noncompliant with tasks in class when agitated. The teacher encouraged Kerry to journal (a coping skill of hers). |
| Acceleration | The student engages in focused behavior designed to elicit a response from others. | Avoid negative interaction and provide clear, concise directions. | When accelerating, Kerry targeted peers by making antagonizing comments to them. The teacher provided clear directions ("It's not OK to talk to peers that way") and provided choices for her ("You can focus and do your work or take time for yourself at your desk"). If Kerry was able to calm herself and participate in class, the teacher would briefly talk with Kerry to help her process her trigger and how she was able to manage it in a positive manner. |

continued

| Phase | Typical Student Actions | Suggested Educator Response | Example |
|---|---|---|---|
| Peak | The student displays aggressive, explosive, or generally unsafe behavior. | Ensure the safety of the student and others. Follow school safety procedures. | Kerry made negative comments to peers, threatened to fight others, and tore up paper or books at her desk. Depending on the severity of the peak phase, the teacher asked Kerry to stay in a certain area in the classroom, call for assistance to remove Kerry from the classroom, or move students out of the classroom to ensure their safety. |
| De-escalation | The student seems unfocused, subdued, or confused. | Allow the student time to return to a calm emotional state. Engage the student in a short debrief to return to the classroom or other setting; ensure any restorative steps (such as those described in the section "Repair Conversations," page 128). | Kerry went to the office if removed or simply stayed at her desk. The teacher or staff instructed Kerry to calm herself using her coping skills and then gave her space to calm down. When she was calm, the teacher checked in about Kerry being able to rejoin the class or activity. ("Do you feel comfortable rejoining us?") |
| Recovery | The student returns to a state of being relatively cooperative and agreeable. | Encourage return to normal routine; conduct more formal problem solving or debrief. | Kerry returned to the class or activity. The teacher and Kerry had a more formal debrief, including any necessary repair conversations. Often, the counselor joined and helped facilitate a discussion with peers whom Kerry had targeted. |

*Source: Adapted from Colvin & Scott, 2015; Harlacher, 2015.*

### Phase One: Calm

During the calm phase, students are compliant and follow the directions and routines of the school day. During this phase, the aim is to keep the student in this phase using the universal practices described already in this book. This includes teaching of prosocial skills, such as expectations and SEL skills and routines, prompting use of those prosocial skills to offset unwanted behavior, acknowledging students' use of those prosocial skills, and building relationships between teacher and students and among the students.

### Phase Two: Trigger

During the trigger phase, the student experiences a trigger that evokes tension and emotional unrest. A trigger in this context is any action or event that begins the escalation cycle (Colvin & Scott, 2015). It can be a single event, such as a disagreement with a friend during lunch, or a gradual buildup of events over time, such as a lack of sleep each night. Triggers usually arise when a student is denied something he or she wants, has an unresolved conflict, or experiences something negative (Colvin & Scott, 2015; Pickens & Tschopp, 2017). Triggers can occur at school, as with peer conflicts, poor grades, or correction procedures, or at home, with health problems, substance abuse, or family conflicts.

Teachers have two general approaches to offset the impact of a trigger (Colvin & Scott, 2015; Harlacher, 2015).

1.  Teachers can have prevention strategies in place to mitigate the impact of a trigger. For example, if a student has conflicts with others at home, then the teacher can check in with the student as he or she enters the classroom or encourage the student to journal. If schoolwork is an ongoing trigger, then the teacher might adjust the work demands or curriculum for the student. Teachers can identify methods to offset triggers, but the nature of the prevention strategy will vary depending on the specific trigger for the individual student.

2.  Teachers can also set up structures to actively teach students coping skills to manage the triggers they encounter. For example, a student may need to learn different ways to manage conflict with peers or to manage emotions when he or she experiences difficulty completing work. Such an approach requires actively teaching students missing skills and can take time. Table 6.3 (page 146) offers strategies.

**Table 6.3: Strategies to Offset Triggers**

| Trigger | Examples of Prevention Strategy | Examples of Skill to Teach |
| --- | --- | --- |
| Difficult task or schoolwork | • Modify or break work into manageable pieces. | • Teach missing academic or self-management skills. |
| Conflict with others | • Check in with the student at the start of class to debrief any conflict.<br>• Allow the student to journal about emotions from conflict. | • Teach conflict resolution or relationship skills. |
| Internalizing emotions (anxiety, depression) | • Check in with the student and allow for journaling or processing of emotions.<br>• Provide space and precorrection to use coping skills. | • Teach coping skills or emotion regulation skills. |
| Stressors at home | • Collaborate with parents or guardians to identify solutions to offset stressors.<br>• Check in with the student at start of the day to process stressors.<br>• Allow breaks for the student to use coping skills.<br>• Ensure adequate communication between home and school by having frequent and two-way communication. | • Teach coping skills to navigate or manage stressors.<br>• Teach healthy ways to navigate stressors, such as self-management or self-awareness.<br>• Discuss the issues with students and identify ways to resolve the situation. |
| Changes in routine or schedule | • Provide plenty of notice for changes in routines using different formats (verbal or written).<br>• Provide daily schedule and start the day by going over the schedule. | • Teach coping skills or emotion-regulation skills. |

## Phase Three: Agitation

In this phase, the teacher (and others) can see the tension actively building up in the student as he or she loses focus and gets off task. The student may become nonresponsive during this phase, withdrawing or becoming less talkative. He or she may also be visibility agitated, as indicated by moving about the room, not being able to sit still, or bouncing his or her leg when seated (Colvin, 2004; McKnight, 2020).

Here, the goal is to avoid a student escalating into the next phase by allowing him or her space and time to use coping skills to de-escalate and refocus on the surroundings. This is a way to offer compassion by allowing adjustment of current classroom routines or work to manage the student's agitated state. It's OK for the student to work on a preferred activity during this time and to allow space to work through the trigger. Offering support and assurances that the student can manage his or her trigger is helpful too (Pickens & Tschopp, 2017). While it may be hard to allow a student to work on a preferred activity rather than the instructional work at the moment, the key is to avoid any escalation into the next phase of the cycle.

The teacher can also connect emotionally with the student and offer encouragement on making an appropriate choice and processing the agitated state. This is where the foundation of a relationship with students is helpful. A teacher with rapport can connect with the student and use humor, empathy, or other skills to de-escalate the student and manage his or her current state. When the student is de-escalated or is more engaged, then he or she can address the missed work or activities (Colvin, 2004; Harlacher, 2015).

## Phase Four: Acceleration

If a student doesn't resolve the trigger well, he or she can enter the acceleration phase. In this phase, there is a rapid or marked increase in the student's behavior. The student may intentionally engage with others to elicit a reaction from them. For example, the student may argue, disagree, make unwanted or inappropriate comments, destroy items or property, or make threats toward others. The student may follow directions but do so in a manner to goad others into engaging with him or her. For example, a student may sit down when asked to do so but will make noises or exasperated sighs to make a demonstration out of it. Or the student may follow directions to write his or her name on an assignment but do so in an aggressive manner, such as writing it abnormally large or illegibly. Overall, the student is intent on targeting others and escalating the situation. As such, attempts to de-escalate or defuse the situation are simply a chance for the student to escalate things (Colvin, 2004).

Consequently, the most effective approach is to remain calm, brief, and direct when engaging with the student. We recommend offering a student a clear choice, outlining the results of either choice, and then disengaging before the student can argue or escalate the situation. For example, the teacher may say, "You can complete your assignment and leave class on time, or you can not complete it and earn time after school to complete it." Once the teacher provides direction, he or she can walk away, attend to other students and provide reinforcement, and allow the affected student time to process the choice provided. Note that the student may be currently trying to engage classmates in a negative way, so the teacher can actively supervise and provide attention or feedback to the class for their on-task or prosocial behavior. After a short time, the teacher comes back to the student. If the student complies with directions, the teacher offers praise, attends to others, and then returns shortly after with more attention for the student's prosocial behavior.

At that point, we suggest debriefing with the student by asking the following questions:

1. What happened?
2. What was your behavior?
3. What was your concern or need?
4. What could you do differently next time that would be acceptable?
5. What are you expected to do next? (Harlacher, 2015, p. 110)

Only conduct this debrief if the student has chosen to comply. If the student does not comply, the teacher can restate the choices the student has and disengage again. If the student's behavior escalates to the next phase, avoid debriefing and instead follow the process for managing students in the peak phase.

### Phase Five: Peak

In the peak phase, the student has escalated to aggressive and destructive behavior. These students are often out of control emotionally and physically and display behavior that is a serious threat to themselves or others. This can include tantrums, assault, physical harm, or destruction of property. During this phase, the goal is to ensure the safety of the student and others while the student regains control.

When escalated, the student will expend energy and eventually come down from his or her peak phase. While the student is escalated, interaction with the student should be limited, as interactions can often prolong the peak phase (Colvin & Scott, 2015). Instead, the teacher should limit interaction, give space, ensure the safety of the student and others, and follow the school's safety procedures. A student's peak phase may include major forms of aggression, which would require removal of the student or others to ensure everyone's safety. In this case, obviously interaction occurs. However, if the student's peak is sulking at his or her desk or aggressively scribbling in a notebook, for example, it may be possible to allow the escalated behavior to run its course and limit interaction with the student. The peak phase can vary in length (Colvin & Scott, 2015). Some students may yell and push a book off a desk, whereas others may destroy property or try to fight others for a lengthy period of time.

## Phase Six: De-escalation

After the peak phase, the student slowly returns to a relatively calmer emotional state. In this phase, the student is often unfocused, confused, or behaves in a subdued manner. Also during this phase, the student is likely to be quiet and isolated or removed from others and slowly regains control over his or her emotions and physical state.

During this phase, it's helpful to give the student space and limit interaction. The student can work on an independent assignment to allow him or her space and time to decompress and refocus on emotions and environment. When the student is calm and responsive, the teacher can meet with him or her to debrief and process the peak phase for reentry into the setting or activity where the peak phase occurred. During this processing and debriefing stage, the teacher can discuss any consequences or restorative steps the student needs to take before reentering the room. For example, the student may have been removed from the group or classroom during the peak phase, so it's important to discuss a reentry plan to repair any harm done by the student.

It's not uncommon for other students to be weary or hurt from the student's peak phase, so discussing how to handle that is critical (that is, repair conversations, discussed on page 128). Allowing the student to rejoin without acknowledging what happened can lead to unresolved feelings or communicate that the escalation was OK (Abry et al., 2017). As such, having a clear reentry plan, even a gradual one where the student displays prosocial behavior to earn his or her way back into the classroom, is appropriate. Of note is that sometimes a student can become agitated and escalated while processing his or her behavior because they are reminded of behavior that they may feel shame about. If this happens, stop the processing and disengage. Continue the discussion when the student is ready to continue (Colvin & Scott, 2015; Harlacher, 2015).

## Phase Seven: Recovery

During this phase, the student has returned to the classroom or setting where the peak phase occurred and is largely cooperative and integrating back into the daily routine or setting. The student may show enthusiasm or an eagerness to join class discussion or do group work. In this phase, the teacher encourages the student's return to the normal routine, as well as having a more extensive debrief in which teacher and student problem solve how to avoid future escalations. Whereas the debrief during the de-escalation phase is about the immediate goal of the student returning to the setting, this debrief is centered on formal problem solving to avoid any future occurrences of escalation.

For this debriefing, the teacher focuses on long-term outcomes. To conduct the debrief, focus on supporting the student in avoiding any future escalations. Make connections to classwide expectations and support the student in creating a safe and positive school climate. We offer questions to work through with the student.

1. What was the action or behavior that wasn't OK?

2. What do you think led to this action? (What were you thinking? What were you feeling? What was your body experiencing?)

3. What can you do differently next time?

4. What help can I (the teacher) or the class offer to support you?

Throughout this debrief, the teacher is looking for a skill to reinforce and strengthen in the student. Additionally, the response to the fourth question can indicate how the teacher can adjust the environment or setting to support the student as well. Following the debrief, the teacher can look to strengthen and reinforce the student's plan and skills that are missing.

## ····▶ Key Points

In this chapter, we outlined ways to offer compassion by adjusting strategies for students with SEB needs, mental health needs, or a history of trauma. We provided practical tips that center on understanding students' needs and providing support to reinforce use of prosocial skills. Other students may display a pattern of escalation and aggressive behavior, and we provide a way for teachers to interact and de-escalate such situations. The general concept when working with students with SEB is to understand students' needs and teach new ways for them to adapt to or handle situations.

# Cooldown Considerations

Directions: Have students complete this worksheet as a prompt to help them process their agitated state and identify positive coping skills. They can identify their feeling and why they feel that way. They then identify what they need to manage their emotion, such as *someone to feel safe with* or *space to process my emotions or calm down*. They can identify what they can do to manage their emotion, such as *journal my emotions*, *talk to the counselor (or peer or teacher)*, or *take a break and take deep breaths*.

| I'm feeling _____ |
| because: |
|  |
|  |
|  |
|  |
| **What I need is** |
|  |
|  |
|  |
|  |
| **What I can do is** |
|  |
|  |
|  |
|  |

# CHAPTER 7

# Using Data Effectively
# to Tie It All Together

U p to this point, we have covered ideas and strategies for understanding student behavior and social and emotional concerns, for preventing concerning behavior with efforts to create a resilient classroom environment, and for responding to challenging behaviors. The purpose of this chapter is to provide a framework that ties together all of these practices. Specifically, we provide guidance for teachers that emphasizes the power of using data (our favorite four-letter word) to recognize classwide patterns of student strengths and to understand when they might need to intensify or shift their instructional practices toward consistency, connection, and compassion in order to better support student social, emotional, and behavioral development. We also examine situations in which student behavioral concerns are more intensive and teachers need help from school-based professionals with particular behavioral expertise, such as school psychologists or school counselors, in order to solve problems and plan for further intervention.

First, we describe how teachers can identify outcomes and envision the types of social-emotional behaviors they want to see in their classrooms. Then, we share sources of data teachers can use to monitor whether students are engaging in resilient behaviors. Finally, we give ideas for how teachers can use classwide data to understand patterns of social and emotional behaviors and to plan strategies that promote consistency, connection, and compassion for the particular needs of their students.

## Identify Outcomes

To help teachers understand how all these pieces fit together for a classroom of students, let's consider behavior experts George Sugai and Robert H. Horner's (2006) pioneering model for organizing social, emotional, and behavioral support structures in classrooms, schools, and districts. These authors outlined the relationships between a classroom, school, or district's overall intended outcomes for students, their use of data to identify and monitor students' instructional needs, the selection and implementation of practices, and the systems and routines that are developed to support staff implementation of practices. Sugai and Horner (2006) recommend that school professionals start with identifying intended outcomes for social and emotional behavior. For the purposes of this chapter, we focus on classrooms. Defining intended outcomes can help teachers identify social and emotional skills that they want to teach students and focus resilience planning for their classrooms overall. Intended outcomes are focused on social, emotional, and behavioral constructs or competency areas.

Consider aspects of resilience or skills specific to this particular classroom community that one would ideally increase, and contrast this with less desirable attributes of the environment and student behavior that one could decrease. Think about developing a specific, relevant, and measurable outcome statement, as gathering data to help determine whether students are achieving or experiencing positive outcomes will be a next step.

Table 7.1 shows some example outcomes statements. You may develop your intended outcomes for your classroom on your own as part of a grade-level team or in conjunction with schoolwide planning. You might initially focus on one area, such as increasing classroom climate, improving social and emotional competencies, or decreasing disciplinary incidents. You then select measurement and instructional practices aligned to these intended outcomes.

## Measure Outcomes

Once you have identified and defined intended outcomes for all students, it is helpful to think concretely about how and when to measure outcomes and how to set more specific goals for needed behavior changes. Measurement of social and emotional behavior can be challenging, as social and emotional development in this domain is less linear than something like early literacy or mathematics-skill development. Furthermore, teachers are incredibly busy, and thinking through another measurement procedure can be taxing.

**Table 7.1: Outcomes Statements**

| Intended Outcome | Example Outcome Statements |
|---|---|
| Improved classroom climate | • Students will experience their classroom as a safe environment.<br>• Students will have increased positive interactions with peers and teachers. |
| Enhanced social and emotional skills | • Students will regulate uncomfortable emotions and use coping strategies with increased frequency.<br>• Students will resolve conflict without adult intervention with increased frequency.<br>• Students will work collaboratively. |
| Enhanced academic behaviors | • Students will demonstrate increased organizational skills.<br>• Students will demonstrate increased ability to pay attention in class. |
| Reduced behavioral challenges | • Students will engage in fewer behaviors that disrupt instruction. |
| Reduced social and emotional challenges | • Students will demonstrate fewer symptoms of anxiety from the beginning to the end of the school year. |

Given these challenges, schoolwide systems that support feasible and useful data collection and use are essential. Such systems help gather population data, whether classwide or schoolwide, to take the so-called temperature of students' social, emotional, and behavioral experiences in the classroom. The data they collect help identify whether instructional efforts are aiding schools in making progress toward their stated intended outcomes. In this section, we describe types of data sources that you can use to make classwide instructional decisions, and ways to select an appropriate measure. Further, we view this discussion through a problem-solving lens, in which we use data to identify and analyze concerns, plan for instructional solutions, and evaluate our efforts.

School psychologist Stephen Kilgus (2020) described the following two data sources that school teams or individual practitioners might use to make decisions.

1. *Performance data* are existing data sources that most schools already gather that can clarify areas of strength and potentially also flag

individual students or groups of students for risk. Examples include attendance data, grades, nurse visits, and disciplinary data.

2. *SEB data* are a bit more specific and can be used to screen, progress monitor, and even diagnose students for social, emotional, and behavioral concerns, such as anxiety, depression, or social-skills deficits. For the purposes of this chapter, we will primarily focus on performance and SEB data used for screening and monitoring, and not diagnostic purposes.

## Performance Data

Existing data can be a useful starting place for teachers or school teams to better understand indicators of strength or risk, as they are already available and, in our experiences, are often underutilized. Most school professionals use these data to identify individual students that may be at risk. For example, a student who is failing classes or frequently tardy or absent may be identified as a student in need of additional supports. Less often, teams or practitioners use such data to identify classwide social, emotional, and behavioral instructional targets for Tier 1 (Means, Chen, DeBarger, & Padilla, 2011).

If your school is already doing this, bravo! If not, consider the particular strengths and challenges of using these data sources presented in table 7.2. Overall, an obvious strength of these data is that they are regularly collected and often aggregated for state reporting. Additionally, they reflect important outcomes for students, such as engagement and achievement. In our experience, there are also limitations to these data sources. For example, nurse visits are often logged as individual health records for legal purposes, so those data are trickier to access meaningfully in aggregate, and aggregated data may be more useful for making classwide decisions.

Office disciplinary referrals may be used to measure an intended outcome focused on reducing problematic behavior in the classroom. Schools use office disciplinary referrals most frequently to understand student social and emotional behavior, so we will share a little more information on the particular strengths and limitations of these data. Referrals are most often made when students engage in a challenging behavior that warrants documentation and response. Often, schools regularly collect and log these data, which can offer good information about patterns of social, emotional, and behavioral concerns happening in a school and classroom. Teachers can notice, for example, if there are particular behaviors or times of day that seem to be most problematic for groups of students.

**Table 7.2: Performance Data**

| Data Source | Outcomes Targeted | Strengths | Limitations |
|---|---|---|---|
| Attendance | Proxy for engagement (National Forum on Education Statistics, 2021) | Objective, reliable data that can be sorted and analyzed to understand group-level behavior | May not reflect a student's motivation to engage but rather other environmental barriers |
| Grades | Indicator of academic achievement (National Forum on Education Statistics, 2021) | Tied to instruction, curricula; can be sorted and analyzed to understand group behavior | May reflect faulty instruction rather than student competence in subject matter |
| Nurse visits | Somatic complaints are often an indicator of internalized concerns, such as anxiety or depression (Tingstedt et al., 2018) | Objective, reliable documentation practices | May not always be a reliable indicator of behavioral health; challenging to look at these data in aggregate |
| Office disciplinary referrals | Indicator of externalized behaviors (Pas, Bradshaw, & Mitchell, 2011) | Regularly collected data that can give a wide range of information about behavior patterns | May reflect biases of referring adult |

While office disciplinary referrals can serve as helpful indicators of behavioral concerns, they also should be interpreted with caution for at least two reasons.

1.  Teachers are most often the individuals documenting referrals, and this documentation reflects their perception of a situation. Such perceptions may be biased for a number of reasons. Research suggests, for example, that teachers are more likely to refer students of color than White students, particularly for behaviors that are more subjectively defined (such as disrupting class) versus objectively defined (such as tardiness; Petrosino, Fronius, Goold, Losen, & Turner, 2017). These referral patterns may reflect implicit bias or overall expectations for student behavior (Santiago-Rosario, Whitcomb, Pearlman, & McIntosh, 2021) rather than what actually occurred in the moment.

2.  Disciplinary data likely do not capture a complete picture of a student's social, emotional, and behavioral health. For instance, students experiencing internalized concerns, like anxiety or depression, may not ever receive a disciplinary referral.

Using performance data such as office disciplinary referrals can be extremely helpful, but as noted, educators must do so with caution. We will provide examples for how to look at classwide data, but it's crucial to take time to reflect on interactions with students. Are teachers using neutralizing routines so that they respond in an instructive rather than reactive way? Also, consider looking at the patterns of referrals. Are teachers more likely to give certain groups of students referrals than other groups of students? Why is that?

## Social, Emotional, and Behavioral (SEB) Data

Kilgus (2020) suggests that social, emotional, and behavioral data can provide more information than performance data and can help practitioners understand student strengths as well as areas in which they may be experiencing symptoms of concerns such as anxiety or depression, or lagging social and emotional skills. Social, emotional, and behavioral screening practices can be particularly useful in helping schools or classrooms to identify needs across a population of students. Screening includes the collection of small amounts of information that enable practitioners to proactively screen students for risk as well as identify overall areas that could become Tier 1 instructional focus areas. Screening measures may supplement office disciplinary referrals and capture students that are experiencing internalized concerns. These tools are not meant to diagnose concerns. Rather, they are indicators of risk and clues that further intervention may be warranted. These measures are often formatted as brief rating scales or surveys.

Schools can screen students a number of ways, but to gather information about an entire population, typically teachers report on student behavior; students who are old enough (for example, third grade and older) can reliably self-report on symptoms or areas of social, emotional, and behavioral skill. In addition to the variety of screening tool response formats (for example, teacher report and self-report), tools also vary in the behaviors they target, the quality of their psychometric properties (for example, reliability and validity), and the recommended frequency of use in a school year (Glover & Albers, 2007; Whitcomb, 2017).

It is important that school teams or teachers choose tools that adequately target the needs of their particular school population or classroom, and that they select high-quality tools that are feasible to implement and use. Screening does involve collecting additional data beyond what currently exists in schools, such as the performance data mentioned here, but it is meant to be an efficient process that is useful for decision making (Whitcomb, 2017).

Schools that have adopted a screening measure must attend to a few considerations prior to implementation.

- **Parental consent or student assent:** Schools must think about what type of parental consent or student assent might be needed to proceed with data collection. According to the Substance Abuse and Mental Health Services Administration (SAMHSA, 2019), it is helpful to provide families with information about why screening may be important, how data will be collected, and how it will be used to better understand students' SEB needs. Often, families are provided with such detail and a passive consent option, where they can opt out if desired. A similar procedure can work with students.

- **How data will be collected:** Schools should consider how they collect data. For example, if teachers will complete brief rating scales for each student in their class, when will they do it? We often work with schools that make time for teachers to complete them during a faculty meeting. Middle and high school students are most often asked to self-report, meaning they must be given time to complete a screener. This often happens in a homeroom or advisory period.

- **How data will be stored and who has access:** Schools must also consider how they will store data and who will have access to data. Access to a student's screening data should be limited to only individuals that have a legitimate educational reason for such access, per the Family Educational Rights and Privacy Act of 1974.

- **Equity:** Schools should consider equity in their screening process to ensure that teachers or students can access the screening tool meaningfully. This may include attending to language, computer access, and so on (SAMHSA, 2019).

Table 7.3 (page 160) includes some commonly used screening tools and the domains, or SEB constructs, they measure. Some tools are available through data management systems for which schools purchase licenses, and others are free. While free measures are appealing, they require that schools set up a routine for data entry and analysis, which takes time and person power that schools may not have. We also encourage users to access the Comprehensive, Integrated, Three-Tiered Model of Prevention website (www.ci3t.org) for further information about screening tools and procedures.

**Table 7.3: Commonly Used Screening Tools**

| Screening Tool | Constructs Measured | Availability |
|---|---|---|
| Social, Academic, and Emotional Behavior Risk Screener (SAEBRS; Kilgus, von der Embse, Chafouleas, & Riley-Tillman, 2014) | Academic, social, and emotional behaviors | www.fastbridge.org/saebrs |
| Devereux Student Strengths Assessment-Mini (DESSA-Mini; Naglieri, Lebuffe, & Shapiro, 2011) | Social and emotional competence | https://bit.ly/3r8Lrwv |
| BASC-3 Behavioral and Emotional Screening System (BESS; Kamphaus & Reynolds, 2015) | Behavioral problems and strengths | https://bit.ly/3jjvroy |
| Strengths and Difficulties Questionnaire (SDQ; Goodman, 1997) | Emotional symptoms, conduct problems, hyperactivity or inattention, peer relationship problems, and prosocial behaviors | www.sdqinfo.org |
| Student Risk Screening Scale—Internalizing and Externalizing (SRSS-IE; Lane et al., 2015) | Internalizing and externalizing problem behaviors | www.ci3t.org/screening |

For a classroom teacher to use performance data or SEB screening data to understand patterns of group behavior, there are a few necessary data collection and management factors to consider. It is important that users can easily access these data and sort them to view classwide data. Ideally, teachers would have access to a data-management system that summarizes or even graphs data, so they could easily see challenges that students may be experiencing (Algozzine et al., 2019). If this is not possible, then it is helpful for school administrators or schoolwide MTSS teams to make such data available to teachers.

# Use the Problem-Solving Model

Once measurement and data management strategies are in place, teachers should regularly access their classwide data, aligned to their intended outcomes, to better understand the needs of their students and adjust practices as needed. Teachers can do this work individually, but it is often helpful to collaborate with grade-level or departmental colleagues, and perhaps even with school professionals who have expertise in social, emotional, and behavioral supports, such as a school counselor or school psychologist. Having data meetings—during which teachers can review their classwide data, note areas for improvement, and plan instructional adjustments with the support of other colleagues—can be helpful. Having data meetings early in the academic year and then again later in the year gives teachers time to identify student needs, adjust instructional practices, and then evaluate student progress.

To gather, review, and use data, we recommend a process that follows the four steps of the problem-solving model (Deno, 2016; McIntosh & Goodman, 2016; Shinn, 2008; Todd et al., 2011; Whitcomb, 2017). The problem-solving model is a four-step heuristic for how schools and educators can identify, define, and ultimately solve problems, and it can be applied at the individual, group, and system levels (Harlacher, Potter, & Weber, 2015; McIntosh & Goodman, 2016). We discuss the problem-solving model as a way of identifying which skills a group of students may need additional instruction in. We list each step before discussing them in depth.

1. **Problem identification:** Define the intended outcomes or preferred social and emotional skills for students to acquire and use, and notice areas of current maladaptive social and emotional behavior.

2. **Problem analysis:** Understand current patterns of social and emotional behavior that may require bolstering.

3. **Solution exploration:** Identify practices that can be enhanced and skills that can be taught to bolster student resilience.

4. **Solution evaluation:** Monitor fidelity of practices and patterns of student behavior and skill use.

## Problem Identification

The purpose of data is to identify classwide strengths and patterns of concerns. The first stage, problem identification, consists of identifying intended outcomes and observing data to identify overall patterns. For example, when considering disciplinary data, teachers may identify overall numbers of referrals given during a particular time period. Using a screening tool such as the Social, Academic, and Emotional Behavior Risk Screener (SAEBRS; https://bit.ly/3ofNEqe)—which includes a total risk score and subscales of questions focused on social behaviors, academic behaviors, and emotional symptoms—teachers may first identify overall numbers of students who present as at risk for SEB concerns given their total scores. During this phase, teachers may also identify particular trends among subscales. For example, they might take note of particular subscales in which large numbers of students seem to struggle with behavior or skill deficits. A large group of students may present with emotional symptoms such as persistent worry or sadness and further challenges with flexible thinking. Figure 7.1 is an example of aggregated data.

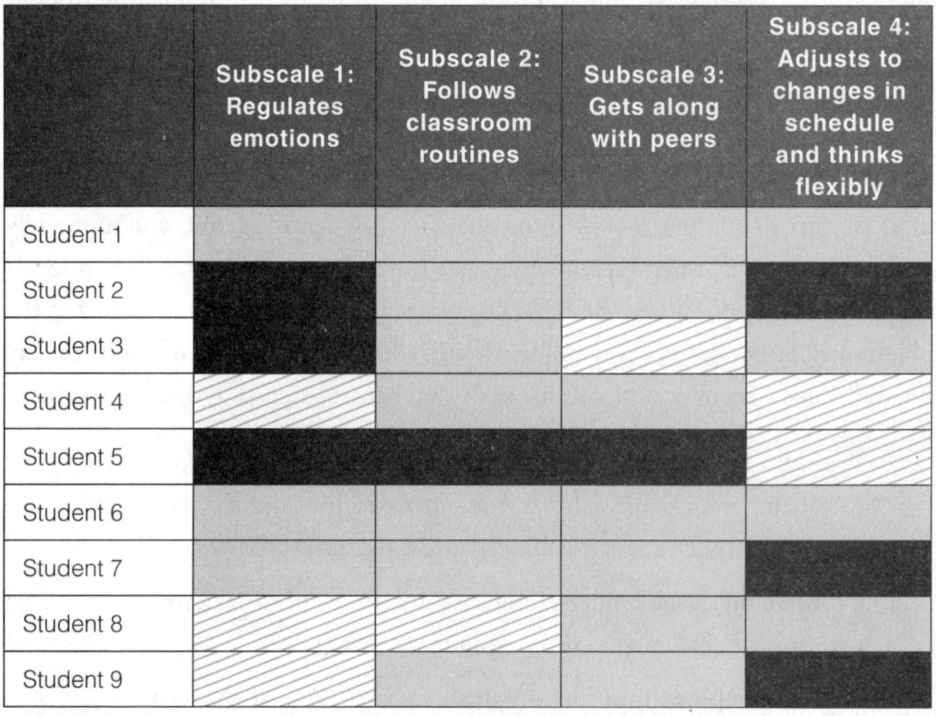

| | Subscale 1: Regulates emotions | Subscale 2: Follows classroom routines | Subscale 3: Gets along with peers | Subscale 4: Adjusts to changes in schedule and thinks flexibly |
|---|---|---|---|---|
| Student 1 | | | | |
| Student 2 | ■ | | | ■ |
| Student 3 | ■ | | ▨ | |
| Student 4 | ▨ | | | ▨ |
| Student 5 | ■ | ■ | ■ | ▨ |
| Student 6 | | | | |
| Student 7 | | | | ■ |
| Student 8 | ▨ | ▨ | | |
| Student 9 | ▨ | | | ■ |

**FIGURE 7.1:** Aggregated screening data.
Black = At risk; Hatched = Some risk; Gray = Low risk

Visualizing data in this way may enable teachers to easily recognize behaviors that the majority of the class is struggling with. For example, based on the scoring and analysis procedures of this fictitious scale, black squares indicate an area of risk, hatched squares indicate some risk, and gray squares indicate low risk. The listed subscales are simply examples of behaviors from a hypothetical screening tool. While one might be tempted to focus in on student 5's multiple areas of concerning behaviors, one can also view this table by column and see patterns of challenges that a large number of students are experiencing—in this case, regulating emotions and adjusting to changes in schedule.

## Problem Analysis

During the problem analysis phase, teachers think a little more deeply to understand the problems or skill gaps they have identified. They might use the W questions (who, what, when, where, why) to guide their thinking.

- Who seems to be struggling the most or the least? Student 5 seems to struggle the most and student 1 the least.

- What behaviors, such as regulates emotions, follows classroom routines, gets along with peers, and adjusts to changes in routine, are documented most often? Students in this class seem to struggle most with regulating emotions and adjusting to changes.

- During what times of day and where—in what locations—are behaviors more or less likely to occur? These data don't tell us, but teachers know. They can likely identify when and where these challenging behaviors are most likely to occur.

- Why do these behaviors seem to be happening? Is it because there seem to be gaps in students' social, emotional, and behavioral skills, or are the expectations in the environment ambiguous? Again, this will be a hypothesis by the teacher, but thinking functionally, as was emphasized in previous chapters, will be helpful here.

*Why* can be a tricky question to answer, as there may be a multitude of factors contributing to why a problem exists and because it's easy to focus on intrapersonal or inalterable factors (Harlacher, Sakelaris, & Kattelman, 2014; Hosp, 2008; Howell & Nolet, 2000; Shinn, 2008). Be sure to focus on what is in your sphere of control. Identify what skills may be missing or delayed and what a student may be trying to communicate when considering why a problem behavior exists.

An example of skill analysis with disciplinary data might sound something like this scenario: the majority of disciplinary documentation for a fifth-grade class includes minor physical aggression and disruptive behaviors. Sixty percent of students in the class have had a referral written for such behavior. The teacher recognizes a pattern: when students come in from lunch or recess, they often have a great deal of excess energy and a hard time settling into the collaborative work projects that usually occur next in the daily schedule. It is during this time when most referrals occur. In considering this pattern, the teacher now can explore potential solutions to reduce this problematic behavior and increase student engagement during collaborative work times. Solutions are developed in the next step of the problem-solving model, but one potential solution here could be reteaching the classroom expectation of being responsible and using active listening during collaborative work times, praising the use of the expectation during collaborative work times, and ensuring variety in the opportunities to respond as a means of increasing engagement.

In a screening example, a teacher who administered the SAEBRS and noticed a large percentage of her students displayed emotional symptoms might also validate these data with an additional source of data. In this case, the teacher looked at nurse visits and noticed several students visiting the nurse due to stomachaches, primarily during longer literacy or mathematics blocks. Stomachaches often are a somatic symptom that masks anxiety and results in frequent nurse visits (Drake, Steward, Muggeo, & Ginsburg, 2015). Based on the information that these data sources provide, the teacher can use additional professional judgment to further reflect on why emotional symptoms—particularly symptoms of anxiety—might be prevalent in students. It may be hard to figure out why students are anxious, but the teacher can consider enhancing Tier 1 supports that will improve students' awareness of emotions and strategies for coping with anxiety.

### Solution Exploration

Once teachers and teams have determined intended outcomes and analyzed related measurement strategies to better understand student social, emotional, and behavioral patterns, they can begin exploring solutions. In this problem-solving step, the goal is for teachers to link what they have learned from their data to target specific Tier 1 instructional practices that encourage consistency, connection, and compassion. When exploring solutions, teachers can consider both prosocial skills and competencies they hope to increase as well as challenging behaviors that they would like to decrease.

We suggest that teachers approach this planning phase by considering practices shared in chapters 2 through 5. In particular, teachers can consider these practices across instruction, curricula, and the environment to see what adjustments might explain why students are not progressing with prosocial skills (Harlacher & Rodriguez, 2018; Hosp, 2008; Howell & Nolet, 2000). For example, do students need more explicit instruction on the classroom expectations? Does the teacher need to adjust the examples and non-examples with the lesson plans or use a different SEL curriculum? Or perhaps there's not a high enough ratio of praise to corrective statements in the classroom.

We offer questions to explore as part of skill analysis across instruction, curricula, and environment in figure 7.2. When considering instruction, curricula, and environment, teachers may find it helpful to also examine the students' acquisition of the skill and to determine if they need more instruction on using the skill accurately, proficiently, or across settings. Once they determine that, the teacher can ascertain if the instruction, curriculum, and environment match students' skill levels.

| Domain | Question |
|---|---|
| Instruction | • Was the instruction explicit enough for students to learn the classroom expectations or SEL competencies?<br>• Was there sufficient opportunity to practice skills? |
| Curriculum | • Is the SEL curriculum appropriate for the students' needs?<br>• Do examples or nonexamples need to be adjusted in the lesson plans? |
| Environment | • Is the ratio of reinforcement to redirects at least five to one?<br>• Does the physical classroom setting support resilience? (Consider using the reproducible "Checklist for a Classroom's Physical Space," page 64.)<br>• Are strategies effective at supporting relationships in the classroom? |

**FIGURE 7.2:** Questions to consider across instruction, curricula, and environment during problem analysis.

Additionally, teachers can think about how to do three things: (1) prevent concerning behaviors, (2) teach new, adaptive behaviors, and (3) respond when students engage in either desired or concerning behaviors.

As teachers of students in an example class from the data in figure 7.1 (page 162), the overall goals may be to increase students' ability to regulate emotions, adjust to changes in routine, and think flexibly. Based on the data provided, we aim to decrease behaviors associated with emotion dysregulation (such as impulsivity, outbursts, and somatic complaints) and rigidity (such as unhelpful thinking patterns). Teachers can use prevention strategies, teaching strategies, and response strategies (discussed in chapter 5, page 101).

## Prevention Strategies

First, it is important to think strategically about practices that prevent concerning behaviors from happening—in this case, dysregulated and rigid behaviors. These behaviors reflect anxiety (Beauchaine & Hinshaw, 2017), so it might be helpful to think about implementing practices that address anxiety. To prevent anxious behaviors, teachers may consider practices that promote consistency and predict-ability, as those reduce ambiguity in the environment.

To increase predictability of classroom routines, teachers can post a daily sched-ule, clarify behavior expectations across all learning contexts and times of day, and include a classroom cooldown area. Teachers may also think about how they use verbal, visual, and physical prompts to remind students of classroom expectations or to use particular social and emotional strategies that they have previously learned. Implementing strategies to build relationships and connections with students, which we cover in chapter 4 (page 83), is excellent for fostering a warm, comfortable climate and will go a long way to help students with anxiety issues. Finally, consider using classwide mood checks as a prevention strategy. As mentioned earlier, mood checks, or emotional check-ins, provide students with the opportunity to identify and com-municate their emotions on a regular basis. This might be built in as a routine at the start of class or the start of the school day. As noted in previous chapters, mood checks not only help students build their own self-awareness, but they aid teachers in adjusting expectations or plans based on the classroom's temperature. Making such adjustments is just one way that teachers may prevent concerning behaviors and also demonstrate compassion by tuning into immediate student needs.

## Teaching Strategies

Based on classwide needs, teachers may also target particular prosocial skills for instruction or review. In this example of the class that seems to be struggling with regulating emotions and adjusting to changes in routines (figure 7.1, page 162), instructional focus areas would likely be on building student awareness of uncom-fortable emotions and strategies to manage these emotions, helping students rec-ognize unhelpful thoughts or behaviors they engage in when feeling anxious, and strengthening coping strategies.

To do this, teachers may use an evidence-based curriculum and focus on lessons that build these skills. These lessons could occur during a regularly scheduled SEL time, and teachers can also prompt practice of these skills during key teachable moments throughout the day. For example, during a disruption to regular classroom routines, such as a fire drill, a teacher might model for students helpful ways of thinking and managing emotions. The teacher may acknowledge student emotions and give some coping tips such as, "I understand that you might be feeling anxious or afraid from the loud noise and disruption to mathematics class, but remember we are safe and if we take deep breaths and focus on what we need to do next, it will help you feel a little better. Let's line up safely and head out the door." Further strategies might include embedding instruction on these focus areas into existing curricula, such as character analysis in literature or history. The overall goal is to focus energy on teaching and prompting a few key skills in which students need ample practice opportunities.

## Response Strategies

As discussed in previous chapters, teacher responses to student behaviors are a critical factor in student learning. When students effectively use a new prosocial skill they have learned, it is especially helpful for teachers to notice and acknowledge it with specific positive feedback (Gage et al., 2018; Reinke et al., 2013; Simonsen & Myers, 2015). For example, if a student effectively uses the cooldown area to cope with a strong emotion, a teacher could take notice and say, "I like that you recognized you needed to take a break on your own. That is an excellent way to manage a strong feeling."

When students don't use a relevant prosocial skill in a particular moment, even if a teacher prompts them to do so, teachers can provide corrective feedback by restating the prompt if they gauge that the student is ready to hear it, or by conferencing with the student after some time has passed to reflect on the missed opportunity for prosocial skill practice and to set a goal for practice during future opportunities. For example, the teacher might first try a prompt, "You seem to be feeling very angry. Please take a moment in the cooldown area to take a couple of deep breaths and help your body feel better." If the student does not respond to this prompt, at some point after the episode, the teacher might say, "When you started to feel really angry and ready to say unkind things, that would have been a great time to take some deep breaths or to use the cooldown area."

## *Solution Evaluation*

In the last phase of the problem-solving model, teachers can work on solution evaluation. In other words, after teachers adjust instruction based on screening data, they might go back and screen students again to see if there are more areas of competency and fewer areas of concern. For example, based on the example threaded throughout this chapter, the teacher might complete the same screening tool in the spring that she did in the fall. During the spring data meeting, she might look at her aggregated classwide data again and pay special attention to if fewer students are flagged for risk or some risk in the areas pertaining to regulating emotions and adjusting to changes in routines. While this is not an experimental design, it's possible that the strategies the teacher has put into place are contributing to students' social, emotional, and behavioral growth. At this point, the teacher may identify other problem areas as indicated by the data and reengage in the problem-solving model. Similarly, if improvements have not occurred in areas previously targeted for further instruction, it might be helpful, once again, for the teacher to engage in problem solving, revisiting what the problem behaviors look like, why they seem to be happening, and what might be an additional solution to try and then to evaluate.

Figure 7.3 provides a summary of the problem-solving model as illustrated by the example classwide data presented in figure 7.1 (page 162). This figure shows how to use the problem-solving model for resilience.

| Step | Description | Example |
|---|---|---|
| Step 1: Identify problem. | Identify overall concerns related to your intended outcomes. | Eighty percent of students score in a normal-low risk range on a screening measure. |
| Step 2: Analyze problem. | Determine who, what, when, where, and why the problem exists. What factors in instruction, curricula, and environment can you adjust to improve the number of students meeting standards (for example, scoring at expected criterion or low risk on SEL measures, displaying expectations)? | Over half of the class seems to have trouble with regulating emotions. This occurs more often during unstructured times, such as coming in from recess. |
| Step 3: Explore solutions. | Determine prevention, teaching, and response strategies that may bolster student resilience. | The teacher institutes a variety of strategies including mood or emotional checks, prompts for expected behavior before recess, teaching emotion recognition and management through morning circle, and providing feedback on progress. |

| Step | Description | Example |
|---|---|---|
| Step 4: Evaluate solutions. | Determine whether instructional adjustments have improved student resilience. | The teacher looks at the next round of screening data and identifies more than 80 percent of students as being in the low range for social and emotional risk, with fewer students showing problems with regulating emotions and adjusting to routines. |

**FIGURE 7.3:** Application of the problem-solving model for resilience in a classroom.

## ⋯▶ Key Points

In this chapter, we addressed how feasibly accessed data sources can help focus Tier 1 social, emotional, and behavioral instruction. Through defining intended outcomes for student behavior, measuring those behaviors, and then using the measurement data to better pinpoint the current overall needs of the class, teachers can target their instruction on a few key prosocial skills. In the next chapter, we focus on planning for individual students with ongoing social, emotional, and behavioral needs.

# CHAPTER 8

# Helping Students With Ongoing Needs

I n this book thus far, we've discussed teaching students prosocial skills, outlined ways to acknowledge and strengthen those skills, and presented methods to build relationships in the classroom. We have shared the supportive discipline framework and ways to adjust your strategies for students with social, emotional, and behavioral needs. Despite your best intentions, you may still have students with ongoing needs that require outside help from a specialist.

In this chapter, we discuss the process for providing students with additional support, including providing a standard intervention and creating an individualized support plan (ISP). In doing so, teachers offer compassion by addressing a student's need for support based on the function of an unwanted behavior or skill.

When using the supportive discipline framework, teachers may identify students who are not adequately responding to universal practices, students who may have ongoing needs, or students who require additional support. If you've used some of the practices we outlined in chapter 5 (page 101), at level three in the supportive discipline framework, and still need to support a student, the next step is seeking outside help from a specialist or team to provide a standard intervention or to develop an ISP for the student.

Standard interventions are evidence-based interventions that can bolster a student's resilience. The majority of students who receive a standard intervention (70–80 percent) responds and doesn't need additional support (Hawken et al., 2021; Vaughn et al., 2012). When students don't respond to a standard intervention or need a customized plan, teachers can use an ISP. The ISP outlines the conditions and context of not only the unwanted skill or student need, but also the new skill for the student to use, along with methods to teach, prompt, and reinforce that skill (O'Neill et al., 2015). Our goal for this chapter is to describe what creating an ISP looks like, but we strongly recommend seeking the assistance of a school psychologist, a school counselor, or your school's individual problem-solving team in order to create an ISP for students.

## Provide Support With Standard Interventions

Because of time constraints, standard interventions may be a useful method for classrooms and schools. Teachers can engage in the problem-solving process and use standard interventions during step 3 of the problem-solving model—exploring solutions. Teachers can also shorten assessment methods for efficiency's sake, such as using a brief functional behavioral assessment rather than a comprehensive one, and then provide a standard intervention based on the function of the student's behavior. By *standardized*, we mean the intervention is the same for all students and uses similar procedures (Harlacher et al., 2014; Hawken et al., 2021). Rather than developing an individual plan for students, this method affords classroom teachers a more efficient process to support students prior to trying an individualized approach.

Possible standard interventions can include SEL group; check-in, check-out (Hawken et al., 2021); and check and connect (Lehr, Sinclair, & Christenson, 2004; Sinclair, Christenson, Lehr, & Anderson, 2003). We describe each of these in the following sections. Teachers may find it helpful to first provide a standard intervention for students needing additional support. If the issue isn't resolved, then teachers can develop individualized support plans. However, in some instances, initially providing an ISP rather than a standard intervention may be preferred (based on the student's need; this is a data-driven, often team-based decision; Arden, Gandhi, Edmonds, & Danielson, 2017; Jimerson et al., 2016).

We also acknowledge that teachers will likely need support from schoolwide structures and teams to use the processes outlined in this chapter (see McIntosh & Goodman, 2016). In fact, standard interventions can be thought of as Tier 2 interventions (also referred to as *targeted interventions*). Accordingly, ISPs can be thought of as Tier 3 interventions (also referred to as *intensive interventions*). Providing additional support can be difficult if teaming and schoolwide systems are not in place to support them (for example, data systems, progress monitoring, leadership teams), but your school psychologist and school principal are good places to start. This book is not focused on creating schoolwide structures for interventions, but we recommend learning more from the following sources: McIntosh and Goodman (2016), the National Implementation Research Network (NIRN; https://nirn.fpg .unc.edu/national-implementation-research-network), and the Center on MTSS (https://mtss4success.org).

## SEL Group

At Tier 2, students who need additional instruction and practice with the classroom expectations or specific SEL competencies can participate weekly or twice per month in SEL group (Frey et al., 2014; Gresham, 2002; Harlacher & Rodriguez, 2018). These groups, which are usually provided by a school counselor or school psychologist, follow an instructional frame of explicitly teaching the steps of a given skill and then practicing the skill in the school setting. These groups typically have between four and six students and meet for twenty or thirty minutes each week. Figure 8.1 offers a general outline for when schools may not have a curriculum to use at Tier 2.

| Step | Description | Example |
|---|---|---|
| List critical SEL competencies. | List classroom expectations and identify between two and five SEL competencies that fall under each expectation. | *Be safe, be respectful, be responsible* |
| Do a task analysis for each skill. | Define the key components or step for each skill. | *Be safe* (Show empathy, be physically safe, provide emotional safety.) *Be respectful* (Show empathy, wait to speak.) *Be responsible* (Manage time well, identify your emotions and actions.) |

**FIGURE 8.1:** Creating an SEL group curriculum based on expectations.

continued →

| Step | Description | Example |
|------|-------------|---------|
| Develop a lesson plan for each skill. | Create a lesson for each skill. Include examples, non-examples, and a way to practice the skill. | Teachers design lessons for each skill with engagement activities, such as role playing, creating a skit, or writing an essay on how students use the skills. |
| Map out a timeline for each skill. | List when each skill will be taught, practiced, and regularly reviewed across the timeline for the Tier 2 group. | Teachers instruct on two skills each month and review each skill after teaching. |
| Communicate with all staff involved with the student. | Clarify a communication plan with the staff involved with the student so they can reinforce the taught skills. | Teachers receive copies of the lessons and the timeline. They monitor and reinforce use of the specific skills after lessons. |

## Check-In, Check-Out

Check-in, check-out (CICO) is a well-researched intervention (Boyd & Anderson, 2013; Drevon, Hixson, Wyse, & Rigney, 2019; Hawken et al., 2021; Turtura, Anderson, & Boyd, 2014). CICO is designed to help with a range of mild behaviors, including disruption, lack of organization, and impulsive behaviors (Hawken et al., 2021). A student's day is structured so that they meet briefly with an adult in the morning (who isn't their classroom teacher), receive feedback from their classroom teacher on their use of the expectations throughout the day, and meet briefly again in the afternoon with the same adult from the morning. Specifically, each morning, students check in with a staff person and review their goals for that day, ensure they have their materials for class, and are provided a daily point card that shows the expectations. Students receive feedback at designated times from their teachers throughout the day (usually between three and six times a day). At the end of the day, students check out and tally their day's points. They can earn rewards based on reaching their goal, and they take the card home to have reviewed and signed by a parent or guardian.

CICO is largely helpful for students who seek adult attention, which is usually determined based on office referral data or a brief functional behavioral assessment (Hawken et al., 2021). However, the intervention is modifiable to benefit students with escape-maintained behavior, such as avoiding work, or behavior driven by peer attention, such as using inappropriate comments to engage with peers (Boyd & Anderson, 2013;

Turtura et al., 2014). Ideally, students see a CICO program as a supportive plan, so the plan can be branded with an empowering name like the one in figure 8.2. Further, staff should celebrate student successes and graduations from the program (Hawken et al., 2021). In addition, use a standard daily point card first (for efficiency's sake), prior to modifying or adjusting the specific nuances of the intervention (Hawken et al., 2021), such as adding more check-in periods or adding explicit descriptors to each expectation. For example, the descriptor *Use positive comments toward others* can be added under the expectation Always Be Safe in figure 8.2.

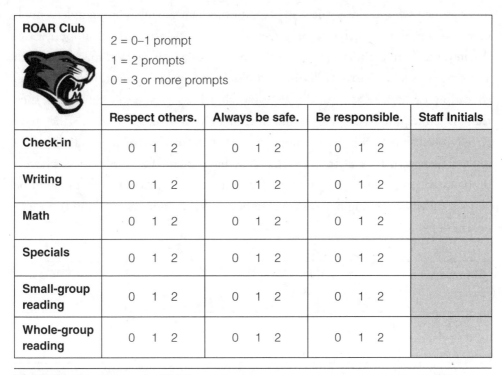

| ROAR Club | Respect others. | Always be safe. | Be responsible. | Staff Initials |
|---|---|---|---|---|
| 2 = 0–1 prompt<br>1 = 2 prompts<br>0 = 3 or more prompts | | | | |
| Check-in | 0  1  2 | 0  1  2 | 0  1  2 | |
| Writing | 0  1  2 | 0  1  2 | 0  1  2 | |
| Math | 0  1  2 | 0  1  2 | 0  1  2 | |
| Specials | 0  1  2 | 0  1  2 | 0  1  2 | |
| Small-group reading | 0  1  2 | 0  1  2 | 0  1  2 | |
| Whole-group reading | 0  1  2 | 0  1  2 | 0  1  2 | |

**FIGURE 8.2:** Example CICO card.

## Check and Connect

Check and connect is designed to increase school engagement, reduce dropouts, and improve attendance. Check and connect provides a platform for the student to develop prosocial skills, building resilience and problem-solving skills (Lehr et al., 2004; Maynard, Kjellstrand, & Thompson, 2014; Sinclair et al., 2003). With check and connect, a mentor from school regularly checks in with an assigned student and communicates with the student's family. Specifically, the mentor regularly checks the student's attendance, academic performance, and behavior referrals and tracks those data on a monitoring form. The mentor also connects with the student's family regularly, communicating the progress in school and in strengthening prosocial skills with them. The basic level entails weekly mentor meetings between the student and the mentor, during which they discuss issues that may have arisen and the importance of attending school. At the intensive level, the school may decide to add interventions such as a small group, tutoring, or counseling. The University of Minnesota (https:// checkandconnect.umn.edu) offers training in the intervention.

## Seek Additional Help

   Each school is different, but we advocate that teachers use whatever systems or routines their schools already have in place for problem solving. For example, schools may have a problem-solving team, a Tier 2 team, or an instructional support team. Whatever the name, these teams typically include an administrator, specialists (such as a school psychologist or school counselor), and special education and general education teachers. When working with individual teachers to solve problems, such teams often require teachers to submit documentation of all the strategies they have already tried. Figure 8.3 is an example of one such form; teachers could also simply use their own records to note what they have tried. If a school doesn't have a problem-solving team or instructional support team in place, this form could be very useful when seeking help or consultation from an individual school counselor or school psychologist.

| Student name: |
| Teacher name: |
| What is the target concern? |
| Disciplinary referrals: |
| Academic concerns: |
| Number of nurse visits and, if possible, why: |
| When is the challenging behavior most likely to occur, and how often? |

| Prevent (Check all that apply.) | Teach | Respond |
|---|---|---|
| **What have I tried to prevent the challenging behavior?** | **What adaptive skills have I taught to reduce the challenging behavior?** | **What does the student seem to be communicating?** |
| ☐ **Change environment.** | ☐ **Define expectations and rules.** | ☐ A need for attention or help |
| • Change seating. | ☐ **Encourage communication skills.** | ☐ A need for a break from a difficult task or situation |
| • Pair students strategically. | • Teach how to ask for help. | ☐ A need for an item or materials |
| ☐ **Increase predictability of routine.** | • Teach how to ask for a break. | **How have I responded to challenging behavior?** |
| • Use visuals. | • Teach how to ask for preferred items, activities, or attention. | ☐ Using planned ignoring |
| • Schedule breaks. | ☐ **Plan for transitions.** | ☐ Giving classwide redirect or warning |
| • Prepare students for changes in routine. | • Signal transition. | ☐ Giving nonverbal redirect or cue |
| ☐ **Provide environmental enrichment.** | • Teach waiting skills. | ☐ Restating expectation |
| • Differentiate instruction. | Other: | ☐ Providing a choice |
| • Employ engagement strategies. | | ☐ Providing in-class break |
| ☐ **Provide instructional choice.** | | ☐ Providing out-of-class break |
| ☐ **Make high-probability requests.** | | ☐ Providing expectation |
| ☐ **Give precorrection.** | | ☐ Restoring environment |
| • Provide clear, concise verbal cues | | ☐ Allowing completion of missed work |
| ☐ **Modify tasks or task length.** | | Other: |
| • Intersperse easier tasks with more difficult tasks. | | |
| • Lessen task demands as appropriate. | | |
| Other: | | |

*Source: Adapted from Whitcomb & Fefer, 2013.*

**FIGURE 8.3:** Requesting support.

Once a teacher has obtained outside assistance, the teacher and the team or specialists use the problem-solving model to support the student. We discussed the problem-solving model in relation to classwide patterns or groups of students in chapter 7 (page 153).

Here, the problem-solving model is applied to individual students. The four steps are the same, though the focus shifts from using it with groups of students to one student.

1. Problem identification: define the unwanted behavior clearly.
2. Problem analysis: understand the behavior's context and function.
3. Solution exploration: devise an individualized support plan.
4. Solution evaluation: monitor the ISP's fidelity and outcome.

### Problem Identification: Define the Unwanted Behavior Clearly

The first step of the problem-solving model for supporting individual students with ongoing needs is to define the unwanted behavior or skill clearly and precisely (Crone et al., 2015). For this, you'll want to define the behavior in observable and measurable terms with such detail that anyone who reads the description will know exactly what the behavior looks like and sounds like. For example, instead of "acting out," one would state that the student "verbally argues with peers and others by disagreeing with what is said." Instead of "won't sit still," the behavior should be defined as, "The student gets out of his seat several times during instruction and leaves his area." Instead of "is disrespectful," the student "argues and rolls her eyes." This step ensures complete clarity on the problematic behavior or skill. Once the teacher and the specialist or team agree on the actual problem, they can move to the next step.

### Problem Analysis: Understand the Behavior's Context and Function

The purpose of this step is to understand the conditions in which the behavior occurs and the contributing factors (Harlacher & Rodriguez, 2018). By understanding what factors contribute to a problem, educators can then develop a hypothesis as to why the problem is occurring (Arden et al., 2017; Deno, 2016; Harlacher et al., 2014). Recall our discussion from chapter 5 (page 101) that behavior is purposeful and is about either getting something or getting away or escaping something (Alberto & Troutman, 2013). By understanding the context where the behavior occurs, educators can determine the antecedents and consequences that contribute to the problem. By knowing the consequences, educators can then identify the function of behavior (is the behavior used to get something or someone or to escape something or someone?). In turn, they can develop an ISP for the student that is aligned to the function of the behavior.

During problem analysis, educators use a specific framework for collecting data. This framework is called the RIOT/ICEL framework (Christ & Aranas, 2014; Hosp, 2008; Howell & Nolet, 2000).

- **RIOT represents assessment methods:** *Review* of records, *interviews* with those close to the issue, *observing* the student or learning environment, and *testing* the student or those around the student

- **ICEL refers to assessment domains:** Instruction, curriculum, environment, and the learner; *instruction* refers to how students are taught, *curriculum* is what students are taught, *environment* is the learning setting and conditions, and *learner* is the student or person being taught.

By examining ICEL using RIOT, teachers and specialists can explore variables related to learning and determine what factors contribute to or inhibit a student's resilience. In doing so, they can form a hypothesis as to why a problem occurs.

During this stage, it's helpful to conduct a functional behavioral assessment to understand the function of the student's behavior (O'Neill et al., 2015). A functional behavioral assessment is a data-driven process in which educators gather data to identify the function of the student's behavior. Specialists such as the school psychologist are well equipped to conduct a functional behavioral assessment, but teachers have a critical role in assisting psychologists with determining the function of behaviors. In fact, teachers can examine or gather data to assist with determining the function of a student's behavior.

Another way to think about function is to identify what students are communicating by behaving the way that they do. Identifying the function first entails having a clear understanding of what happens after the behavior is performed. From the consequences of the behavior, a teacher can analyze the data to determine the most likely function ("most likely" because the teacher is taking a data-informed guess at this point). One way to determine the function is to use a behavior chain tracking form, such as the reproducible "Antecedent and Consequence Tracking Form" (page 190). This form enables a teacher to gather information on what happens prior to a behavior and what happens following the behavior. After several instances in which a pattern is clear in the data, the teacher can analyze the data to estimate the most likely function of the behavior. With this form, the teacher could tally each category and determine which is the most common antecedent and the most likely function of behavior.

There are other ways to determine the function of students' behavior, including analyzing the perceived motivation as reported on behavior referrals or having a school psychologist observe the behavior directly. For the latter, a teacher could ask a colleague to come and observe the student or even record the student for a few minutes so the teacher can watch it later. In addition to identifying the function, the teacher can also identify the context and antecedents that prompt the behavior, thereby gaining not only an understanding of the conditions that lead to the behavior, but also circumstances that maintain the function of the behavior (Crone et al., 2015).

The end result of the problem analysis is understanding the context of the student's need in a summary statement; figure 8.4 provides the summary statement example of Jeremy, a fifth-grade student displaying difficulty with emotion regulation by arguing and destroying property when he feels escalated. This statement summarizes the presumed function of the student's unwanted behavior, along with information about the instruction, curriculum, and environment that contribute to the student's unwanted behavior or skill (Crone et al., 2015).

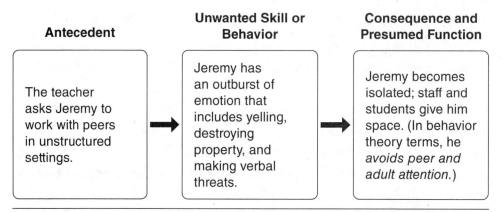

**FIGURE 8.4:** Summary statement example.

## Solution Exploration: Devise an Individualized Support Plan

Once educators complete a summary statement and feel that they understand the context and function of the student's behavior, they can discuss the skills or behaviors the student needs to learn. The skills that the student should learn, and the summary statement, are encapsulated in a competing behavior pathway.

### Competing Behavior Pathway

The competing behavior pathway illustrates the factors that contribute to the student's behavior and the conditions under which an unwanted behavior or skill occurs, as well as the desired skill or behavior that the staff would like the student to use more often (Crone et al., 2015). A competing behavior pathway centers on a summary statement of the student's unwanted skill or behavior. In the example in figure 8.5, the function is related to a sensory need in terms of tension release: Jeremy reports he feels better after the escalation. However, the function also leads to isolation and peers

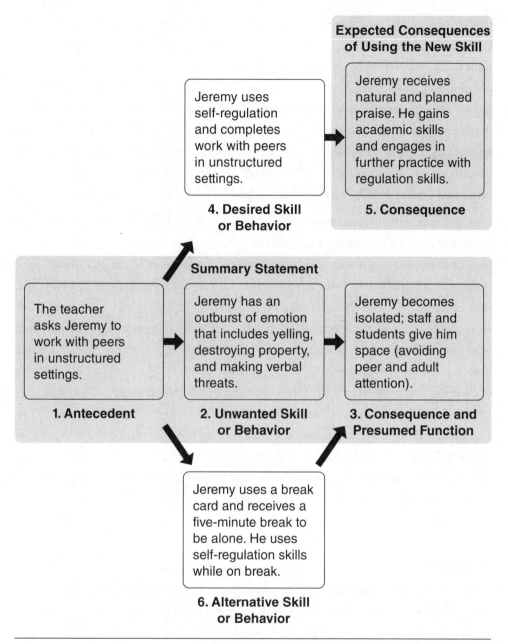

**FIGURE 8.5:** Example of a competing behavior pathway.

avoiding interacting with him. Thus, the primary function is to avoid adult and peer attention, including any demands others may place on him at that time.

Box 5 (Consequence) indicates the expected consequences of using the new skill. For example, the teacher asks Jeremy to complete his work with peers and to stay in the unstructured setting, during which he receives natural reinforcement. *Natural reinforcement* refers to the everyday consequences and reactions that result from per-forming the desired skill, in this case increased interaction with peers, acquisition of skills from completing his work, and praise that results from displaying the skill. In addition to natural consequences, the support for Jeremy includes planned praise, as Jeremy's teacher monitors his behavior and provides a higher rate of praise for using the desired skill shown in box 4; doing so also strengthens his use of the skill. Also, by working through his emotions and completing his work in the unstructured set-ting with peers, Jeremy will use self-regulation skills that are more prosocial than the unwanted skill in box 2, thus replacing an old behavior with a new one.

In addition, students may need a temporary alternative behavior that is more pleas-ing to use but that also serves the same function, as illustrated by box 6 (Alternative Skill or Behavior). An alternative behavior is helpful because it can be difficult for a student to suddenly stop using a habitual skill (even if it's detrimental to them) and start using a new skill. As such, teachers can transition the student to the new skill with temporary use of an alternative behavior. Here, Jeremy can use a break pass when he's feeling overwhelmed from the antecedent. He still experiences the same function as using the target skill, but the pathway is less destructive than his outburst of emotion and more socially adaptive than the undesired behavior (as shown in fig-ure 8.5, by following the pathway from box 1 to 6 to 3 instead of the pathway from 1 to 2 to 3). Once they have outlined the competing behavior pathway by identifying the antecedent, unwanted behavior, desired behavior, alternative behavior, and the consequences associated with those behaviors, the educators working with the stu-dent can develop a clear ISP that includes strategies to teach and reinforce new skills, including antecedent and consequence strategies to use with the student.

## Individualized Support Plan (ISP)

The ISP is a comprehensive approach in which a student learns a new behavior and the teacher makes changes in the environment to prompt the newly taught skill and reinforces the student's use of the skill. We use the words *prevention*, *teaching*, and *response* to capture the various aspects of the ISP (Dunlap et al., 2010). Specifically, an ISP includes the following.

- Prevention strategies modify antecedents in order to prompt the desired behavior and offset triggering the unwanted behavior.

- Teaching strategies teach the student a skill or behavior that replaces the unwanted skill or behavior.

- Response strategies modify the consequences to reinforce the newly taught skill and also include corrective consequences to redirect use of the unwanted skill or behavior (Bambara & Kern, 2005, 2021; Crone et al., 2015).

We outline the specifics of the ISP in table 8.1.

**Table 8.1: Individualized Support Plan and Components**

| Component | Description | Examples |
|---|---|---|
| Prevention strategies | Prompt the desired behavior and avoid or prevent the unwanted behavior. | • The teacher provides precorrection and reminds student of a break pass when he or she feels escalated. |
| Teaching strategies | Teach the new behavior that replaces the unwanted behavior but serves the same function. | • The teacher actively teaches the student how to use the break pass and the parameters for its use.<br>• The student learns emotion regulation skills with examples and nonexamples.<br>• The student practices emotion regulation skills or coping skills each day before beginning work. |
| Response strategies | Reinforce the taught skill and use corrective consequences to correct any use of the unwanted behavior. | • The student earns minutes toward screen time by practicing the new skill each day. The student can also earn minutes for appropriate use of break pass.<br>• The student receives consistent attention, praise, and support for engaging in class and using coping skills. |

Generally speaking, teachers can teach a new skill or behavior using a lesson-plan structure similar to the one outlined in chapter 2 (page 33) that includes explicit instruction and examples and nonexamples of the taught skill. Following teaching of the skill, the teacher then prompts the new skill by adjusting antecedents and further strengthens the skill by modifying the consequences. During ISP development, the notion is to make the unwanted behavior *irrelevant*, *inefficient*, and *ineffective* (Crone et al., 2015; O'Neill et al., 2015).

Consider the following.

- Teachers or staff make a behavior *irrelevant* by preventing antecedents from triggering it and instead prompting the taught behavior.

- Teachers or staff also make a behavior *inefficient* by teaching the student a new skill that is more efficient to use (for instance, one that requires less energy to use) to replace the old behavior.

- Teachers or staff make an old behavior *ineffective* by not allowing it to access the previous function. Recall that function is the purpose of a behavior to either get something or someone or to escape something or someone (see figure 5.2, page 105). Instead, the new behavior is more efficient and effective at accessing reinforcement (Crone et al., 2015).

Teachers will want to match a selected strategy with the function of the behavior. There are numerous ways to do this, but we offer examples of prevention and response strategies in tables 8.2 and 8.3, respectively.

**Table 8.2: Examples of Prevention Strategies by Function**

| Function | Examples |
|---|---|
| To get or obtain others' attention | • Provide individualized attention when the student arrives to class. With front-loaded attention, the student is less inclined to use unwanted behavior to get attention.<br>• Allow peer or group work for certain activities.<br>• Provide leadership opportunities as a means to access attention prior to using an unwanted behavior or skill. |
| To escape or avoid others' attention | • Remind the student that it is OK to take a break to use noise-canceling headphones or access a space in the room away from others.<br>• Use visual or written prompts versus verbal directions, or give one-to-one attention. |
| To get or obtain an activity or item | • Remind the student that displays of the expected behavior or skills mean access to the preferred item. |
| To escape or avoid an activity or item | • Embed easier requests throughout more difficult ones to offset frustration with completing work.<br>• Preteach content or teach missing skills related to task demands. |

| Function | Examples |
|---|---|
| To manage a sensory need | • Check in with students as they arrive to determine any sensory needs they may have.<br>• Provide a space in the classroom that is quiet before students begin class to reduce overstimulation the student may have.<br>• Have the student use a coping skill at the start of class to ensure a calmer emotional state.<br>• Allow flexibility in seating arrangement or temperature to provide relief for sensory needs. |

**Table 8.3: Examples of Response Strategies by Function**

| Function | Examples |
|---|---|
| To get or obtain others' attention | • Provide regular interaction and attention contingent on skill use.<br>• Allow students to earn time with peers or adults (for example, work for *x* minutes, take a brief break to talk with peers or adults). |
| To escape or avoid others' attention | • Allow extended alone time for skill use.<br>• Allow intermittent breaks from others for skill use (for example, the student can take a water break or take something to the office). |
| To get or obtain an activity or item | • Allow access to the item or activity as a reward for skill use. |
| To escape or avoid an activity or item | • Provide breaks as a reward for skill use.<br>• Allow use of a break pass for brief breaks during work time. |
| To manage a sensory need | • Allow time to use a coping skill to return to a normal emotional state. |

Returning to Jeremy, we depict his ISP in figure 8.6 (page 186). In this example, the school counselor teaches Jeremy the new skill explicitly in a one-to-one setting and includes examples and nonexamples as well as practice of the new skill. Jeremy also learns how to recognize the physiology of feeling stressed and overwhelmed and coping skills to manage his anxious feelings by going to a quiet space in the room and writing or using breathing techniques. Specifically, Jeremy had four thirty-minute sessions with the school counselor, with the first session focused on being responsible, the second session on self-regulation, and the next two sessions spent practicing the skills in the classroom. Following those four sessions, Jeremy also met with the school counselor for fifteen minutes each week to check in and receive support on continued use of his self-regulation skills.

**Desired behavior:** The student completes work in unstructured settings with peers. The student uses self-regulation skills as needed.

**Alternative behavior:** The student uses a break card and receives a five-minute break to be alone. The student uses self-regulation skills while on break.

| Prevention Strategies | Teaching Strategies | Response Strategies |
|---|---|---|
| • Greet student at the door as he enters the classroom. <br> • Provide regular positive contact. <br> • Precorrect by reminding the student to use self-regulation skills and break card if he feels overwhelmed, particularly before peer group work. <br> • Give the student a break card to use. <br> • Place a visual card of steps to self-regulate on his desk. | • Hold over four thirty-minute sessions with the counselor, and reteach being responsible with examples and nonexamples that target using self-regulation and managing emotions. <br> • Provide weekly fifteen-minute meetings with the counselor for support with self-regulation. <br> • Teach student how to use the break card and parameters for its use. | • Increase praise and feedback to the student relative to peers for self-regulating and being responsible. <br> • Engage the student in brief (one- to two-minute) teacher feedback sessions each hour on use of desired skills. <br> • Remind the student when he or she escalates or feels frustrated to use the break card or self-regulation skills, giving brief error correction, and prompt to use appropriate skills. |

**FIGURE 8.6:** ISP example.

For prevention strategies, the classroom teacher greets Jeremy warmly at the door as he enters. The teacher checks in with him, welcomes him to the classroom, and reminds him to use his self-regulation skills. The teacher also gives Jeremy a card on his desk that depicts the steps of self-regulation. He also has a break card that he can use two to three times per class period that allows him a five-minute break away from others when he holds up the card. The teacher also provides a quiet space in the classroom (in this case, a carpeted area in the corner of the classroom) for Jeremy to use his self-regulation skills.

For response strategies, the teacher praises Jeremy throughout his time in class on using the self-regulation skill, for completing his work, and for staying in the unstructured settings with peers. He also earns points toward a reward for using those skills. The reward is based on the function of the unwanted behavior; in this case, Jeremy can earn a quiet break doing a preferred activity with no adult or peer attention.

### Solution Evaluation: Monitor the ISP's Fidelity and Outcome

In this last step of the problem-solving model, the teacher monitors the ISP for fidelity of implementation and whether it benefits the student. In particular, the teacher gathers data on two things: (1) a measurement of the fidelity with which student and teacher are following the ISP and (2) student outcome data to determine the impact of the plan.

*Fidelity* is the extent to which a plan is implemented as intended (Wilkinson, 2007; Wolery, 2011). A good analogy is a doctor's instruction to follow her medical advice. For example, your doctor may ask you to take a pill once daily as part of a health plan. Fidelity refers to the extent to which you take your pill daily—that is, how well you follow the doctor's plan. In this example, an easy fidelity measure could be recording in a journal whether you took your pill that day or not. You could then use this information to determine if your fidelity was high or low.

In a classroom, fidelity can be measured by either observing ISP components or self-reporting if components were implemented (Harlacher & Rodriguez, 2018). For example, the teacher can measure adherence to the plan by documenting if all the strategies listed in the ISP occurred. (Did the student receive teaching of the new skill? Were the prevention strategies used? Were the response strategies used?) The teacher or other involved staff can record these data daily. Conversely, other staff, such as the counselor or school administrator, could take brief moments throughout the week to observe and record if ISP components were implemented. For example, the administrator could observe the teaching strategies and indicate if they were implemented as intended; in this example, the administrator can document implementation with a simple *Yes, it was implemented* or *No, it wasn't*.

For the ISP illustrated in figure 8.7 (page 188), the school counselor created a checklist of the listed prevention, teaching, and response strategies (figure 8.6). The counselor then asked the teacher to rate once per week the extent to which the strategy was used on a scale of 1 (not used at all) to 5 (used each day). These data are averaged across all strategies to give a percentage of strategies used. Broadly speaking, teachers should be happy with at least 90–95 percent fidelity of implementation (see Hawken et al., 2021; Vaughn et al., 2012).

| Person recording data: | Date: | | | | |
|---|---|---|---|---|---|
| **Prevention Strategies** | **Level of Implementation**<br>**1 = Not implemented or didn't occur**<br>**5 = Implemented well** | | | | |
| Greet student at the door as he enters the classroom. | 1 | 2 | 3 | 4 | 5 |
| | N/A or didn't observe | | | | |
| Provide regular positive contact. | 1 | 2 | 3 | 4 | 5 |
| | N/A or didn't observe | | | | |
| Precorrect by reminding the student to use self-regulation skills and break card if he feels overwhelmed, particularly before peer group work. | 1 | 2 | 3 | 4 | 5 |
| | N/A or didn't observe | | | | |
| Give the student a break card to use. | 1 | 2 | 3 | 4 | 5 |
| | N/A or didn't observe | | | | |
| Place a visual card of steps to self-regulate on his desk. | 1 | 2 | 3 | 4 | 5 |
| | N/A or didn't observe | | | | |
| **Teaching Strategies** | | | | | |
| Over four thirty-minute sessions with the counselor, reteach being responsible with examples and nonexamples that target using self-regulation and managing emotions. | 1 | 2 | 3 | 4 | 5 |
| | N/A or didn't observe | | | | |
| Provide weekly fifteen-minute meetings with the counselor for support with self-regulation. | 1 | 2 | 3 | 4 | 5 |
| | N/A or didn't observe | | | | |
| Teach student how to use the break card and parameters for its use. | 1 | 2 | 3 | 4 | 5 |
| | N/A or didn't observe | | | | |
| **Response Strategies** | | | | | |
| Increase praise and feedback to the student relative to peers for self-regulating and being responsible. | 1 | 2 | 3 | 4 | 5 |
| | N/A or didn't observe | | | | |
| Engage the student in brief (one- to two-minute) teacher feedback sessions each hour on his use of desired skills. | 1 | 2 | 3 | 4 | 5 |
| | N/A or didn't observe | | | | |
| Remind the student when he escalates or feels frustrated to use the break card or self-regulation skills, giving brief error correction, and prompt to use appropriate skills. | 1 | 2 | 3 | 4 | 5 |
| | N/A or didn't observe | | | | |

**FIGURE 8.7:** Example ISP fidelity checklist.

## ····▶ Key Points

This chapter and the previous chapters outlined how to show compassion for students by adjusting strategies to meet their needs and matching the teacher's response to the student's response. In this chapter, we described an intensive support process using the problem-solving model to support students with ongoing needs. By matching supports to a student's need, teachers and specialists can teach a student a beneficial prosocial skill. As illustrated in this chapter, the process follows the problem-solving model and aligns with behavior theory principles that were outlined in chapter 5 (page 101).

# Antecedent and Consequence Tracking Form

To use this form, record each instance of the behavior with the date and time that it occurred, and then place checkmarks next to all of the antecedents (listed in the Antecedents column) and the consequences (listed in the Consequences column). You will need one copy of this form for each instance of the behavior.

Note: This is just an example of a tracking form. You may wish to alter the options for the antecedents and consequences based on your classroom.

Behavior to track (defined in observable and measurable terms): _____

| | Antecedents | | Consequences | |
| --- | --- | --- | --- | --- |
| Date and Time | Activity or Setting | Task | With Whom | Get or Obtain Responses | Avoid or Escape Responses |
| | ☐ Reading<br>☐ Writing<br>☐ Mathematics<br>☐ Science<br>☐ Social studies<br>☐ Transition<br>☐ Lunchtime<br>☐ Recess<br>☐ Study hall<br>☐ Library<br>☐ Computer<br>☐ Other: | ☐ Work demand or request<br>☐ Verbal direction or request<br>☐ Removal of item<br>☐ Writing task<br>☐ Reading task<br>☐ Spelling task<br>☐ Noisy room<br>☐ Errors or correction with work<br>☐ Change from routine<br>☐ Other: | ☐ Alone (no attention)<br>☐ Whole-class instruction<br>☐ Small group<br>☐ Independent work<br>☐ With one peer<br>☐ Other: | ☐ Teacher talked with student<br>☐ Peer(s) interacted with student<br>☐ Worked on another activity or a preferred activity<br>☐ Obtained an item (for example, a preferred book)<br>☐ Obtained a task (for example, computer time)<br>☐ Other: | ☐ Did not complete work or avoided work<br>☐ Spent time in hallway or area alone (removed attention)<br>☐ Moved into a different area or setting<br>☐ Other: |

*Harlacher, J. E. (2015). Designing effective classroom management. Bloomington, IN: Marzano Resources.*

# EPILOGUE

With this book, we wanted to create a common thread among the various approaches that support a welcoming environment for students. In doing so, we hope our readers have seen that a classroom built on consistency, connection, and compassion can bolster resilience and create a fair and equitable environment. See figure E.1 for a visual summary of the three Cs. By creating consistency through the teaching of expectations and routines, teachers can establish an environment that is structured and safe. Teachers can explicitly create connection among their students and have them understand they are important and valued. And teachers can adjust their structure to be flexible to meet the needs of their students, showing them compassion. As a result, teachers can build a classroom that uses best practices and ultimately creates a more positive climate.

We know the amount of work and stress teachers face in doing this work. It's not easy to teach students academic content as well as meet their social and emotional needs. By anchoring a classroom to consistency, connection, and compassion, we hope things are manageable and practical for teachers.

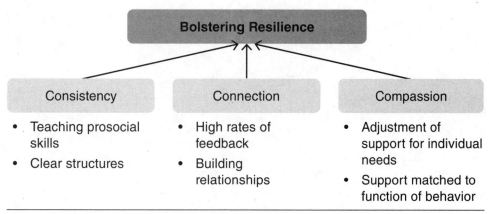

**FIGURE E.1:** Visual conceptualization of bolstering resilience.

We began work on this book in mid-2019. It was our goal to honor our mentor's legacy by providing teachers with a handbook on how to create environments that bolster resilience. Little did we know that we, like the rest of the world, would enter a pandemic exacerbated by political strife and social justice violations. We watched with the rest of the population as students and young people rallied to say, "Enough is enough" and to advocate for a better world and safer schools. We want this book to be a part of that message. In fact, 2020 and the COVID-19 pandemic only served to highlight our message that students need to know that they matter. That their voices, needs, and paths in life are important.

We believe that strengthening students' social and emotional competencies and bolstering their resilience lead to an equitable and fair school climate. We advocate that all students should feel valued by and connected to school, so this book is our step toward that ideal.

# REFERENCES AND RESOURCES

Abry, T., Rimm-Kaufman, S. E., & Curby, T. W. (2017). Are all program elements created equal? Relations between specific social and emotional learning components and teacher-student classroom interaction quality. *Prevention Science, 18*(1), 193–203.

Akin-Little, K. A., Eckert, T. L., Lovett, B. J., & Little, S. G. (2004). Extrinsic reinforcement in the classroom: Bribery or best practice. *School Psychology Review, 33*(3), 344–362.

Alberto, P. A., & Troutman, A. C. (2013). *Applied behavior analysis for teachers* (9th ed.). Boston: Pearson.

Albright, M. I., Weissberg, R. P., & Dusenbury, L. A. (2011). *School-family partnership strategies to enhance children's social, emotional, and academic growth.* Newton, MA: National Center for Mental Health Promotion and Youth Violence Prevention, Education Development Center. Accessed at https://casel.org/wp-content/uploads /2016/06/school-family-partnership-strategies-to-enhance-childrens-social-emotional -and-academic-growth.pdf on June 2, 2021.

Algozzine, B., Barrett, S., Eber, L., George, H., Horner, R., Lewis, T., et al. (2019). *School-wide PBIS tiered fidelity inventory.* Eugene, OR: OSEP Technical Assistance Center on Positive Behavioral Interventions and Supports. Accessed at www.pbis.org/resource/tfi on June 2, 2021.

Algozzine, B., Cooke, N., White, R., Helf, S., Algozzine, K., & McClanahan, T. (2008). The North Carolina Reading and Behavior Center's K–3 prevention model: Eastside Elementary School case study. In C. R. Greenwood, T. R. Kratochwill, & M. Clements (Eds.), *Schoolwide prevention models: Lessons learned in elementary schools* (pp. 173–214). New York: Guilford Press.

Algozzine, B., Newton, J. S., Horner, R. H., Todd, A. W., & Algozzine, K. (2012). Development and technical characteristics of a team decision-making assessment tool: Decision observation, recording, and analysis (DORA). *Journal of Psychoeducational Assessment, 30*(3), 237–249.

Allday, R. A., Hinkson-Lee, K., Hudson, T., Neilsen-Gatti, S., Kleinke, A., & Russel, C. S. (2012). Training general educators to increase behavior-specific praise: Effects on students with EBD. *Behavioral Disorders, 37*(2), 87–98.

Anderson, A. R., Christenson, S. L., Sinclair, M. F., & Lehr, C. A. (2004). Check & Connect: The importance of relationships for promoting engagement with school. *Journal of School Psychology, 42*(2), 95–113.

Anderson, C. M., & Borgmeier, C. (2010). Tier II interventions within the framework of school-wide positive behavior support: Essential features for design, implementation, and maintenance. *Behavior Analysis in Practice, 3*(1), 33–45.

Anhalt, K., McNeil, C. B., & Bahl, A. B. (1998). The ADHD Classroom Kit: A whole-classroom approach for managing disruptive behavior. *Psychology in the Schools, 35*(1), 67–79.

Arden, S. V., Gandhi, A. G., Edmonds, R., Z., & Danielson, L. (2017). Toward more effective tiered systems: Lessons from national implementation efforts. *Exceptional Children, 83*(3), 269–280.

Aronson, E., & Patnoe, S. (2011). *Cooperation in the classroom: The jigsaw method.* London: Pinter & Martin.

Aronson, E., Stephan, C., Sikes, J., Blaney, N., & Snapp, M. (1978). *The jigsaw classroom.* Beverly Hills, CA: SAGE.

Baer, D. M., Wolf, M. M., & Risley, T. R. (1968). Some current dimensions of applied behavior analysis. *Journal of Applied Behavior Analysis, 1*(1), 91–97.

Bambara, L. M., & Kern, L. (Eds.). (2005). *Individualized supports for students with problem behaviors: Designing positive behavior plans.* New York: Guilford Press.

Bambara, L. M., & Kern, L. (Eds.). (2021). *Individualized supports for students with problem behaviors: Designing positive behavior plans* (2nd ed.). New York: Guilford Press.

Bandura, A. (1986). *Social foundations of thought and action: A social cognitive theory.* Englewood Cliffs, NJ: Prentice Hall.

Barlow, D. H. (2002). *Anxiety and its disorders.* New York: Guilford Press.

Barrett, S., Eber, L., McIntosh, K., Perales, K., & Romer, N. (2018). *Teaching social-emotional competencies within a PBIS framework.* Eugene, OR: OSEP Technical Assistance Center on Positive Behavioral Interventions and Supports. Accessed at www.pbis.org/resource/teaching-social-emotional-competencies-within-a-pbis-framework on June 2, 2021.

Barrish, H. H., Saunders, M., & Wolf, M. M. (1969). Good behavior game: Effects of individual contingencies for group consequences on disruptive behavior in a classroom. *Journal of Applied Behavior Analysis, 2*(2), 119–124.

Bear, G. G. (2010). *School discipline and self-discipline: A practical guide to promoting prosocial student behavior*. New York: Guilford Press.

Beauchaine, T. P., & Hinshaw, S. P. (2017). *Child and adolescent psychopathology* (3rd ed.). Hoboken, NJ: Wiley.

Berger, R., Rugen, L., & Woodfin, L. (2014). *Leaders of their own learning: Transforming schools through student-engaged assessment*. London: Jossey-Bass.

Bergin, C. A., & Bergin, D. A. (2009). Attachment in the classroom. *Educational Psychology Review, 21*(2), 141–170.

Bettenhausen, S. (1998). Make proactive modifications to your classroom. *Intervention in School and Clinic, 33*(3), 182–183.

Biglan, A., Flay, B. R., Embry, D. D., & Sandler, I. R. (2012). The critical role of nurturing environments for promoting human wellbeing. *American Psychologist, 67*(4), 257–271.

Bitsko, R. H., Holbrook, J. R., Ghandour, R. M., Blumberg, S. J., Visser, S. N., Perou, R., et al. (2018). Epidemiology and impact of health care provider: Diagnosed anxiety and depression among US children. *Journal of Developmental and Behavioral Pediatrics, 39*(5), 395–403.

Blase, K., Van Dyke, M., & Fixsen, D. (2013). *Stages of implementation analysis: Where are we?* Chapel Hill, NC: National Implementation Research Network, Frank Porter Graham Child Development Institute, University of North Carolina at Chapel Hill.

Blum, R. W., McNeely, C. A., & Rinehart, P. M. (2002). *Improving the odds: The untapped power of schools to improve the health of teens*. Minneapolis: Center for Adolescent Health and Development, University of Minnesota.

Bondy, E., & Ketts, S. (2001). "Like being at the breakfast table": The power of classroom morning meeting. *Childhood Education, 77*(3), 144–149.

Bornstein, M. H., Putnick, D. L., Gartstein, M. A., Hahn, C., Auestad, N., & O'Connor, D. L. (2015). Infant temperament: Stability by age, gender, birth order, term status, and SES. *Child Development, 86*(3), 844–863.

Bosworth, K., & Judkins, M. (2014). Tapping into the power of school climate to prevent bullying: One application of schoolwide positive behavior interventions and supports. *Theory Into Practice, 53*(4), 300–307.

Bowen, J. M., Jenson, W. R., & Clark, E. (2004). *School-based interventions for students with behavior problems*. New York: Kluwer Academic/Plenum.

Boyd, R. J., & Anderson, C. M. (2013). Breaks are better: A Tier II social behavior intervention. *Journal of Behavioral Education, 22*(4), 348–365.

Brackett, M. (2020, January 19). *The colors of our emotions* [Blog post]. Accessed at www.marcbrackett.com/the-colors-of-our-emotions on June 1, 2021.

Bradshaw, C. P., Mitchell, M. M., & Leaf, P. J. (2010). Examining the effects of schoolwide positive behavioral interventions and supports on student outcomes: Results from a randomized controlled effectiveness trial in elementary schools. *Journal of Positive Behavior Interventions, 12*(3), 133–148.

Bradshaw, C. P., Waasdorp, T. E., & Leaf, P. J. (2012). Effects of school-wide positive behavioral interventions and supports on child behavior problems. *Pediatrics, 130*(5), e1136–e1145.

Bronfenbrenner, U. (1979). *The ecology of human development: Experiments by nature and design.* Cambridge, MA: Harvard University Press.

Brophy, J., & Good, T. L. (1986). Teacher behavior and student achievement. In M. Wittrock (Ed.), *Handbook of research on teaching* (3rd ed., pp. 328–375). New York: Macmillan.

Bross, L. A., Common, E. A., & Oakes, W. P. (2018). High-probability request sequence: An effective, efficient low-intensity strategy to support student success. *Beyond Behavior, 27*(3), 140–145.

Buchanan, A. (2014). Risk and protective factors in child development and the development of resilience. *Open Journal of Social Sciences, 2*(4), 244–249.

Buck, G. H. (1999). Smoothing the rough edges of classroom transitions. *Intervention in School and Clinic, 34*(4), 224–227, 235.

Burns, M. K., Riley-Tillman, T. C., & Rathvon, N. (2017). *Effective school interventions: Evidence-based strategies for improving student outcomes* (3rd ed.). New York: Guilford Press.

Burns, M. K., VanDerHeyden, A. M., & Zaslofsky, A. F. (2014). Best practices in delivering intensive academic interventions with a skill-by-treatment interaction. In A. Thomas & J. Grimes (Eds.), *Best practices in school psychology: Student level services* (6th ed., pp. 129–142). Bethesda, MD: National Association of School Psychologists.

Cairns, K. E., Yap, M. B. H., Pilkington, P. D., & Jorm, A. F. (2014). Risk and protective factors for depression that adolescents can modify: A systematic review and meta-analysis of longitudinal studies. *Journal of Affective Disorders, 169*, 61–75.

Cameron, J., Banko, K. M., & Pierce, W. D. (2001). Pervasive negative effects of rewards on intrinsic motivation: The myth continues. *Behavior Analyst, 24*(1), 1–44.

Cameron, J., & Pierce, W. D. (1994). Reinforcement, reward, and intrinsic motivation: A meta-analysis. *Review of Educational Research, 64*(3), 363–423.

Cannon, W. B. (1927). The James-Lange theory of emotions: A critical examination and an alternative theory. *American Journal of Psychology, 39*, 106–124.

Center on Positive Behavioral Interventions and Supports. (n.d.a). *Getting started.* Accessed at www.pbis.org/pbis/getting-started on August 25, 2021.

Center on Positive Behavioral Interventions and Supports. (2020). *Guidance on adapting check-in check-out (CICO) for distance learning.* Accessed at www.pbis.org/resource /guidance-on-adapting-check-in-check-out-cico-for-distance-learning on June 1, 2021.

Center on Positive Behavioral Interventions and Supports, & Center for Parent Information and Resources. (2020). *Supporting families with PBIS at home.* Accessed at www.pbis .org/resource/supporting-families-with-pbis-at-home on June 2, 2021.

Center on the Developing Child at Harvard University. (n.d.). *ACEs and toxic stress: Frequently asked questions.* Accessed at https://developingchild.harvard.edu/resources /aces-and-toxic-stress-frequently-asked-questions on June 2, 2021.

Centre for Education Statistics and Evaluation. (2020). *Classroom management: Creating and maintaining positive environments.* Parramatta, New South Wales, Australia: NSW Department of Education. Accessed at www.cese.nsw.gov.au/publications-filter /classroom-management on January 4, 2022.

Chambers, C. R. (2006). High-probability request strategies: Practical guidelines. *Young Exceptional Children, 9*, 20–28.

Christ, T., & Aranas, Y. A. (2014). Best practices in problem analysis. In P. Harrison & A. Thomas (Eds.), *Best practices in school psychology VI: Data-based and collaborative decision making* (pp. 87–98). Bethesda, MD: National Association of School Psychologists.

Chung, K. K. H., Lam, C. B., & Liew, J. (2020). Studying children's social-emotional development in school and at home through a cultural lens. *Early Education and Development, 31*(6), 927–929.

Clark, M. D. (2018, May 31). *Butler County teachers learn to plug bullet holes as part of active shooter training.* Accessed at www.journal-news.com/news/butler-county-teachers-learn -plug-bullet-holes-part-active-shooter-training/RHnRUTOiYzKMbT88zCHB6M on June 1, 2021.

Clarke, A., Sorgenfrei, M., McMurphy, J., Davie, P., Freidrich, C., & McBride, T. (2021). *Adolescent mental health: A systematic review on the effectiveness of school-based interventions.* London: Early Intervention Foundation. Accessed at www.eif.org.uk/report/adolescent -mental-health-a-systematic-review-on-the-effectiveness-of-school-based-interventions on January 4, 2022.

Collaborative for Academic, Social, and Emotional Learning. (n.d.). *CASEL program guides: Effective social and emotional learning programs.* Accessed at https://casel.org/guide on November 11, 2020.

Collaborative for Academic, Social, and Emotional Learning. (2020). *CASEL's SEL framework: What are the core competence areas and where are they promoted?* Accessed at https://casel.org/wp-content/uploads/2020/12/CASEL-SEL-Framework-11.2020.pdf on June 1, 2021.

Collaborative for Academic, Social, and Emotional Learning. (2021). *Indicators of schoolwide SEL*. Accessed at https://schoolguide.casel.org/what-is-sel/indicators-of-schoolwide-sel on November 4, 2020.

Collins, T. A., Cook, C. R., Dart, E. H., Socie, D. G., Renshaw, T. L., & Long, A. C. (2016). Improving classroom engagement among high school students with disruptive behavior: Evaluation of the class pass intervention. *Psychology in the Schools*, *53*(2), 204–219.

Colvin, G., & Scott, T. M. (2015). *Managing the cycle of acting-out behavior in the classroom* (2nd ed.). Thousand Oaks, CA: Corwin Press.

Colvin, G., Sugai, G., & Patching, B. (1993). Precorrection: An instructional approach for managing predictable problem behaviors. *Intervention in School and Clinic*, *28*(3), 143–150.

Cook, C. R., Coco, S., Zhang, Y., Fiat, A. E., Duong, M. T., Renshaw, T. L., et al. (2018a). Cultivating positive teacher-student relationships: Preliminary evaluation of the establish-maintain-restore (EMR) method. *School Psychology Review*, *47*(3), 226–243.

Cook, C. R., Collins, T. A., Dart, E., Vance, M. J., McIntosh, K., Grady, E. A., et al. (2014). Evaluation of the class pass intervention for typically developing students with hypothesized escape-motivated disruptive classroom behavior. *Psychology in the Schools*, *51*(2), 107–125.

Cook, C. R., Fiat, A. E., Larson, M., Daikos, C., Slemrod, T., Holland, E. A., et al. (2018b). Positive greetings at the door: Evaluation of a low-cost, high-yield proactive classroom management strategy. *Journal of Positive Behavior Interventions*, *20*(3), 149–159.

Costello, B., Wachtel, J., & Wachtel, T. (2009). *The restorative practices handbook for teachers, disciplinarians and administrators*. Bethlehem, PA: International Institute for Restorative Practices.

Crone, D. A., Hawken, L. S., & Horner, R. H. (2010). *Responding to problem behavior in schools: The behavior education program* (2nd ed.). New York: Guilford Press.

Crone, D. A., Hawken, L. S., & Horner, R. H. (2015). *Building positive behavior support systems in schools: Functional behavioral assessment* (2nd ed.). New York: Guilford Press.

Cummings, K. P., Addante, S., Swindell, J., & Meadan, H. (2017). Creating supportive environments for children who have had exposure to traumatic events. *Journal of Child and Family Studies*, *26*(1), 2728–2741.

Curwin, R. (2014, October 28). *It's a mistake not to use mistakes as part of the learning process* [Blog post]. Accessed at www.edutopia.org/blog/use-mistakes-in-learning-process-richard-curwin on January 9, 2022.

Daly, E. J., Lentz, F. E., & Boyer, J. (1996). The instructional hierarchy: A conceptual model for understanding the effective components of reading interventions. *School Psychology Quarterly*, *11*(4), 369–386.

Darch, C. B., & Kame'enui, E. J. (2003). *Instructional classroom management: A proactive approach to behavior management* (2nd ed.). Upper Saddle River, NJ: Merrill.

Davis, C. A., Brady, M. P., Williams, R. E., & Hamilton, R. (1992). Effects of high-probability requests on the acquisition and generalization of responses to requests in young children with behavior disorders. *Journal of Applied Behavior Analysis, 25*(4), 905–916.

Decker, D. M., Dona, D. P., & Christenson, S. L. (2007). Behaviorally at-risk African American students: The importance of student-teacher relationships for student outcomes. *Journal of School Psychology, 45*(1), 83–109.

Deitz, D. E. D., & Repp, A. C. (1983). Reducing behavior through reinforcement. *Exceptional Education Quarterly, 3*(4), 34–46.

Dement, W. C., & Vaughan, C. (1999). *The promise of sleep: A pioneer in sleep medicine explores the vital connection between health, happiness, and a good night's sleep.* New York: Delacorte Press.

Denham, S. A., Wyatt, T. M., Bassett, H. H., Echeverria, D., & Knox, S. S. (2009). Assessing social-emotional development in children from a longitudinal perspective. *Journal of Epidemiology and Community Health, 63*(1), 37–52.

Deno, S. L. (1985). Curriculum-based measurement: The emerging alternative. *Exceptional Children, 52*(3), 219–232.

Deno, S. L. (2016). Data-based decision making. In S. R. Jimerson, M. K. Burns, & A. M. VanDerHeyden (Eds.), *Handbook of response to intervention: The science and practice of multi-tiered systems of support* (pp. 9–28). New York: Springer.

De Pry, R. L., & Sugai, G. (2002). The effect of active supervision and pre-correction on minor behavioral incidents in a sixth grade general education classroom. *Journal of Behavioral Education, 11*(4), 255–267.

Dietz, S. M., & Repp, A. C. (1973). Decreasing classroom misbehavior through the use of DRL schedules of reinforcement. *Journal of Applied Behavior Analysis, 6*(3), 457–463.

Doll, B., Brehm, K., & Zucker, S. (2014). *Resilient classrooms: Creating healthy environments for learning* (2nd ed.). New York: Guilford Press.

Doll, B., & Lyon, M. A. (1998). Risk and resilience: Implications for the delivery of educational and mental health services in schools. *School Psychology Review, 27*(3), 348–363.

Doyle, P. D., Jenson, W. R., Clark, E., & Gates, G. (1999). Free time and dots as negative reinforcement to improve academic completion and accuracy for mildly disabled students. *Proven Practice, 2*, 10–15.

Drake, K. L., Steward, C. E., Muggeo, M. A., & Ginsburg, G. S. (2015). Enhancing the capacity of school nurses to reduce excessive anxiety in children: Development of the CALM intervention. *Journal of Child and Adolescent Psychiatric Nursing, 28*, 121–130.

Drevon, D. D., Hixson, M. D., Wyse, R. D., & Rigney, A. M. (2019). A meta-analytic review of the evidence for check-in check-out. *Psychology in the Schools*, *56*(1), 393–412.

Driscoll, K. C., & Pianta, R. C. (2010). Banking time in Head Start: Early efficacy of an intervention designed to promote supportive teacher-child relationships. *Early Education and Development*, *21*(1), 38–64.

Drummond, T. (1994). *The Student Risk Screening Scale (SRSS)*. Grants Pass, OR: Josephine County Mental Health Program.

Duckworth, A. (2016). *Grit: The power of passion and perseverance*. New York: Scribner.

Dufrene, B. A., Lestremau, L., & Zoder-Martell, K. (2014). Direct behavioral consultation: Effects on teachers' praise and student disruptive behavior. *Psychology in the Schools*, *51*(6), 567–580.

Dunlap, G., dePerczel, M., Clarke, S., Wilson, D., Wright, S., White, R., et al. (1994). Choice making to promote adaptive behavior for students with emotional and behavioral challenges. *Journal of Applied Behavior Analysis*, *27*(3), 505–518.

Dunlap, G., Harrower, J., & Fox, L. (2005). Understanding the environmental determinants of problem behaviors. In L. M. Bambara & L. Kern (Eds.), *Individualized supports for students with problem behaviors: Designing positive behavior plans* (pp. 25–46). New York: Guilford Press.

Dunlap, G., Iovannone, R., Kincaid, D., Wilson, K., Christiansen, K., & Strain, P. S. (2019). *Prevent-teach-reinforce: The school-based model of individualized positive behavior support* (2nd ed.). Baltimore: Brookes.

Dunlap, G., Iovannone, R., Kincaid, D., Wilson, K., Christiansen, K., Strain, P. S., et al. (2010). *Prevent-teach-reinforce: The school-based model of individualized positive behavior support*. Baltimore: Brookes.

Dunlap, G., Sailor, W., Horner, R. H., & Sugai, G. (2009). Overview and history of positive behavior support. In W. Sailor, G. Dunlop, G. Sugai, & R. Horner (Eds.), *Handbook of positive behavior support* (pp. 3–16). New York: Springer.

Durlak, J. A., Weissberg, R. P., Dymnicki, A. B., Taylor, R. D., & Schellinger, K. B. (2011). The impact of enhancing students' social and emotional learning: A meta-analysis of school-based universal interventions. *Child Development*, *82*(1), 405–432.

Dusenbury, L. A., Calin, S., Domitrovich, C. E., & Weissberg, R. P. (2015). *What does evidence-based instruction in social and emotional learning actually look like in practice?* Accessed at www.casel.org/wp-content/uploads/2016/08/PDF-25-CASEL-Brief-What-Does-SEL-Look-Like-in-Practice-11-1-15.pdf on June 1, 2021.

Dweck, C. (2006). *Mindset: The new psychology of success*. New York: Ballantine Books.

Dweck, C. (2015). *Carol Dweck revisits the "growth mindset"*. Accessed at www.edweek.org /leadership/opinion-carol-dweck-revisits-the-growth-mindset/2015/09 on January 9, 2022.

Eber, L., Barrett, S., Scheel, N., Flammini, A., & Pohlman, K. (2020). *Integrating a trauma-informed approach within a PBIS framework*. Eugene: Center on PBIS, University of Oregon.

Edutopia. (2015). *Creating a culture of trust and safety in every class*. Accessed at www .edutopia.org/practice/morning-meetings-creating-safe-space-learning on January 4, 2022.

Eisenberg, N., & Spinrad, T. L. (2014). Multidimensionality of prosocial behavior: Rethinking the conceptualization and development of prosocial behavior. In L. M. Padilla-Walker & G. Carlo (Eds.), *Prosocial development: A multidimensional approach* (pp. 17–39). Oxford, UK: Oxford University Press.

Elmore, R. F. (2000). *Building a new structure for school leadership*. Accessed at www.aft.org /pdfs/americaneducator/winter9900/NewStructureWint99_00.pdf on June 1, 2021.

Estrapala, S., Rila, A., & Bruhn, A..L. (2021). A systematic review of Tier 1 PBIS implementation in high schools. *Journal of Positive Behavior Interventions, 23*(4), 288–302.

Fefer, S., DeMagistris, J., & Shuttleton, C. (2016). Assessing adolescent praise and reward preferences for academic behavior. *Translational Issues in Psychological Science, 2*(2), 153–162.

Felitti, V. J., Anda, R. F., Nordenberg, D., Williamson, D. F., Spitz, A. M., Edwards, V., et al. (1998). Relationship of childhood abuse and household dysfunction to many of the leading causes of death in adults: The adverse childhood experiences (ACE) study. *American Journal of Preventive Medicine, 14*(4), 245–258.

Feuerborn, L. L., Wallace, C., & Tyre, A. D. (2013). Gaining staff support for schoolwide positive behavior supports: A guide for teams. *Beyond Behavior, 22*(2), 27–34.

Fisher, D., & Frey, N. (2008). *Better learning through structured teaching: A framework for the gradual release of responsibility*. Alexandria, VA: Association for Supervision and Curriculum Development.

Fisher, D., & Frey, N. (2014). *Better learning through structured teaching: A framework for the gradual release of responsibility* (2nd ed.). Alexandria, VA: Association for Supervision and Curriculum Development.

Fisher, D., & Frey, N. (2021). *Better learning through structured teaching: A framework for the gradual release of responsibility* (3rd ed.). Alexandria, VA: Association for Supervision and Curriculum Development.

Fonollosa, J., Neftci, E., & Rabinovich, M. (2015). *Learning of chunking sequences in cognition and behavior.* Accessed at http://journals.plos.org/ploscompbiol/article?id=10.1371/journal.pcbi.1004592 on October 18, 2021.

Fixsen, D. L., Naoom, S. F., Blase, K. A., Friedman, R. M., & Wallace, F. (2005). *Implementation research: A synthesis of the literature* (Florida Mental Health Institute Publication No. 231). Tampa: Louis de la Parte Florida Mental Health Institute, National Implementation Research Network, University of South Florida.

Floress, M. T., Beschta, S. L., Meyer, K. L., & Reinke, W. M. (2017). Praise research trends and future directions: Characteristics and teacher training. *Behavioral Disorders, 43*(1), 227–243.

Forehand, R. L., & McMahon, R. J. (1981). *Helping the noncompliant child: A clinician's guide to parent training.* New York: Guilford Press.

Frank, A. (1993). *Anne Frank: The diary of a young girl.* New York: Bantam. (Original work published 1952)

Frey, J. R., Elliot, S. N., & Miller, C. F. (2014). Best practices in social skills training. In A. Thomas & P. Harrison (Eds.), *Best practices in school psychology* (pp. 214–224). Bethesda, MD: National Association of School Psychologists.

Gage, N. A., Grasley-Boy, N. M., & MacSuga-Gage, A. S. (2018). Professional development to increase teacher behavior-specific praise: A single-case design replication. *Psychology in the Schools, 55*(3), 264–277.

Galton, F. (1869). *Hereditary genius: An inquiry into its laws and consequences.* New York: Macmillan.

George, H. (2009, June). *Schoolwide positive behavioral interventions and supports training.* In-service training provided at Washoe County School District, Reno, NV.

George, H., Kincaid, D., & Pollard-Sage, J. (2009). Primary-tier interventions and supports. In W. Sailor, G. Dunlap, G. Sugai, & R. H. Horner (Eds.), *Handbook of positive behavior support* (pp. 375–394). New York: Springer.

Gest, S. D., Madill, R. A., Zadzora, K. M., Miller, A. M., & Rodkin, P. C. (2014). Teacher management of elementary classroom school dynamics: Associations with changes in student adjustment. *Journal of Emotional and Behavioral Disorders, 22*(2), 107–118.

Ghandour, R. M., Sherman, L. J., Vladutiu, C. J., Ali, M. M., Lynch, S. E., Bitsko, R. H., et al. (2019). Prevalence and treatment of depression, anxiety, and conduct problems in US children. *Journal of Pediatrics, 206*(1), 256–267.

Glenz, T. (2014). *The importance of learning students' names.* Accessed at http://teachingonpurpose.org/wp-content/uploads/2015/03/Glenz-T.-2014.-The-importance-of-learning-students-names.pdf on October 2, 2021.

Glover, T. A., & Albers, C. A. (2007). Considerations for evaluating universal screening assessments. *Journal of School Psychology, 45*(2), 117–135.

Goldstein, S., & Brooks, R. B. (Eds.). (2013). *Handbook of resilience in children* (2nd ed.). New York: Springer.

Goleman, D. (2005). *Emotional intelligence.* New York: Bantam Books.

Gonzalez, L., Brown, M. S., & Slate, J. R. (2008). Teachers who left the teaching profession: A qualitative understanding. *The Qualitative Report, 13*(1), 1–11.

Goodman, R. (1997). The strengths and difficulties questionnaire: A research note. *Journal of Child Psychology and Psychiatry, 38*(5), 581–586.

Gottman, J. M. (1994). *Why marriages succeed or fail: And how you can make yours last.* New York: Simon & Schuster.

Gray, L., & Taie, S. (2015). *Public school teacher attrition and mobility in the first five years: Results from the first through fifth waves of the 2007–08 Beginning Teacher Longitudinal Study* (NCES 2015–337). Washington, DC: National Center for Education Statistics. Accessed at https://nces.ed.gov/pubs2015/2015337.pdf on August 1, 2020.

Greenberg, J., Putman, H., & Walsh, K. (2014). *Training our future teachers: Classroom management.* Accessed at https://files.eric.ed.gov/fulltext/ED556312.pdf on March 8, 2022.

Gresham, F. M. (2002). Teaching social skills to high-risk children and youth: Preventive and remedial strategies. In M. R. Shinn, H. M. Walker, & G. Stoner (Eds.), *Interventions for academic and behavior problems II: Preventive and remedial approaches* (pp. 403–432). Bethesda, MD: National Association of School Psychologists.

Gresham, F. M., & Elliott, S. N. (1990). *Social skills rating system manual.* Circle Pines, MN: American Guidance Service.

Gresham, F. M., Sugai, G., & Horner, R. H. (2001). Interpreting outcomes of social skills training for students with high-incidence disabilities. *Exceptional Children, 67*(3), 331–344.

Gresham, F. M., Van, M. B., & Cook, C. R. (2006). Social skills training for teaching replacement behaviors: Remediating acquisition deficits in at-risk students. *Behavioral Disorders, 31*(4), 363–377.

Grskovic, J. A., Hall, A. M., Montgomery, D. J., Vargas, A. U., Zentall, S. S., & Belfiore, P. J. (2004). Reducing time-out assignments for students with emotional/behavioral disorders in a self-contained classroom. *Journal of Behavioral Education, 13*(1), 25–36.

Gueldner, B. A., Feuerborn, L. L., Merrell, K. W., & Weissberg, R. P. (2020). *Social and emotional learning in the classroom* (2nd ed.). New York: Guilford Press.

Hanna Institute. (n.d.). *Alternative ACEs*. Accessed at www.hannainstitute.org/research /alternative-aces on January 3, 2022.

Hardy, J. K., & McLeod, R. H. (2020). Using positive reinforcement with young children. *Beyond Behavior, 29*(2), 95–107.

Haring, N. G., Lovitt, T. C., Eaton, M. D., & Hansen, C. L. (1978). *The fourth R: Research in the classroom*. Columbus, OH: Merrill.

Harlacher, J. E. (2015). *Designing effective classroom management*. Bloomington, IN: Marzano Resources.

Harlacher, J. E., Potter, J. B., & Weber, J. M. (2015). A team-based approach to improving core instructional reading practices within response to intervention. *Intervention in School and Clinic, 50*(4), 210–220.

Harlacher, J. E., Roberts, N. E., & Merrell, K. W. (2006). Classwide interventions for students with ADHD: A summary of teacher options beneficial for the whole class. *Teaching Exceptional Children, 39*(2), 6–12.

Harlacher, J. E., & Rodriguez, B. J. (2018). *An educator's guide to schoolwide positive behavioral interventions and supports: Integrating all three tiers*. Bloomington, IN: Marzano Resources.

Harlacher, J. E., Sakelaris, T. L., & Kattelman, N. M. (2014). *Practitioner's guide to curriculum-based evaluation in reading*. New York: Springer.

Harvard Health Publishing. (2020, July 6). *Understanding the stress response*. Accessed at www .health.harvard.edu/staying healthy/understanding-the-stress-response on June 1, 2021.

Hawken, L. S., Crone, D. A., Bundock, K., & Horner, R. H. (2021). *Responding to problem behavior in schools: The check-in, check-out intervention*. New York: Guilford Press.

Hawkins, S. M., & Heflin, L. J. (2011). Increasing secondary teachers' behavior-specific praise using a video self-modeling and visual performance feedback intervention. *Journal of Positive Behavior Interventions, 13*(2), 97–108.

Haydon, T., & Kroeger, S. D. (2016). Active supervision, precorrection, and explicit timing: A high school case study on classroom behavior. *Preventing School Failure: Alternative Education for Children and Youth, 60*(1), 70–78.

Haydon, T., Conroy, M. A., Scott, T. M., Sindelar, P. T., Barber, B. R., & Orlando, A. (2010). A comparison of three types of opportunities to respond on student academic and social behaviors. *Journal of Emotional and Behavioral Disorders, 18*(1), 27–40.

Heppen, J. B., & Therriault, S. B. (2008). *Developing early warning systems to identify potential high school dropouts*. Arlington, VA: National High School Center, American Institutes for Research.

Hester, T. (2013, September 11). *7 tips for better classroom management* [Blog post]. Accessed at www.edutopia.org/blog/7-tips-better-classroom-management-tyler-hester on August 30, 2021.

Hoffman, J. B., & DuPaul, G. J. (2000). Psychoeducational interventions for children and adolescents with attention-deficit/hyperactivity disorder. *Child and Adolescent Psychiatric Clinics of North America, 9*(3), 647–661.

Hollingsworth, J. R., & Ybarra, S. E. (2017). *Explicit direction instruction: The power of the well-crafted, well-taught lesson.* Thousand Oaks, CA: Corwin Press.

Horner, R. H., Sugai, G., Todd, A. W., & Lewis-Palmer, T. (2005). Schoolwide positive behavior support. In L. M. Bambara & L. Kern (Eds.), *Individualized supports for students with problem behaviors: Designing positive behavior plans* (pp. 359–390). New York: Guilford Press.

Hosp, J. L. (2008). Best practices in aligning academic assessment with instruction. In A. Thomas & J. Grimes (Eds.), *Best practices in school psychology V* (pp. 363–376). Bethesda, MD: National Association of School Psychologists.

Howell, K. W., & Nolet, V. (2000). *Curriculum-based evaluation: Teaching and decision making* (3rd ed.). Belmont, CA: Wadsworth.

Ingersoll, R. M. (2002). The teacher shortage: A case of wrong diagnosis and wrong prescription. *NASSP Bulletin, 86*(631), 16–31.

Ingersoll, R. M., Merrill, E., Stuckey, D., & Collins, G. (2018). *Seven trends: The transformation of the teaching force.* Accessed at https://repository.upenn.edu/cgi/viewcontent.cgi?article=1109&context=cpre_researchreports on January 4, 2022.

Ingram, B. (n.d.). *Trauma informed approaches to classroom management.* Accessed at www.yvc.org/wp-content/uploads/2019/06/Trauma-Informed-Approaches-to-Classroom-Management.pdf on June 2, 2021.

Intervention Central. (n.d.a). *How to: Reduce time-outs with active response beads.* Accessed at www.interventioncentral.org/node/963272 on June 1, 2021.

Intervention Central. (n.d.b). *'Rubber band' intervention.* Accessed at www.interventioncentral.org/behavioral-interventions/challenging-students/problem-student-behaviors on June 1, 2021.

James, A. G., Noltemeyer, A., Ritchie, R., & Palmer, K. (2019). Longitudinal disciplinary and achievement outcomes associated with school-wide PBIS implementation level. *Psychology in the Schools, 56*(9), 1512–1521.

Jenkins, L. N., Floress, M. T., & Reinke, W. (2015). Rates and types of teacher praise: A review and future directions. *Psychology in the Schools, 52*(5), 463–476.

Jennings, P. A., & Greenberg, M. T. (2009). The prosocial classroom: Teacher social and emotional competence in relation to student and classroom outcomes. *Review of Educational Research*, *79*(1), 491–525.

Jenson, W. R., Rhode, G., Williams, N. A., & Reavis, H. K. (2020). *The tough kid tool box*. Eugene, OR: Ancora.

Jimerson, S. R., Burns, M. K., & VanDerHeyden, A. (Eds.). (2016). *Handbook of response to intervention: The science and practice of multi-tiered systems of support* (2nd ed.). New York: Springer.

Jones, S. M., & Kahn, J. (2017). *The evidence base for how we learn: Supporting students' social, emotional, and academic development*. Accessed at www.aspeninstitute.org/publications /evidence-base-learn on January 4, 2022.

Jones, J. L., Jones, K. A., & Vermette, P. J. (2009). Using social and emotional learning to foster academic achievement in secondary mathematics. *American Secondary Education*, *37*(3), 4–9.

Jones, S., Bailey, R., Brush, K., & Kahn, J. (2018). *Preparing for effective SEL implementation*. Cambridge, MA: Harvard Graduate School of Education. Accessed at www.wallacefoundation.org/knowledge-center/pages/preparing-for-effective -sel-implementation.aspx on January 4, 2022.

Jones, S. M., & Bouffard, S. M. (2012). Social and emotional learning in schools: From programs to strategies. *Social Policy Report*, *26*(4), 3–22.

Jurbergs, N., Palcic, J., & Kelley, M. L. (2007). School-home notes with and without response cost: Increasing attention and academic performance in low-income children with attention-deficit/hyperactivity disorder. *School Psychology Quarterly*, *22*(3), 358–379.

Kame'enui, E. J., & Simmons, D. C. (1990). *Designing instructional strategies: The prevention of academic learning problems*. Columbus, OH: Merrill.

Kamphaus, R. W., & Reynolds, C. R. (2015). *Behavior Assessment System for Children (BASC-3) Behavioral and Emotional Screening System (BESS)*. New York: Pearson.

Kann, L., Kinchen, S., Shanklin, S. L., Flint, K. H., Kawkins, J., Harris, W. A., et al. (2014). Youth risk behavior surveillance: United States, 2013. *Morbidity and Mortality Weekly Report Supplements*, *63*(4), 1–168.

Katznelson, I. (n.d.). *Quick dose: Why do I feel tired mid-afternoon?* Accessed at www.nm.org /healthbeat/healthy-tips/quick-dose-why-do-i-feel-tired-mid-afternoon on January 10, 2022.

Kemp, J. (2020). *Using consultation with performance feedback to align classroom management strategies with a social emotional learning curriculum in early childhood.* Doctoral dissertation, University of Massachusetts Amherst. Accessed at https://scholarworks.umass.edu/dissertations_2/1925 on August 9, 2021.

Kennedy, M. (n.d.). *Homegrown SW-PBIS videos.* Accessed at https://vimeo.com/groups/pbisvideos on August 25, 2021.

Kern, L., White, G. P., & Gresham, F. M. (2007). Educating students with behavioral challenges. *Principal, 86*(4), 56–59.

Khan-Baker, A. (2016). *Why pronouncing students' names is important to building relationships.* Accessed at www.nbpts.org/why-pronouncing-students-names-is-important-to-building-relationships on January 4, 2022.

Kien, K., Chung, H., Lam, C. B., & Liew, J. (2020). Studying children's social-emotional development in school and at home through a cultural lens. *Early Education and Development, 31*(6), 927–929.

Kilgus, S. (2020). *Get the whole picture: Using social, emotional and behavioral assessments to support student success.* Accessed at www.fastbridge.org/wp-content/uploads/2020/09/seb-ebook.pdf on June 1, 2021.

Kilgus, S., von der Embse, N. P., Chafouleas, S. M., & Riley-Tillman, T. C. (2014). *Social, academic, and emotional behavior risk screener: Teacher rating scale.* Accessed at www.rand.org/education-and-labor/projects/assessments/tool/2013/saebrs-teacher-version.html on January 10, 2022.

Kim, B. K. E., Oesterle, S., Hawkins, J. D., & Shapiro, V. B. (2015). Assessing sustained effects of *Communities That Care* on youth protective factors. *Journal of the Society for Social Work and Research, 6*(4), 565–589.

Kincade, L., Cook, C. R., & Goerdt, A. (2020). Meta-analysis and common practice elements of universal approaches to improving student-teacher relationships. *Review of Educational Research, 90*(5), 710–748.

Kincaid, D., Childs, K., & George, H. (2010). *Tier 1 benchmarks of quality (BoQ).* Accessed at https://assets-global.website-files.com/5d3725188825e071f1670246/60303de04f17fab0bc5d854c_Tier_1_Benchmarks_of_Quality.pdf on January 10, 2022.

Knight, C. (2019). Trauma informed practice and care: Implications for field instruction. *Clinical Social Work Journal, 47*(1), 79–89.

Kovacs, M. (2010). *Children's depression inventory 2.* New York: Pearson.

Kratochwill, T. R., Elliott, S. N., & Callan-Stoiber, K. (2002). Best practices in school-based problem-solving consultation. In A. Thomas & J. Grimes (Eds.), *Best practices in school psychology IV* (pp. 583–608). Bethesda, MD: National Association of School Psychologists.

Kriete, R., & Davis, C. (2014). *The morning meeting book* (3rd ed.). Turners Falls, MA: Northeast Foundation for Children.

Labrie, K. (2014, November 8). *Student-led PBIS* [Blog post]. Accessed at www.corelaboratewa.org/blog/teacher-leaders/single/~board/teacher-leaders-archive/post/student-led-pbis on May 15, 2020.

Lane, K. L., Menzies, H. M., Parks, R. E., Oakes, W. P., & Lane, K. S. (2018). Instructional choice: An effective, efficient, low-intensity strategy to support student success. *Beyond Behavior, 27*(3), 160–167.

Lane, K. L., Oakes, W. P., Swogger, E. D., Schatschneider, C., Menzies, H. M., & Sanchez, J. (2015). Student Risk Screening Scale for internalizing and externalizing behaviors: Preliminary cut scores to support data-informed decision making in middle and high schools. *Behavioral Disorders, 40*(3), 159–170.

Langland, S., Lewis-Palmer, T., & Sugai, G. (1998). Teaching respect in the classroom: An instructional approach. *Journal of Behavioral Education, 8*(2), 245–262.

La Salle, T. P., McIntosh, K., & Eliason, B. M. (2018). *School climate survey suite administration manual.* Accessed at www.pbis.org/resource/school-climate-survey-suite on June 2, 2021.

LeBuffe, P. A., Shapiro, V. B., & Naglieri, J. A. (2014). *The Devereux Student Strengths Assessment (DESSA): Assessment, technical manual, and user's guide.* Cerritos, CA: Apperson.

Ledford, G. E., Jr., Gerhart, B., & Fang, M. (2013). Negative effects of extrinsic rewards on intrinsic motivation: More smoke than fire. *World at Work, 22*(2), 17–29.

Lee, H. (1960). *To kill a mockingbird.* New York: Lippincott.

Lee, H. Y., Jamieson, J. P., Miu, A. S., Josephs, R. A., & Yeager, D. S. (2018). An entity theory of intelligence predicts higher cortisol levels when high school grades are declining. *Child Development, 90*(6), e849–e867.

Lehr, C. A., Sinclair, M. F., & Christenson, S. L. (2004). Addressing student engagement and truancy prevention during the elementary school years: A replication study of the Check & Connect model. *Journal of Education for Students Placed at Risk, 9*(3), 279–301.

Leverson, M., Smith, K., McIntosh, K., Rose, J., & Pinkelman, S. (2021). *PBIS cultural responsiveness field guide: Resources for trainers and coaches.* Accessed at www.delawarepbs.org/wp-content/uploads/2020/07/Leverson-et-al-2019-PBIS-Cultural-Responsiveness-Field-Guide_-Resources-for-Trainers-and-Coaches.pdf on January 3, 2022.

Lewis, B. (2019). *How to create behavior contracts: Your most challenging students require creative discipline solutions.* Accessed at www.thoughtco.com/how-to-create-behavior-contracts-2080989 on March 8, 2022.

Lewis, T. J., Colvin, G., & Sugai, G. (2000). The effects of pre-correction and active supervision on the recess behavior of elementary students. *Education and Treatment of Children, 23*(2), 109–121.

Lewis, T. J., Hudson, S., Richter, M., & Johnson, N. (2004). Scientifically supported practices in emotional and behavioral disorders: A proposed approach and brief review of current practices. *Behavioral Disorders, 29*(3), 247–259.

Loftin, R. L., Gibb, A. C., & Skiba, R. J. (2005). Using self-monitoring strategies to address behavior and academic issues. *Impact, 18*(2), 12–13.

Losada, M., & Heaphy, E. (2004). The role of positivity and connectivity in the performance of business teams: A nonlinear dynamics model. *American Behavioral Scientist, 47*(6), 740–765.

Mackay, S., McLaughlin, T. F., Weber, K., & Derby, K. M. (2001). The use of precision requests to decrease noncompliance in the home and neighborhood: A case study. *Child and Family Behavior Therapy, 23*(3), 41–50.

March, J. S. (2012). *Multidimensional anxiety scale for children* (2nd ed.). New York: Pearson.

Martinelli, K. (2021). *Are time-outs harmful to children?* Accessed at https://childmind.org /article/are-time-outs-harmful-kids on January 4, 2022.

Marzano, R. J. (2003). *What works in schools: Translating research into action.* Alexandria, VA: Association for Supervision and Curriculum Development.

Maynard, B. R., Kjellstrand, E. K., & Thompson, A. M. (2014). Effects of Check and Connect on attendance, behavior, and academics: A randomized effectiveness trial. *Research on Social Work Practice, 24*(3), 296–309.

Maynard, N., & Weinstein, B. (2020). *Hacking school discipline: 9 ways to create a culture of empathy and responsibility using restorative justice.* Highland Heights, OH: Times 10.

McCammon, B. (2020). *Restorative practices at school: An educator's guided workbook to nurture professional wellness, support student growth, and build engaged classroom communities.* Berkeley, CA: Ulysses Press.

McIntosh, K. (2020, December 1). *An equity-focused PBIS approach for increasing racial equity in school discipline* [Webinar]. Arlington, VA: Council for Exceptional Children.

McIntosh, K., & Goodman, S. (2016). *Integrated multi-tiered systems of support: Blending RTI and PBIS.* New York: Guilford Press.

McKevitt, B. C., & Braaksma, A. (2008). Best practices in developing a positive behavior support system at the school level. In A. Thomas & J. Grimes (Eds.), *Best practices in school psychology V* (pp. 735–747). Bethesda, MD: National Association of School Psychologists.

McKnight, S. E. (2020). *De-escalating violence in healthcare: Strategies to reduce emotional tension and aggression*. Accessed at https://sigma.nursingrepository.org/bitstream /handle/10755/17096/Chapter3.pdf?sequence=3 on March 8, 2022.

McLaughlin, K. A., & Lambert, H. K. (2017). Child trauma exposure and psychopathology: Mechanisms of risk and resilience. *Current Opinion in Psychology, 14*, 29–34.

McNeely, C. A., Nonnemaker, J. M., & Blum, R. W. (2002). Promoting school connectedness: Evidence from the National Longitudinal Study of Adolescent Health. *Journal of School Health, 72*(4), 138–146.

Means, B., Chen, E., DeBarger, A., & Padilla, C. (2011). *Teachers' ability to use data to inform instruction: Challenges and supports*. Washington, DC: U.S. Department of Education.

Mercurio, M. A., Schmitt, A. J., Loftus-Rattan, S. M., & McCallum, E. (2021). Reducing classroom transition time using a music-infused video modeling intervention. *Psychology in the Schools, 58*(9), 1741–1752.

Merrell, K. W., Cohn, B. P., & Tom, K. M. (2011). Development and validation of a teacher report measure for assessing social-emotional strengths of children and adolescents. *School Psychology Review, 40*(2), 226–241.

Metz, A., & Louison, L. (2019). *The hexagon tool: Exploring context*. Accessed at https://nirn .fpg.unc.edu/sites/nirn.fpg.unc.edu/files/imce/documents/Hexagon.Education.Kentucky .May2019.pdf on June 2, 2021.

Meyer, A. M., & Bartels, L. K. (2017). The impact of onboarding levels on perceived utility, organizational commitment, organizational support, and job satisfaction. *Journal of Organizational Psychology, 17*(5), 10–27.

Midwest PBIS Network. (n.d.). *Classroom practices*. Accessed at www.midwestpbis.org /materials/classroom-practices on June 1, 2021.

Minahan, J. (2019). Trauma-informed teaching strategies. *Educational Leadership, 77*(2), 30–35.

Missouri School-Wide Positive Behavior Support. (n.d.). *Chapter 3: Student identification process*. Accessed at https://pbismissouri.org/wp-content/uploads/2018/08/Tier-2-2018_ Ch.-3.pdf on June 1, 2021.

Moroz, K. B., & Jones, K. M. (2002). The effects of positive peer reporting on children's social involvement. *School Psychology Review, 31*(2), 235–245.

Murphy, J., & Zlomke, K. (2014). Positive peer reporting in the classroom: A review of intervention procedures. *Behavior Analysis in Practice, 7*(2), 126–137.

Musti-Rao, S., & Haydon, T. (2011). Strategies to increase behavior-specific teacher praise in an inclusive environment. *Intervention in School and Clinic, 47*(2), 91–97.

Naglieri, J. A., Lebuffe, P., & Shapiro, V. B. (2011). *The Devereux Student Strengths Assessment-Mini (DESSA-Mini) assessment, technical manual, and user's guide.* Cerritos, CA: Apperson.

National Commission on Excellence in Education. (1983). *A nation at risk: The imperative for educational reform.* Washington, DC: Author. Accessed at https://edreform.com /wp-content/uploads/2013/02/A_Nation_At_Risk_1983.pdf on November 9, 2020.

National Forum on Education Statistics. (2021). *Forum guide to attendance, participation, and engagement data in virtual and hybrid learning models* (NFES2021058). Accessed at https://ies.ed.gov/pubsearch/pubsinfo.asp?pubid=NFES2021058 on January 10, 2022.

National School Climate Center. (n.d.). *What is school climate?* Accessed at www .schoolclimate.org/about/our-approach/what-is-school-climate on June 1, 2021.

Nelson, J. R., & Carr, B. A. (1996). *The think time strategy for schools: Bringing order to the classroom* [Video recording]. Longmont, CO: Sopris West.

Netsi, E., Pearson, R. M., Murray, L., Cooper, P., Craske, M. G., & Stein, A. (2018). Association of persistent and severe postnatal depression with child outcomes. *JAMA Psychiatry, 75*(3), 247–253.

Newmann, F. M., Smith, B., Allensworth, E., & Bryk, A. S. (2001). Instructional program coherence: What it is and why it should guide school improvement policy. *Educational Evaluation and Policy Analysis, 23*(4), 297–321.

Newton, J. S., Horner, R. H., Algozzine, R. F., Todd, A. W., & Algozzine, K. M. (2009). Using a problem-solving model to enhance data-based decision making in schools. In W. Sailor, G. Dunlap, G. Sugai, & R. H. Horner (Eds.), *Handbook of positive behavior support* (pp. 551–580). New York: Springer.

Nimocks, J. (2011). *Intervention name: Positive peer reporting.* Accessed at https://education .missouri.edu/wp-content/uploads/sites/21/2013/04/Positive-Peer-Reporting.pdf on January 10, 2022.

Noell, G. H., Duhon, G. J., Gatti, S. L., & Connell, J. E. (2002). Consultation, follow-up, and implementation of behavior management interventions in general education. *School Psychology Review, 31*(2), 217–234.

Norris, J. A. (2003). Looking at classroom management through a social and emotional learning lens. *Theory Into Practice, 42*(4), 313–318.

Oliver, R. M., Lambert, M. C., & Mason, W. A. (2019). A pilot study for improving classroom systems within schoolwide positive behavior support. *Journal of Emotional and Behavioral Disorders, 27*(1), 25–36.

Oliver, R. M., Wehby, J. H., & Reschly, D. J. (2011). Teacher classroom management practices: Effects on disruptive or aggressive student behavior. *Campbell Systematic Reviews, 7*(4), 1–55.

O'Neill, R. E., Albin, R. W., Storey, K., Horner, R. H., & Sprague, J. R. (2015). *Functional assessment and program development for problem behavior: A practical handbook* (3rd ed.). Stamford, CT: Cengage Learning.

O'Neill, R. E., Horner, R. H., Albin, R. W., Sprague, J. R., Storey, K., & Newton, J. S. (1997). *Functional assessment and program development for problem behavior: A practical handbook* (2nd ed.). Pacific Grove, CA: Brooks/Cole.

Osterman, K. F. (2000). Students' need for belonging in the school community. *Review of Educational Research, 70*(3), 323–367.

Partin, T. C. M., Robertson, R. E., Maggin, D. M., Oliver, R. M., & Wehby, J. H. (2010). Using teacher praise and opportunities to respond to promote appropriate student behavior. *Preventing School Failure, 54*(3), 172–178.

Pas, E. T., Bradshaw, C. P., & Mitchell, M. M. (2011). Examining the validity of office discipline referrals as an indicator of student behavior problems. *Psychology in the Schools, 48*(6), 541–555.

Patrikakou, E. N. (2016). Contexts of family-school partnerships: A synthesis. In S. M. Sheridan & E. M. Kim (Eds.), *Family-school partnerships in context* (pp. 109–120). New York: Springer.

Payton, J., Weissberg, R. P., Durlak, J. A., Dymnicki, A. B., Taylor, R. D., Schellinger, K. B., et al. (2008). *The positive impact of social and emotional learning for kindergarten to eighth-grade students: Findings from three scientific reviews.* Accessed at https://casel.org /the-positive-impact-of-social-and-emotional-learning-for-kindergarten-to-eighth-grade -students-findings-from-three-scientific-reviews on June 2, 2021.

Perou, R., Bitsko, R. H., Blumberg, S. J., Pastor, P., Ghandour, R. M., Gfroerer, J. C., et al. (2013). Mental health surveillance among children: United States, 2005–2011. *Morbidity and Mortality Weekly Report Supplement, 62*(2), 1–35.

Petrosino, A., Fronius, T., Goold, C. C., Losen, D. J., & Turner, H. M. (2017). *Analyzing student-level disciplinary data: A guide for districts.* Washington, DC: Institute of Education Sciences.

Pickens, I. B., & Tschopp, N. (2017). *Trauma-informed classrooms.* Accessed at www.ncjfcj .org/wp-content/uploads/2017/10/NCJFCJ_SJP_Trauma_Informed_Classrooms_Final .pdf on June 1, 2021.

Pierce, J. M., Spriggs, A. D., Gast, D. L., & Luscre, D. (2013). Effects of visual activity schedules on independent classroom transitions for students with autism. *International Journal of Disability, Development, and Education, 60*(3), 253–269.

Pisacreta, J., Tincani, M., Connell, J. E., & Axelrod, S. (2011). Increasing teachers' use of a 1:1 praise-to-behavior correction ratio to decrease student disruption in general education classrooms. *Behavioral Interventions, 26*(4), 243–260.

Plomin, R., DeFries, J. C., Knopik, V. S., & Neiderhiser, J. M. (2016). Top 10 replicated findings from behavioral genetics. *Perspectives in Psychological Science, 11*(1), 3–23.

Public Health Management Corporation. (2013). *Findings from the Philadelphia Urban ACE Survey.* Accessed at www.rwjf.org/en/library/research/2013/09/findings-from-the -philadelphia-urban-ace-survey.html January 10, 2022.

Quinn, M. M., Kavale, K. A., Mathur, S. R., Rutherford, R. B., Jr., & Forness, S. R. (1999). A meta-analysis of social skill interventions for students with emotional or behavioral disorders. *Journal of Emotional and Behavioral Disorders, 7*(1), 54–64.

Rafferty, L. A. (2010). Step-by-step: Teaching students to self-monitor. *Teaching Exceptional Children, 43*(2), 50–58.

Rathel, J. M., Drasgow, E., Brown, W. H., & Marshall, K. J. (2014). Increasing induction-level teachers' positive-to-negative communication ratio and use of behavior-specific praise through e-mailed performance feedback and its effect on students' task engagement. *Journal of Positive Behavior Interventions, 16*(4), 219–233.

Reinke, W. M., Herman, K. C., & Stormont, M. (2013). Classroom-level positive behavior supports in schools implementing SW-PBIS: Identifying areas for enhancement. *Journal of Positive Behavior Interventions, 15*(1), 39–50.

Reinke, W. M., Lewis-Palmer, T., & Martin, E. (2007). The effect of visual performance feedback on teacher use of behavior-specific praise. *Behavior Modification, 31*(3), 247–263.

Responsive Classroom. (2015, July 29). *Our hopes and dreams for school.* Accessed at www .responsiveclassroom.org/our-hopes-and-dreams-for-school on June 2, 2021.

Robichaux, N. M. (2016). *Effects of various seating arrangements on disruptive classroom behavior.* Doctoral dissertation, Louisiana State University, Baton Rouge. Accessed at https://digitalcommons.lsu.edu/gradschool_dissertations/3696 on August 9, 2021.

Rothbart, M. K. (2012). Advances in temperament: History, concepts, and measures. In M. Zentner & R. L. Shiner (Eds.), *Handbook of temperament* (pp. 3–20). New York: Guilford Press.

Rothbart, M. K., & Rueda, M. R. (2005). The development of effortful control. In U. Mayr, E. Awh, & S. Keele (Eds.), *Developing individuality in the human brain: A tribute to Michael I. Posner* (pp. 167–188). Washington, DC: American Psychological Association.

Rucinski, C. L., Brown, J. L., & Downer, J. T. (2018). Teacher–child relationships, classroom climate, and children's social-emotional and academic development. *Journal of Educational Psychology, 110*(7), 992–1004.

Rutter, M. (1985). Resilience in the face of adversity: Protective factors and resistance to psychiatric-disorder. *British Journal of Psychiatry, 147*(6), 598–611.

Ryan, J. B., Sanders, S., Katsiyannis, A., & Yell, M. L. (2007). Using time-out effectively in the classroom. *Teaching Exceptional Children, 39*(4), 60–67.

Sailor, W., Dunlap, G., Sugai, G., & Horner, R. H. (Eds.). (2009). *Handbook of positive behavior support*. New York: Springer.

Samek, D. R., & Hicks, B. M. (2014). Externalizing disorders and environmental risk: Mechanisms of gene-environment interplay and strategies for intervention. *Clinical Practice, 11*(5), 537–547.

Santa Clara University. (n.d.). *Theoretical framework*. Accessed at www.scu.edu/oml/about-us /theoretical-framework on September 26, 2021.

Santiago-Rosario, M. R., Whitcomb, S. A., Pearlman, J., & McIntosh, K. (2021). Associations between teacher expectations and racial disproportionality in discipline referrals. *Journal of School Psychology, 85*(3), 80–93.

SBSK. (2018). *Normalizing the diversity of the human condition*. Accessed at https://sbsk.org on August 31, 2021.

Schlund, J., Jagers, R. J., & Schlinger, M. (2020). *Emerging insights: Advancing social and emotional learning (SEL) as a lever for equity and excellence*. Accessed at https://casel .s3.us-east-2.amazonaws.com/CASEL-Gateway-Advancing-SEL-for-Equity-Excellence .pdf on January 4, 2022.

Schmoker, M. (2006). *Results now: How we can achieve unprecedented improvements in teaching and learning*. Alexandria, VA: Association for Supervision and Curriculum Development.

Scholastic, & Bill & Melinda Gates Foundation. (2013). *Primary sources: America's teachers on teaching in an era of change* (3rd ed.). Accessed at www.scholastic.com/primarysources /PrimarySources3rdEditionWithAppendix.pdf on January 4, 2022.

Schonert-Reichl, K. A., Hanson-Peterson, J. L., & Hymel, S. (2015). SEL and preservice teacher education. In J. A. Durlak, C. E. Domitrovich, R. P. Weissberg, & T. P. Gullotta (Eds.), *Handbook of social and emotional learning: Research and practice* (pp. 406–421). New York: Guilford Press.

Sharma, S., Mustanski, B., Dick, D., Bolland, J., & Kertes, D. A. (2019). Protective factors buffer life stress and behavioral health outcomes among high-risk youth. *Journal of Abnormal Child Psychology, 47*(8), 1289–1301.

Sheldrick, R. C., Schlichtung, L. E., Berger, B., Clyde, A., Ni, P., Perrin, E. C., et al. (2019). Establishing new norms for developmental milestones. *Pediatrics, 144*(6), e20190374.

Sheridan, S. M., Smith, T. E., Kim, E. M., Beretvas, S. N., & Park, S. (2019). A meta-analysis of family-school interventions and children's social-emotional functioning: Moderators and components of efficacy. *Review of Educational Research, 89*(2), 296–332.

Shinn, M. R. (2008). Best practices in curriculum-based measurement and its use in a problem-solving model. In A. Thomas & J. Grimes (Eds.), *Best practices in school psychology V* (pp. 243–262). Bethesda, MD: National Association of School Psychologists.

Siegel, D. J., & Bryson, T. P. (2016). *No-drama discipline: The whole-brain way to calm the chaos and nurture your child's developing mind.* New York: Bantam Books.

Simonsen, B., Fairbanks, S., Briesch, A., Myers, D., & Sugai, G. (2008). Evidence-based practices in classroom management: Considerations for research to practice. *Education and Treatment of Children, 31*(3), 351–380.

Simonsen, B., Freeman, J., Goodman, S., Mitchell, B., Swain-Bradway, J., Flannery, B., et al. (2015). *Supporting and responding to student behavior: Evidence-based classroom strategies for teachers* (OSEP Technical Assistance Brief). Accessed at https://osepideasthatwork.org /sites/default/files/ClassroomPBIS_508.pdf on January 4, 2022.

Simonsen, B., MacSuga, A. S., Fallon, L. M., & Sugai, G. (2013). The effects of self-monitoring on teachers' use of specific praise. *Journal of Positive Behavior Interventions, 15*(1), 5–15.

Simonsen, B., & Myers, D. (2015). *Classwide positive behavior interventions and supports: A guide to proactive classroom management.* New York: Guilford Press.

Simonsen, B., Myers, D., & DeLuca, C. (2010). Teaching teachers to use prompts, opportunities to respond, and specific praise. *Teacher Education and Special Education, 33*(4), 300–318.

Sinclair, M. F., Christenson, S. L., Lehr, C. A., & Anderson, A. R. (2003). Facilitating student engagement: Lessons learned from Check & Connect longitudinal studies. *California School Psychologist, 8*(1), 29–41.

Skiba, R., Ormiston, H., Martinez, S., & Cummings, J. (2016). Teaching the social curriculum: Classroom management as behavioral instruction. *Theory Into Practice, 55*(2), 120–128.

Skinner, B. F. (1953). *Science and human behavior.* New York: Free Press.

Skinner, B. F. (1976). *About behaviorism.* New York: Random House.

Smith, T. E., Sheridan, S. M., Kim, E. M., Park, S., & Beretvas, S. N. (2020). The effects of family-school partnership interventions on academic and social-emotional functioning: A meta-analysis exploring what works for whom. *Educational Psychology Review, 32*(2), 511–544.

Song, H., Kim, J., & Luo, W. (2016). Teacher-student relationships in online classes. *Computers in Human Behavior, 54,* 436–443.

Stage, S. A., & Quiroz, D. R. (1997). A meta-analysis of interventions to decrease disruptive classroom behavior in public education settings. *School Psychology Review, 26*(3), 333–368.

Stronge, J. H., Ward, T. J., & Grant, L. W. (2011). What makes good teachers good? A cross-case analysis of the connection between teacher effectiveness and student achievement. *Journal of Teacher Education, 62*(4), 339–355.

Substance Abuse and Mental Health Services Administration. (2019). *Ready, set, go, review: Screening for behavioral health risk in schools.* Accessed at www.samhsa.gov/sites/default/files/ready_set_go_review_mh_screening_in_schools_508.pdf on March 8, 2022.

Sugai, G., & Colvin, G. (1997). Debriefing: A transition step for promoting acceptable behavior. *Education and Treatment of Children, 20*(2), 209–221.

Sugai, G., & Horner, R. H. (2006). A promising approach for expanding and sustaining school-wide positive behavior support. *School Psychology Review, 35*(2), 245–259.

Sutherland, K. S., & Wehby, J. H. (2001). Exploring the relationship between increased opportunities to respond to academic requests and the academic and behavioral outcomes of students with EBD: A review. *Remedial and Special Education, 22*(2), 113–121.

Sutherland, K. S., Wehby, J. H., & Copeland, S. R. (2000). Effect of varying rates of behavior-specific praise on the on-task behavior of students with EBD. *Journal of Emotional and Behavioral Disorders, 8*(1), 2–8, 26.

Taylor, R. D., Oberle, E., Durlak, J. A., & Weissberg, R. P. (2017). Promoting positive youth development through school-based social and emotional learning interventions: A meta-analysis of follow-up effects. *Child Development, 88*(4), 1156–1171.

Taylor-Greene, S., Brown, D., Nelson, L., Longton, J., Gassman, T., Cohen, J., et al. (1997). School-wide behavioral support: Starting the year off right. *Journal of Behavior Education, 7*(1), 99–112.

Thapa, A., Cohen, J., Guffey, S., & Higgins-D'Alessandro, A. (2013). A review of school climate research. *Review of Educational Research, 83*(3), 357–385.

Theodore, L. A., Bray, M. A., Kehle, T. J., & Jensen, W. R. (2001). Randomization of group contingencies and reinforcers to reduce classroom disruptive behavior. *Journal of School Psychology, 39*(3), 267–277.

Tilly, W. D. (2008). The evolution of school psychology to science-based practice: Problem solving and the three-tiered model. In A. Thomas & J. Grimes (Eds.), *Best practices in school psychology V* (pp. 17–35). Bethesda, MD: National Association of School Psychologists.

Tingstedt, O., Lindblad, F., Koposov, R., Blatný, M., Hrdlička, M., Stickley, A., et al. (2018). *Somatic symptoms and internalizing problems in urban youth: A cross-cultural comparison of Czech and Russian adolescents.* Accessed at https://academic.oup.com/eurpub/article/28/3/480/4823625 on March 8, 2022.

Todd, A. W., Horner, R. H., Newton, J. S., Algozzine, R. F., Algozzine, K. M., & Frank, J. L. (2011). Effects of team-initiated problem solving on decision making by schoolwide behavior support teams. *Journal of Applied School Psychology, 27*(1), 42–59.

Todd, A. W., Horner, R. H., & Sugai, G. (1999). Self-monitoring and self-recruited praise: Effects on problem behavior, academic engagement, and work completion in a typical classroom. *Journal of Positive Behavior Interventions, 1*(2), 66–76.

Todd, A. W., Horner, R. H., & Tobin, T. (2006). *Referral form definitions: Version 4.0.* Accessed at www.pbis.org/common/cms/files/NewTeam/Data/ReferralFormDefinitions .pdf on December 2, 2014.

Trussell, R. P. (2008). Classroom universals to prevent problem behaviors. *Intervention in School and Clinic, 43*(3), 179–185.

Turtura, J. E., Anderson, C. M., & Boyd, R. J. (2014). Addressing task avoidance in middle school students: Academic behavior check-in/check-out. *Journal of Positive Behavior Interventions, 16*(3), 159–167.

Valenti, M. W., & Kerr, M. M. (2014). Addressing individual perspectives in the development of schoolwide rules: A data-informed process. *Journal of Positive Behavior Interventions, 17*(4), 245–253.

Van Droogenbroeck, F., Spruyt, B., & Vanroelen, C. (2014). Burnout among senior teachers: Investigating the role of workload and interpersonal relationships at work. *Teaching and Teacher Education, 43*, 99–109.

Vaughn, S., Wexler, J., Roberts, G., Barth, A. A., Cirino, P. T., Romain, M. A., et al. (2011). Effects of individualized and standardized interventions on middle school students with reading disabilities. *Exceptional Child, 77*(4), 391–407.

Venet, A. S. (2021). *Equity-centered trauma-informed education.* New York: Norton.

von Ravensburg, H. (2020). *Remote learning for families: Keeping it positive, keeping it accessible.* Accessed at www.pbis.org/resource/remote-learning-for-families-keeping-it -accessible-keeping-it-positive on January 4, 2022.

Waguespack, A. M., Moore, L. A., Wickstrom, K. F., Witt, J. C., & Gaydos, G. R. (1994). Mystery Motivator: An effective and time efficient intervention. *School Psychology Review, 23*(1), 106–118.

Waldman, I. D., Rhee, S. H., LoParo, D., & Park, Y. (2018). Genetic and environmental influences on psychopathy and antisocial behavior. In C. J. Patrick (Ed.), *Handbook of psychopathy* (pp. 335–353). New York: Guilford Press.

Walker, H. M. (1979). *The acting-out child: Coping with classroom disruption.* Boston: Allyn & Bacon.

Walker, H. M., Small, J. W., Severson, H. H., Seeley, J. R., & Feil, E. G. (2014). Multiple-gating approaches in universal screening within school and community settings. In R. J. Kettler, T. A. Glover, C. A. Albers, & K. A. Feeney-Kettler (Eds.), *Universal screening in educational settings: Evidence-based decision making for schools* (pp. 47–75). Washington, DC: American Psychological Association.

Walker, P. (2013). *Complex PTSD: From surviving to thriving.* Lafayette, CA: Azure Coyote.

Wang, C., Hatzigianni, M., Shahaeian, A., Murray, E., & Harrison, L. J. (2016). The combined effects of teacher-child and peer relationships on children's social-emotional adjustment. *Journal of School Psychology, 59,* 1–11.

Watkins, C., & Slocum, T. A. (2004). The components of direct instruction. In N. E. Marchand-Martella, T. A. Slocum, & R. C. Martella (Eds.), *Introduction to direct instruction* (pp. 28–65). Boston: Allyn & Bacon.

Watson, J. B. (1913). Psychology as the behaviorist views it. *Psychological Review, 20*(2), 158–177.

Webber, J., Scheuermann, B., McCall, C., & Coleman, M. (1993). Research on self-monitoring as a behavior management technique in special education classrooms: A descriptive review. *Remedial and Special Education, 14*(2), 38–56.

Webster-Stratton, C. (2019). *The Incredible Years: A trouble-shooting guide for parents of children aged 3–8 years* (3rd ed.). Seattle: The Incredible Years.

Whitcomb, S. (2017). *Behavioral, social, and emotional assessment of children and adolescents* (5th ed.). New York: Taylor & Francis.

Whitcomb, S. A., & Fefer, S. (2013). *Request for assistance* [Unpublished resource]. Amherst, MA: Author.

Whiting, S. B., Wass, S. V., Green, S., & Thomas, M. S. C. (2021). Stress and learning in pupils: Neuroscience evidence and its relevance for teachers. *Mind, Brain, and Education, 15*(2), 177–188.

Wilkinson, L. A. (2007). Assessing treatment integrity in behavioral consultation. *International Journal of Behavioral Consultation and Therapy, 3*(3), 420–432.

Wolery, M. (2011). Intervention research: The importance of fidelity measurement. *Topics in Early Childhood Special Education, 31*(3), 155–157.

Wolery, M., Bailey, D. B., Jr., & Sugai, G. (1988). *Effective teaching: Principles and procedures of applied behavior analysis with exceptional students.* Boston: Allyn & Bacon.

Wong, H. K., & Wong, R. T. (2009). *The first days of school: How to be an effective teacher* (4th ed.). Mountain View, CA: Harry K. Wong.

Wong, H. K., & Wong, R. T. (2018). *The first days of school: How to be an effective teacher* (5th ed.). Mountain View, CA: Harry K. Wong.

Wong, H. K., Wong, R. T., Jondahl, S. F., & Ferguson, O. F. (2018). *The classroom management book*. Mountain View, CA: Harry K. Wong.

Yarbrough, J. L., Skinner, C. H., Lee, Y. J., & Lemmons, C. (2004). Decreasing transition times in a second grade classroom: Scientific support for the Timely Transitions Game. In C. H. Skinner (Ed.), *Single-subject designs for school psychologists* (pp. 85–107). Binghamton, NY: Haworth Press.

Yeager, D. S. (2017). Social and emotional learning programs for adolescents. *Future of Children, 27*(1), 73–94.

Yeager, D. S., Hanselman, P., Walton, G. M., Murray, J. S., Crosnoe, R., Muller, C., et al. (2019). A national experiment reveals where a growth mindset improves achievement. *Nature, 573*, 364–369.

Yeager, D. S., Purdie-Vaughns, V., Garcia, J., Apfel, N., Brzustoski, P., Master, A., et al. (2014). Breaking the cycle of mistrust: Wise interventions to provide critical feedback across the racial divide. *Journal of Experimental Psychology: General, 143*(2), 804–824.

Yoder, N., & Gurke, D. (2017). *Social and emotional learning coaching toolkit: Keeping SEL at the center*. Accessed at www.air.org/sites/default/files/downloads/report/Social-and-Emotional-Learning-SEL-Coaching-Toolkit-August-2017.pdf on June 2, 2021.

Yoder, N., & Nolan, L. (2018). What does SEL look like in the classroom? *The Learning Professional, 39*(4), 60–66.

Zenger, J., & Folkman, J. (2013). *The ideal praise-to-criticism ratio*. Accessed at https://hbr.org/2013/03/the-ideal-praise-to-criticism on October 20, 2021.

Zolkoski, S. M. (2019). The importance of teacher-student relationships for students with emotional and behavioral disorders. *Preventing School Failure: Alternative Education for Children and Youth, 63*(3), 236–241.

# INDEX

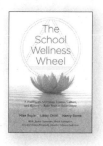

### The School Wellness Wheel
*Mike Ruyle, Libby Child, and Nancy Dome*
Your school can evolve to address trauma, promote well-being, and elevate learning. *The School Wellness Wheel* will show you how. Backed by educational, psychological, and medical research, the resource introduces a comprehensive framework for supporting students' cognitive, social, and emotional needs.
**BKL064**

### Designing Effective Classroom Management
*Jason E. Harlacher*
Discover the components of proactive classroom management. With this practical, step-by-step guide, teachers and school administrators will uncover five components that help improve student achievement: create clear expectations and rules, establish procedures and structure, reinforce expectations, actively engage students, and manage misbehavior.
**BKF830**

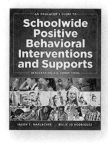

### An Educator's Guide to Schoolwide Positive Behavioral Interventions and Supports
*Jason E. Harlacher and Billie Jo Rodriguez*
Discover how to create an encouraging, productive school culture using the Schoolwide Positive Behavioral Interventions and Supports (SWPBIS) framework. This book includes the authors' personal experiences in applying SWPBIS and explores practical examples of what the elements and tiers of this model look like in practice.
**BKL030**

### Teaching Self-Regulation
*Amy S. Gaumer Erickson and Patricia M. Noonan*
Self-regulation fuels students to become socially and emotionally engaged, lifelong learners. With this timely resource you'll gain 75 instructional activities to teach self-regulation in any secondary classroom. Ample teacher-tested tools and templates are also included to help you create authentic learning experiences and deliver effective feedback.
**BKF988**

**MARZANO** Research

Visit MarzanoResources.com or call 888.849.0851 to order.

# Professional Development Designed for Success

Empower your staff to tap into their full potential as educators. As an all-inclusive research-into-practice resource center, we are committed to helping your school or district become highly effective at preparing every student for his or her future.

Choose from our wide range of customized professional development opportunities for teachers, administrators, and district leaders. Each session offers hands-on support, personalized answers, and accessible strategies that can be put into practice immediately.

## Bring Marzano Resources experts to your school for results-oriented training on:

- ▶ Assessment & Grading
- ▶ Curriculum
- ▶ Instruction
- ▶ School Leadership

- ▶ Teacher Effectiveness
- ▶ Student Engagement
- ▶ Vocabulary
- ▶ Competency-Based Education

**LEARN MORE at** MarzanoResources.com/PD